# Writing Essays
## about Literature
### A Guide and Style Sheet

#### FIFTH EDITION

# Writing Essays
## about Literature
### A Guide and Style Sheet

FIFTH EDITION

## KELLEY GRIFFITH
*University of North Carolina at Greensboro*

HARCOURT BRACE COLLEGE PUBLISHERS

Fort Worth  Philadelphia  San Diego  New York  Orlando  Austin  San Antonio
Toronto  Montreal  London  Sydney  Tokyo

| | |
|---|---|
| Publisher: | Earl McPeek |
| Executive Editor: | Michael Rosenberg |
| Acquisitions Editor: | John Meyers |
| Product Manager: | Ilse Wolfe-West |
| Developmental Editor: | Helen Triller |
| Project Editors: | Betsy Ener and Travis Tyre |
| Art Director: | Vicki Whistler |
| Text Designer: | Linda Harper |
| Production Managers: | Melinda Esco and Andrea Johnson |
| Cover Photo: | Kevin Tolman |
| Cover Photo Tinting: | Donna Buie |
| ISBN: | 0-15-503708-0 |

Library of Congress Catalog Card Number: 97-71993

Address for orders:
Harcourt Brace College Publishers
6277 Sea Harbor Drive
Orlando, FL 32887-6777
1-800-782-4479

Address for editorial correspondence:
Harcourt Brace College Publishers
301 Commerce Street, Suite 3700
Fort Worth, TX 76102

Web site address:
http://www.hbcollege.com

Harcourt Brace & Company will provide complimentary supplements or supplement packages to those adopters qualified under our adoption policy. Please contact your sales representative to learn how you qualify. If as an adopter or potential user you receive supplements you do not need, please return them to your sales representative or send them to: Attn: Returns Department, Troy Warehouse, 465 South Lincoln Drive, Troy, MO 63379.

Printed in the United States of America

0 1 2 3 4 5 6 066 9 8 7 6 5 4 3

for *Gareth* and *Bronwen*

# *Preface*

I wrote this book in response to needs that constantly arose in my literature courses. When I assigned out-of-class essays, students would respond with perplexity and even panic: "What should I look for?" "What do you want?" "How long should the essay be?" "Do we have to use outside sources?" Some students had never written essays about literature, and others hadn't for a long time. They were at a loss about how to get started. After answering these questions again and again, I realized I wanted a book that would not only meet my students' immediate needs but also would cover most aspects of writing about literature. It would introduce students to the study of literature, define key critical terms, explain details of usage, and include whole essays that would serve as useful illustrations of good student writing.

Although *Writing Essays about Literature: A Guide and Style Sheet* has evolved over its five editions, it still accomplishes these purposes in three general ways. First, it provides guidance about reading literature. Reading well is rewarding in itself, but it is essential for writing well. Part One of the book—Chapters 1 through 7—focuses on reading literature. Chapter 1 (Strategies for Reading Literature) serves as the introduction and poses the question: How can we interpret literature? Chapters 2-5 are discussions of the nature of literature and of the three major literary genres—fiction, drama, and poetry. These chapters define the elements of literature, but they also provide *heuristics*—questions and "thinking-on-paper" exercises—that lead readers toward their own interpretations. Chapter 6 suggests criteria for evaluating the quality of literary works, and Chapter 7, with its discussions of critical approaches, invites readers to expand their studies beyond the scope of the book.

Second, the book offers comprehensive guidance for writing about literature. Chapter 8 (Writing about Literature) serves as an introduction to Part Two and poses two questions: Why write about literature? Why write essays about literature? Although this chapter emphasizes the interpretive essay, it also discusses more "personal" kinds of writing, such as notes and journals. By bringing in personal writing here, I urge writers to connect their own lives to the literature they read and write about. Chapters 9-14 explore the four stages of the writing process: inventing, drafting, revising, and editing. Chapter 9 (Choosing Topics) suggests strategies for generating topics, and Chapter 10 (Drafting the Essay) emphasizes the argumentative nature of most essays about literature. It includes suggested ways for students to develop the reasoning and organization of their essays as they move from early to final drafts.

Third, the book serves as a style guide. As such it deals with the third and fourth stages of the writing process: revising and editing. Chapter 11 (Documenting Sources) explains what research papers are, how to find information and opinion, how to incorporate them into essays, and how to document sources using the MLA style. Chapter 12 (Revising and Editing) offers general advice about revising, provides rules for quotations and other matters of usage common to essays about literature, and it gives guidelines for the essay's appearance and format. The book concludes with a chapter on taking essay tests and a chapter containing six student essays—two each on a short story, a poem, and a play. All of these essays illustrate effective principles of literary interpretation and serve as useful examples of student writing.

Several things are new in this edition. With the ever-growing pool of materials available on computers, students and instructors are often bewildered about what's out there and how to find it. In Chapter 11 (Documenting Sources), I have added new information about how to find research materials available on computer databases and on the Internet. But once you find this information, how do you document it? Here, too, I provide guidelines for documenting computer and Internet resources. In Chapter 7 (Specialized Approaches to Analyzing Literature), I expand the overview of feminist criticism to include gender criticism, and I provide a new discussion of New Historicism. A number of people requested sample essays that illustrate a work in progesss. Chapter 10 (Drafting the Essay) now concludes with a student essay in two drafts. I streamlined the beginning of the book to give greater emphasis to its two-part organization: reading literature and writing about literature. Thus, Chapter 1 in the fourth edition is now

Chapter 8, where it serves as the introduction to Part Two. Finally, I have made editorial changes throughout the book to make it more *hermeneutic,* to highlight the most rewarding task of thoughtful readers and writers: interpretation.

The book is not meant to be an all-inclusive treatment of the study of literature. It does, however, explain succinctly how to go about the rewarding task of thinking about and discussing literature. Instructors may use it in many ways, as a textbook in introductory courses or as a supplement in more advanced ones. Students may use it on their own as an introduction to the study of literature, as a guide to writing essays about literature, and as a reference manual.

I welcome any comments and suggestions from users of this book who may see ways for making it better. My e-mail address is <griffitk@fagan.uncg.edu>. Snail mail is English Department, University of North Carolina at Greensboro, Greensboro, NC 27412.

## ACKNOWLEDGMENTS

I owe many people gratitude for their help. I am indebted to the writers whose works I have consulted. I thank my colleagues Walter Beale and William Tucker for reading and criticizing this work in its initial stages and for making suggestions for improvement once it was published. During the writing of previous editions, I incorporated the valuable comments of Laurence Perrine, Frank Garratt (Tacoma Community College), George Gleason (Southwest Missouri State University), John Hanes (Duquesne University), Jacqueline Hartwich (Bellevue Community College), Irving Howe (Hunter College), Edward Pixley (State University of New York at Oneaonta), Dexter Westrum (Ottawa University), Jeff Bagato (Virginia Polytechnic Institute), Helen O'Grady (University of Wyoming), Karen Meyers (University of North Carolina at Greensboro), Thomas C. Bonner (Midlands Technical College), Nancy Hume (Essex Community College), Gretchen Lutz (San Jacinto College), Robbie Clifton Pinter (Belmont University), and Wallace Watson (Duquesne University).

For this edition I wish to acknowledge the valuable suggestions of Judy Brown (University of British Columbia), Gaye Elder (Abraham Baldwin Agricultural College), Albert J. Griffith (Our Lady of the Lake University), James M. Hutchisson (The Citadel), Ellen N. Moody (George Mason University), John David Moore (Eastern Illinois University), and Tyler Smith (Midlands Technical College).

At Harcourt Brace, I thank John Meyers, who shepherded the book to completion with good humor, skill, and patience. I would also like to thank Helen Triller, Melinda Esco, Andrea Johnson, Betsy Ener, Travis Tyre, and Vicki Whistler.

Finally, I am deeply grateful to my family for the encouragement they always give me.

# Contents

# $\mathcal{I}$NTRODUCTION

L ike all art, literature gives pleasure. It has a certain magic that transports us from the "real" world to seemingly remote and enjoyable places. We can feel this quality without thinking about it. But literature also poses intellectual challenges that do demand thought. For most readers, grappling with these challenges enhances the pleasure of literature. By studying literature, we "see" more of it to appreciate. And we often learn that, far from being remote from life, literature reflects and clarifies the real world and helps us define our places in it.

This book addresses two related questions: How can we read literature? How can we write about it? In order to write well about literature we have to read it well. In turn, writing about literature helps us understand what we have read.

There are many ways to read and write about literature, but this book focuses largely on one way—interpretation. By "interpretation" I mean the act of making sense of something, of establishing its meaning. When we read literature this way, we try to discover its meaning. When we write about it, we attempt to communicate that meaning. You might ask, Why concentrate on interpretation? Why not something else? The reason is that interpretation is the most widely practiced, most rewarding, most challenging, and most interesting way to read and write about literature. We often read literature for other purposes as well—for information or pleasure—but most people who like to read literature want to make sense of it. To interpret well, furthermore, requires skill. Most people can interpret at some level, but to interpret so as to satisfy our craving for meaning and to interest other people, we have to employ strategies of discovery, analysis, and reasoning. Exploring those strategies—both for reading and writing—is the subject of this book.

Part One of the book takes up the first question, how to read. It begins with basic strategies of interpretation and then focuses on one widely practiced strategy: analyzing the "formal" elements of literature, those elements that constitute the "form" of literature. Knowing what some of these elements are gives us places to look for meaning. We next consider another strategy for interpretation: evaluating the quality of works of literature. We conclude Part One with brief discussions of other, more specialized strategies.

Part Two considers the question of how to write about literature. Its organization follows a "natural" process that many writers use: Inventing (deciding what to write about), drafting (writing first drafts), revising (writing more drafts), and editing (producing a final draft for "publication"). Throughout Part Two, and most notably in the final chapter, samples of student writing illustrate interpretative writing.

Although each part of the book follows an orderly path—a step-by-step process for reading and writing—you can also use them as "handbooks." Part One covers such things as the elements of literature and of genres (fiction, drama, and poetry), as well as theoretical approaches such as historicism, New Criticism, structuralism, poststructuralism, New Historicism, feminist, and gender criticism. Part Two gives information about such things as generating topics, organizing essays, using logic, doing research, documenting sources, using quotations, and taking tests. All of this material is easy to find, especially when you use the Index of Concepts and Terms located at the back of the book. If you don't remember where a definition or explanation is, just look in the Index for its location.

We begin, then, with reading.

# PART ONE

## Reading Literature

# 1

# *Strategies for Reading Literature*

## WHY DO PEOPLE READ LITERATURE?

People read literature for many reasons. Some read it for information (about cults, or exotic locales, or historical events, or specialized skills, or emotionally troubled people). Others read it because other people do—it's popular or their friends read it. Others because they have to read it (their teachers require it). But probably the two major reasons people read literature—outside classrooms, anyway—are for pleasure and for meaning. People read literature because it's fun and because it speaks to them about important things.

Reading purely for pleasure is something that almost all of us who like to read do. I, for example, even though I've taught literature for years, constantly read just for pleasure. When I do this, I don't necessarily care what the work means. I simply want to escape from the concerns of the day and let the work have its magical effect on me. I sometimes ask my students to describe their first great reading experience. Almost all of them tell about a time—usually in early adolescence—when they read something that was so wonderful to them that they never wanted it to end. For me this happened in the ninth grade with Arthur Conan Doyle's stories about Sherlock Holmes. For other people, it was *The Secret Garden,* or *Jane Eyre,* or *Tom Sawyer,* or *The Wind in the Willows,* or well, what was your first great reading experience?

The other major reason for reading literature is the focus of this book: reading for meaning. Reading for pleasure and reading for meaning are, of course, related. Part of the pleasure of reading comes from the meaning it gives us. Ever since I first read those Sherlock Holmes stories, I have loved detective fiction. One of my favorite writers of detective fiction is Raymond Chandler. When I read my first Chandler novel, all I wanted to know was what was going to happen next. I was so wrapped up in the excitement of the plot that I didn't even notice if there was meaning in it or not, but when I read my next Chandler novel, and especially when I went back and reread the ones I had previously read, I began to discover a richness that I hadn't noticed before. I began to notice how he uses the elements of the detective story—wiseguy dialogue, intrigue, suspense, urban settings, stereotyped characters, savvy hero—to give his fictional world a moral dimension that goes far beyond the intricacies of his plots. I even came to feel that his plots were sometimes not so good, after all; they can be clunky and confusing. Far more important, I discovered, were his poetic language, his mastery of tone, his insights about American cities, about American obsessions, about the connection between highlife and lowlife, wealth and poverty, innocence and crime. As I continued to read Chandler, I found myself moving from one level of enjoyment—reading for escape—to another—reading for meaning. Or, put another way, I found myself reading not just for pleasure *and* meaning but for pleasure *because of* meaning.

The "meaning" of a work of literature is its ideas. These ideas can be its "themes"—its comments about the real world (our world, the world outside the work)—as well as its handling of such things as characters (their motivations, inner conflicts), settings (their effects on characters, on the action), and language devices (patterns of sound or metaphor). The ideas of a work can be ideas the author intended to convey. They can be ideas the author did not intend but that readers have discovered. They can be ideas that you see in the work but that nobody else has seen. When a work has more than one main idea, which is almost always, some readers may think that one idea is important, and other readers may favor another idea. Meaning in literature, in short, is partly personal and subjective. Even if many people agree about what the ideas of a work are, you, the individual reader, still have to decide which ideas are the most important for you. The way we discover ideas in literature is through interpretation.

## WHAT IS INTERPRETATION?

*Interpretation* is a process. It is the process of discovering meaning in works of literature by examining details in the works. Most people do this even when they read a work for the first time. When they read, they encounter details in the work and begin to formulate ideas about what they mean. As they encounter more details, they either confirm their ideas or change them. John Ellis, the literary theorist, says that an interpretation "is a hypothesis about the most general organization and coherence of all the elements that form a literary text." This "organization and coherence" emerges from a synthesis between a work's ideas and its details. "The most satisfying interpretation will be that which is the most inclusive. The procedure of investigation will be that of any inquiry: a continual move between general notions of the coherence of the text, and consideration of the function within the whole of particular parts of it. General conceptions will change in the light of particular observations, and new particular observations will then become necessary in the light of the changed conceptions" (*The Theory of Literature: A Logical Analysis.* Berkeley: University of California Press, 1974. 202).

Many critics today would disagree with Ellis that the best interpretation "covers" or accounts for the most details in a work or that it establishes a "coherence" that unifies the whole work. For one thing, it's hard to say which interpretation covers the most details. For another, the most comprehensive interpretation may not be the most satisfying to a particular reader. For still another, many works stubbornly resist complete "coherence." But Ellis is right about how the process of interpretation works. Interpretation means questing for ideas that are manifested by the work's details. To make your ideas believable and convincing, you must ground them in the details of the text. If you encounter details that contradict your ideas, you must adjust them to accommodate those details.

Interpretation is not something we do only with literature. It is an unavoidable process in any thinking person's life: Why is Miriam angry at me? Why did Jonathan go to pieces when he took the test? Would this job be better for me than that one? How will my blowup with Lucy affect our relationship? Is O. J. guilty? Should we legalize late-term abortions? What were the causes of World War II? Do human beings have free will? Answering questions like these, from the trivial to the profound, requires interpretation.

A crime scene, for example, demands the same kind of interpretation that a work of literature does. As you examine the details of the scene, you begin to formulate hypotheses about what happened and who's responsible. With the discovery of new evidence, you adjust your hypotheses until, finally, you reach accurate and just decisions. Literature, however, is different from crime scenes and other real-life circumstances. Unlike a crime scene, a work of literature has an author who intends to convey ideas. Yet authors of literature usually don't state their ideas directly. Instead, they use literary devices such as metaphor, symbol, plot, connotation, rhyme, and meter to convey meaning. It's up to us to determine what meanings such devices communicate in works of literature. Our way of doing that is interpretation. The craft of interpreting literature is called *literary criticism.* Anytime you interpret literature, then, you are a literary critic.

## HOW CAN WE INTERPRET?

Generally speaking, the definition of "interpretation" states how to do it: Interpreting means looking at a work's details to decide on its meaning. The following are basic suggestions about how to interpret works of literature as you read and reread them.

1. **Get the Facts Straight.** In order to come up with believable interpretations of a work, we have to comprehend what's in the work, its "facts." For some works, this is easy to do; their facts seem completely accessible and understandable. But for other works, getting the facts straight is difficult. The poetry of seventeenth-century poets like John Donne and George Herbert is notoriously dense and requires close study to understand. Modernist authors such as T. S. Eliot, Wallace Stevens, Virginia Wolfe, and James Joyce employ innovative techniques that make their works seem like complicated puzzles. The language of Chaucer and Shakespeare is not quite our language. To understand it we have to rely on the glosses (definitions) that editors often conveniently place at the bottom of the page. In short, we have to work hard just to get the "facts" of many literary works. When you read, then, look up words you don't know. Inform yourself about the allusions in the texts (to myths, the Bible, historical and biographical events). Read slowly. Reread.

2. **Connect the Work with Yourself.** For you, the most important meanings of works of literature will be your own. This does not mean that the reasons other people find authors like Sophocles, Sappho, Virgil, Dante, Shakespeare, Goethe, Emily Dickinson, and George Eliot "great" are unimportant. Such reasons are part of our cultural heritage. Not to be interested in them is to deny ourselves the wisdom of that heritage. Even worse, to care only about our own meanings is to cut ourselves off from the rest of humankind. But, that said, even if people you respect love a work, unless you can connect it to your own experiences and interests, the work won't live for you. It may live for other people, but not for you. A strategy

for interpreting literature, especially those works you can't seem to get into or can't seem to like, is to relate them to your own life.

One way to do this is to project yourself *into* the work. Imagine that you actually inhabit the world of the work. Ask yourself, "What would my life be like in these circumstances?" Students of American literature, for example, typically find the writings of the New England Puritans forbidding. I admit that reading Puritan sermons and didactic poetry is not most people's idea of fun. However, if you use your imagination to place yourself in the world of the Puritans, at least some of their writing might seem more relevant to your life. How would you think and feel had you lived then—about your family, the wilderness around you, the difficulty of scraping out a living, the harsh winters, the imperatives of your religion? What would your psychological makeup—emotional conflicts and tensions—have been? Authors like Nathaniel Hawthorne and Arthur Miller have done this kind of self-projection into Puritan culture and have produced highly imaginative rethinkings of it. By projecting yourself into a work or culture, you may not be able to produce works like *The Scarlet Letter* and *The Crucible,* but you can at least recover the appeal of works of literature that may seem remote from your own life.

Another approach is to pay attention to your own reactions to the work. As you read, answer questions like these:

- How are things in the work (characters, incidents, places) similar to things in your life?
- How might people you know react to this work? Would they be shocked? Pleased? Would they approve of your reading it?
- How does this work challenge your beliefs?
- What new things does the work bring up for you? Do you like them?
- How does this work give you pleasure?
- What is upsetting or unpleasant about it?

3. **Develop Hypotheses as You Read.** When you read a work of literature, even for the first time, you probably generate ideas about it automatically. In fact, some scholars claim that you can't read at all without doing *some* interpreting. The strategy I'm suggesting here, however, is that you make the interpretive process conscious and constant. As you read, raise questions about what the details you encounter mean: Why does this character act in that way? Why does the author keep using that image? Why is this character so blind about her sister's good qualities? Why does the author use this

rhyme scheme? As you read, don't feel that you have to give final answers to these questions. Plan to come back to them later. Such questions and tentative answers get you thinking, help you pick up on important details that pop up later, and make the inevitable rereading or review much easier.

4. **Write as You Read.** I like to own works I want to read carefully. That way, I can write in them. I underline passages, circle words, draw arrows from one passage to another. In the margins, I write questions, summaries, definitions, topics the author addresses, interpretations. If something is repeated in a work, I try to find where it first appeared and write "See page xxx" so I can make comparisons later. I do these things because it helps me think—and remember. My notations allow me to easily review the work—find the important parts of the work—and to synthesize my thoughts about it. In Part Two (Chapter Eight) we will look at how informal writing can help you write essays, but informal writing can also help you interpret *as* you read. You can do what I do— write in the book itself (*your* book, not the library's or someone else's). You can keep a reading notebook or a journal. Some people like to keep double entry notebooks: on one side of each page they write down details of a work—quotations, summaries of scenes, descriptions, facts about a character, and so forth; on the other side they make comments about each one. Informal writing makes you an active, rather than a passive reader. And it helps you claim the work as your own.

5. **Solicit Ideas from Other People.** Sometimes we can interpret works better if we know what other people think about them. We don't have to agree with their ideas, but having an inkling about the work's subject matter and possible meanings before we read or reread often helps us develop our own interpretations. Other people's ideas give us a grounding, an orientation, a place to begin. You can, of course, go to the library and read what critics have said about a work. You can also ask people you know what they think. You might even form a discussion group, an informal gathering for coffee or lunch. Such opportunities to exchange opinion can be beneficial and fun for all participants. One critic wrote that even blurbs on book covers helped him get his bearings in a work.

6. **Analyze the Work.** *Analysis* means breaking something down into its components and discovering the relationships among them that give unity and coherence to the whole or major parts of the whole. Analysis is a powerful, probably necessary, strategy for generating

and communicating interpretations of anything, not just literature. If, for example, you need to sell computers, you will do it better if you can analyze them. Knowing how they work and what they can do lets you know what they "mean" (how, for example, they can help your customers). The same is true for interpreting literature. Being able to analyze literature helps us see how each part contributes to the meaning of a work. As we read individual works, we can be alert to how their authors use elements to signal meaning.

Analyzing literature is too complicated a subject to cover in just a few paragraphs. In the next four chapters, we will consider how some of the best known elements of literature can lead us toward interpretations. The first of these chapters (Chapter 2) focuses on analyzing literature itself. Chapters 3, 4, and 5 deal with analyzing fiction, drama, and poetry.

# 2

# Analyzing Literature

As a reader, you may have been pleased by a work of literature but could not say why. Or someone may have asked you why you like to read literature, and, again, you could not say why. Or you may have wondered what literature is, anyway, and could not think what. Analyzing the nature of literature—not just works of literature but literature itself—helps us answer these questions. Knowing the components of literature, furthermore, helps us interpret it by giving us places to look for meaning. This chapter describes some of these components. As you read, try to spot them and assess their effect on you. Which of them seem especially important in making a work pleasurable and meaningful to you?

## THE NATURE OF LITERATURE

There are enough mysterious elements in literature to make a complete definition impossible. Many critics who have tried to define it, however, have pointed to a few common elements.

### Literature Is Language

The medium of literature is language, both oral and written. But not everything written or spoken is literature. Creators of literature use language in a special way, a way different from that of scientists or people using everyday speech. Scientists use language for its *denotative* value, its ability to provide symbols (words) that mean one thing precisely. For scientists, the thing that the symbol represents—the referent—is more important than the symbol itself. Any symbol will do, as long as it represents the referent clearly and exactly. Because emotions render meanings imprecise, scientists try to use symbols that eliminate the emotional, the irrational, the subjective.

Writers of literature, in contrast, use language *connotatively*. They may at times—as in realistic novels—emphasize denotation, but usually they employ the connotative meanings of language. Connotation is the meaning that attaches to words in addition to their explicit referents. A good example of the difference between denotation and connotation is the word *mother*, whose denotation is simply "female parent" but whose connotations include nurturance, warmth, unqualified love, tenderness, devotion, protection, mercy, intercession, home, childhood, the happier past. The connotative meanings of words are subjective, multiple, and sometimes arbitrary. Even scientific language becomes connotative once it enters everyday speech. When we see Einstein's formula $E = mc^2$, we no longer think just of "Energy equals mass times the speed of light squared" but of mushroom clouds, ruined cities, and a sad-eyed, long-haired genius padding about his house in bedroom slippers.

Writers of literature use language, in short, for its expressive and emotional qualities. But they also use it for itself. They are fascinated by its sounds, its rhythms, even its appearance on the page. Sometimes they become so interested in these qualities that they subordinate meaning to them. People who use language in everyday speech and writing also display a sensitivity to its sounds and subjective qualities, but writers of literature exploit these qualities more fully, more consciously, and more systematically.

As you read, then, pay attention to the way the author uses language. Is there anything unusual or purposeful in the author's choice of words *(diction)*? Does the author, for example, employ connotations and double meanings? Does the author use words you do not know? If so, look them up, especially if the work is poetry. Does the sentence structure *(syntax)* of the work seem unusual or especially appropriate for the work's other qualities? What *is* the syntax—can you analyze it? Are there sound qualities of the author's language that seem important? Does the author use punctuation in odd ways? Does the author write in an archaic style—that is, archaic even for the author's day? Why? Does the author speak in dialect or have characters do so? What does this add to the work? For a look at how questions like these can help develop arguments, see the sample essays on poetry in Chapter 14, both of which explain how authors use language.

## Literature Is Aesthetic

Literature is "aesthetic"; that is, it gives pleasure. This quality is hard to define and describe. In a sense, it just *is*. Like various other pleasures— music, patterns of color, sunsets, dance—literature is an end in itself.

All the elements of literature contribute to the pleasure it gives. But probably the most important is *form,* the order the writer imposes on the material—on language, characters, events, details, all of which he or she draws from the usually disorderly realm of real life. Take, for example, events. In real life, events are not necessarily related by cause and effect. Or if some events are related, many are not. Events do not necessarily lead to a conclusion. The murderer may not be caught, the cruel parent may continue to be cruel, the economic crisis may not be resolved, the poor but honest youth may not be rewarded. So many things happen to us that it is hard to remember or even be aware of them all. We do not always know which events are important, which trivial. But literature can give order to events in the form of a *plot.* Unimportant events will be excluded, cause-and-effect relationships established, conflicts introduced and resolved. Events will be arranged in logical order so that they form a sequence with a beginning, a middle, and an end. They may even have suspense, so that we fearfully or gleefully anticipate what happens next. Plot, of course, is only one of a multitude of ways in which artists give order to material. They may also arrange language into orderly patterns, reduce characters to recognizable types, offer ideas that guide the reader toward a certain interpretation of the material, describe settings in a selective, logical way. In a good work of literature, all of the elements combine to create an *overall* order, an *overall* coherence.

As you read, look for anything that gives pattern or structure to the work. If the work is poetry, is it governed by traditional forms such as the sonnet or ballad? What are the patterns that inevitably emerge from these forms? If it is a play, does it have act and scene divisions? How long are these? What happens in each? If it is a narrative, does it have chapter divisions or sectional divisions of other kinds (indicated by the use of double spacings, numbers, or even paragraph indentations)? Does the author divide the work according to a time scheme— hours, days, months, years? Does the repetition of phrases, words, images, and metaphors mark sections of a work or tie the work together thematically? More subjectively, why does the work give you pleasure? What qualities in it appeal to you?

## Literature Is Fictional

We commonly use the term *fiction* to describe prose works that tell a story (short stories and novels). In fact, however, all works of literature are "fictional" in the sense that the reader sets them apart from the facts of real life.

A work can be fictional in two ways. First, the writer makes up some of the materials. Some of the characters, events, dialogue, and settings exist only in the writer's imagination. He or she may draw upon real-life observations and experiences to create them; but when these appear in the finished work, they have been so altered that no one-to-one correlation can be said to exist between them and anything that actually exists or existed. Furthermore, the writer may ignore laws that govern the real world. An obvious example is fantasy fiction, wherein human beings fly, perform magic, confront dragons, remain young, travel through time, discover utopian kingdoms, metamorphose, or live happily ever after, or where animals or other "creatures" take on human traits such as speech and intelligence. Even historical fiction, which relies on actual events for some of its material, is fictional. It includes characters, dialogue, events, and settings that do not exist in history.

Second, the fictionality of literature lies also in the artistic control the writer exercises over the work. This artistic control has the effect of stylizing the materials of the work and thus setting the work apart from the context of the real. This effect occurs even when the material of the work *does* accurately mirror the facts of real life or when it states ideas that can be verified in actual experience. Such works would include autobiographies such as those by Benjamin Franklin and Frederick Douglass and "true crime" narratives such as Truman Capote's *In Cold Blood* and Norman Mailer's *The Executioner's Song*. Compare, for example, accounts of the same event written by a newspaper reporter and by a poet. Both writers may describe the event accurately, but the reporter makes his or her account correspond as exactly as possible to the event so that the reader will experience the details of the event, not the report of it. The poet, in contrast, makes his or her *poem* the object of experience. Through the use of language, the selection of details, the interpretation—stated or implied—of the event, the inclusion of devices such as metaphor, irony, and imagery, the poet makes the work an artifact, an object of enjoyment and contemplation in itself. The reader instinctively, if not consciously, recognizes it as different from the event itself. In this way, the work becomes "fictional." Because of this element of fictionality, you can experience and even enjoy works whose subject matter would in real life be so depressing or horrifying as to be unendurable.

Consider, for example, two famous autobiographical works, Henry David Thoreau's *Walden* (1854) and Richard Wright's *Black Boy* (1945). Thoreau really did live in a cabin at Walden Pond, and we can be fairly sure the events he records in *Walden* really did happen. But Thoreau does so many "literary" things with those events that he causes us to conceive of them in aesthetic and thematic terms. His prose style is highly stylized and poetic. He emphasizes his own feelings. He collapses the two years he actually spent at Walden into one year, and organizes that year around the four seasons of the year, thus giving the book a kind of plot. He retells events to illustrate philosophical themes. The text is heavily metaphoric and symbolic. As with Thoreau, Richard Wright no doubt records events that actually happened. But here, too, the author employs "literary" devices to make these events vivid. He conveys his intense feelings by means of a first person point of view similar to what a fiction writer would use. His language is charged with emotional intensity. Perhaps most striking, he constructs novelistic scenes. These scenes, which have extensive dialogue and minute descriptions of physical actions and details, are almost certainly fictional in that there's no way the author could have remembered the exact words these people said and the physical details he records. The scenes no doubt happened, but Wright is filling in details to give them aesthetic power.

You can detect the fictional quality of a work most obviously by watching for those elements that depart from the facts of the real world. What historical facts does the author distort or add to? What facts about the physical world and physical laws does the author alter? Why does the author do this? Do these changes or additions destroy the plausibility or enjoyableness of the work?

Less obvious, but equally important, are those elements that make the work an object of scrutiny in and of itself, such as its use of language and its ordering of material. One of the most important effects of the fictionality of literature is the distance it creates between you and the material presented. This distance is both physical and psychological. You know, as you read, that you are not actually involved in the work's events. They are safely removed from you. Thus you can give freer rein to your emotional reactions than you can for real events. It would be difficult to control your emotions were you to meet a real vampire, werewolf, or homicidal maniac, but you can indulge in, enjoy, and yet control your feelings of fright by confronting yourself with fictional ones. Some authors, however, try to reduce as much as they can the psychological distance between their fictional events and you. They want to draw you into the events so fully that, at least for the moment, you imagine you are involved in real events. In contrast, other authors, such as Nikolai Gogol, Henry Fielding, Washington Irving, and W. M. Thackeray, constantly remind you that their events are fictional. What, then, is the psychological distance between you and the material of the work? Does the author make you feel objective about it? Or are you deeply and emotionally caught up in it? How does the author minimize or emphasize this distance? Why does the author do it?

## Literature Is True

Even though works of literature are "fictional," they have the capacity for being "true." This paradox creates one of the most important and pleasurable tensions in literature: the fictionality of literature against its truthfulness in conveying the reality of human experience. Literature can be faithful to the facts of reality, as in descriptive prose and poetry. It also can be true in two other, more important, ways. First, it speaks about the real world even when it distorts, ignores, or alters facts. Simple examples of this "thematic" quality of literature are fables and fairy tales, whose characters and events may be fantastic but whose lessons (themes) are true to our own experience. Aesop's animal characters are like no animals in real life: They can reason and use language. They behave like real persons in similar circumstances, and the lessons we learn from their behavior are shrewd commentaries on human nature.

Unlike fables, however, most literature does not present its concepts about life in the form of a moral tacked on at the end. Rather, the total form of a work represents its interpretation. A work of literature uses literary devices such as plot, metaphor, irony, musical language, and suspense to create an imaginary "world," and this world embodies a theory about how the real world works. That is, it embodies a "world view." Authors may or may not be consciously aware of this theory, but their views of the real world inevitably influence their construction of an imaginary one. In turn, we must infer the authors' world views from the details of their created worlds. Thus, the world of George Orwell's *Nineteen Eighty-Four* is filled with crumbling buildings, frightened people, children who spitefully turn their parents over to the police, procedures whereby truth is systematically altered, masses of people trapped by their ignorance and selfishness, and officials who justify any deed to achieve power. It is a world without love, compassion, justice, joy, tradition, altruism, idealism, or hope. The facts of this world are patently imaginary—Orwell himself placed them in the future—but they communicate Orwell's extremely pessimistic view of human nature and human institutions. Orwell shows that, given what he observed of his world, the terrible society he describes in *Nineteen Eighty-Four* could become a reality.

Authors use numerous literary devices to convey their world views. Two notable ones are the representation of *typical characters* and of *probable actions*. Because works of literature often clothe their worlds in manifold detail, they create the illusion of being real and thus unique. But the characters and events of literature cannot be unique if they are to be meaningful. We often encounter freakish, inexplicable events and people in real life, and they disturb us because we cannot place them within an orderly context. However, we expect literature to give order to the chaos of real life, and it does so partly by exposing patterns of meaning in life. To do this, literature must conform to generally recognizable patterns of behavior and probability. J. R. R. Tolkien, for example, offers an array of fantasy creatures and kingdoms in *The Hobbit* and its sequel, *The Lord of the Rings*. Yet his characters, whatever they may look like, represent types of human behavior, and the events in which they participate represent human activities we recognize as characteristic of individuals, clans, organizations, and nations. The protagonists, Bilbo and Frodo Baggins, typify those gentle, kindly people who would much prefer to live in domestic obscurity but who are called on to play heroic roles in cataclysmic dramas. And the way they behave is probable, because it fits the types of people they are. They don't suddenly become supermen with supernatural powers. Like average people, they are vulnerable to superior strength and to their own fears and temptations. They succeed because they exhibit the strengths of average people: perseverance, shrewdness, unselfishness, courage, and honesty.

Of course, world views expressed in works of literature are subjective. The authors are expressing *their* views of what the real world is like. Orwell's view is very different from Tolkien's. Orwell shows an average man rebelling against social corruption and failing miserably to do anything about it. He is weak, ineffective, and controlled by forces outside himself. In Orwell's world, good loses because people are too stupid or too greedy or too weak to overcome evil. Like Orwell, Tolkien also shows the average man as weak, but in his world view, the average person is innately good and potentially strong; such individuals can band together with others like themselves and overthrow evil. Orwell is pessimistic about human nature and the future of humanity; Tolkien is optimistic.

In addition to offering a world view, literature can be true by presenting the *experience* of reality. The experience may be new or old, unique or shared by many people. Whatever it is, the author uses his or her imagination to put us in the midst of it, to make us feel it. The result is that we understand it better. Scientists don't often write novels about their research, but one who did was Björn Kurtén, the Swedish paleontologist. His novel *Dance of the Tiger: A Novel of the Ice Age* (New York: Pantheon, 1980) features the interaction of *Homo sapiens* and Neanderthal peoples during the Ice Age. Kurtén has published many scholarly books on Ice Age peoples. Why, he asks in his preface, "write a novel about prehistoric man?" He answers as follows:

> In the last three decades, it has been my privilege to be immersed in the life of the Ice Age. More and more, I have felt there is much to be told that simply cannot be formulated in scientific reports. How did it feel to live then? How did the world look to you? What were your beliefs? Above all, what was it like to meet humans not of your own species? That is an experience denied to us, for we are all *Homo sapiens*. (xxiii)

Kurtén brilliantly succeeds in bringing Ice Age peoples alive for us. Through the thoughts, conflicts, and daily activities of his characters, we feel what it was like to live 35,000 years ago.

Another example is Jessamyn West's novel *The Massacre at Fall Creek*. In the afterword she says she had long been intrigued by a historical event that occurred in Indiana in 1824. A white judge and jury convicted four white men of killing Indians, and the men were hanged. As far as West could discover, this event marked the first time in United States history that white men convicted other white men for killing Indians. But she was unable to find much historical information on this episode. She wondered what it was like to be condemned to death for something that had up to then been approved, or at least tolerated. How must the people, Indians and whites alike, have felt about the event? West's novel is an answer to these questions. We do not have a record of what these people experienced, but through an act of imagination, West shows us what they *probably* experienced, because she can assess what most people would go through under those circumstances. Furthermore, she causes us to *feel* what they experienced. We live through the killings themselves, with all their gruesome details. We share with the whites the fear of Indian reprisal. We see the callousness of hardened Indian killers. We experience the dawning realization of some whites that Indians are human beings and have rights. We suffer the alienation felt by those who take unpopular moral stands. We partake of the circuslike atmosphere of the crowd who come to see the hangings. We puzzle over the ambiguity of the ethical problem confronting the judge. We stand on the scaffold with the condemned.

An idea that underlies Jessamyn West's world view is that it is wrong to kill Indians. Or, to put it more generally, she shows that all human life is precious and therefore should not be wantonly destroyed. Like the ideas in most works of literature, this idea is not new or unusual. Compare it, for example, with Orwell's in *Nineteen Eighty-Four* (totalitarianism is dehumanizing) and Tolkien's in *The Lord of the Rings* (eternal vigilance is the price of freedom). But the abstract ideas that underlie works of literature almost *have* to be commonplace in order to be recognizable and thus universal. The profundity of literature lies in its imaginative reconstruction of the experience of commonplace ideas. We don't have to read *Anna Karenina* to learn that circumstances and moral blindness can drive a person to despair. We read it because Tolstoy, through Anna, makes us *feel what it is like* to have everything we care about taken from us little by little because of flaws in our character or because of blind chance.

Here are some questions that should help you analyze the "truths" within a work:

1. What are the work's basic ideas? Sometimes the author states them or has a character state them. Usually, however, authors present themes indirectly; you have to infer them from details in the works. Underline or mark events, dialogue, aspects of setting, or whatever seems to develop a theme. For an extended treatment of theme in a work, see the next chapter (pages 35–39).

2. What is typical about the characters in the work? What do they do and say that identify them as typical? What ideas do the characters represent? That is, do their character types, attitudes, or philosophies represent a way of looking at the world that is important in the work? One character, for example, may be worldly, wise, and tolerant, another naïve and thoughtless, another greedy and miserly, still another fatalistic and pessimistic. To which of these views does the author seem sympathetic? Which predominates at the end of the work?

3. Sometimes authors deliberately depart from the typical and probable. Why do they do so? How does this departure reflect the author's

ideas? For example, if a character is extraordinarily beautiful and graceful, the author may be using these traits to glamorize ideas the character expresses or believes.

4. What are the implications of titles and epigraphs? (An epigraph is a pertinent quotation put at the beginning of a work or chapter.) *The Grapes of Wrath* (taken from a line in "The Battle Hymn of the Republic"), *All the King's Men* (from the nursery rhyme "Humpty-Dumpty"), *Pride and Prejudice, Great Expectations,* and *Measure for Measure* are examples of titles that represent the authors' judgment of what their works are about. What do these titles mean when applied to the contents of the work?

5. What themes does the author develop in other works? Sometimes you must read more than one work by an author to reconstruct the author's world view. Reading literary criticism is helpful here, because often the critics have already done the work for you; they have read an author's works and have drawn conclusions about themes.

6. What has the author said about the work—in speeches, interviews, lectures, and essays? These may be worth seeking out, especially if the work is puzzling. Flannery O'Connor's comments about "A Good Man Is Hard to Find" are very revealing about the story's possible meaning.

7. What has your instructor said about the meaning of the work? These comments, of course, also provide insights into the work's meaning. Mark those sections the instructor calls to your attention in class and reread them.

## Literature Is Expressive

Literature is an expression of the individuals who write it. Their personalities, emotions, and beliefs are bound up in their works. Some authors may try to reduce their presence as much as possible, so that the work seems to be merely that of a faceless observer who transcribes or mirrors reality. Shakespeare's plays and Daniel Defoe's novels have this quality. Other authors make themselves and their feelings the obvious subject matter of their work. William Wordsworth, who wrote that poetry "is the spontaneous overflow of powerful feelings," is one example. Lord Byron and Thomas Wolfe are others but whatever authors decide about the relationship between themselves and their subject matter, they inevitably stamp it with those qualities that belong uniquely to them. When we read their works, we feel the force of their character and personality.

One result of the expressive aspect of literature is that we may be drawn to a work because we are drawn to the author. We are charmed or impressed by the author's presence in the work, and we may read other works by that writer because we want to experience more of him or her. We may read Jane Austen to experience Jane Austen, Ernest Hemingway to experience Ernest Hemingway. Another result—sometimes intended by the author—is that, through the work, we experience events and emotional reactions that may be outside our own experience. The work thus broadens the range of our experience.

The expressive element in works of literature is often elusive. It may be solely a matter of language, whereby the author maintains a consistent style from work to work. Jane Austen, for example, is witty and ironic. Or it may be a philosophical outlook that carries over from work to work. Or it may be an autobiographical treatment of events in the author's life. If the expressive aspect of literature interests you, your best bet is to read more than one work by an author and to read more about the author. What similarities of style, ideas, and events do you see present in the author's works? How would you characterize the author's "voice"—the author's unique way of writing? Where and how in the work does the writer make his or her presence felt and his or her ideas known?

## Literature Is Affective

Often related to the expressive aspect of literature is its *affective* aspect—that is, its ability to create an emotional response in the reader. The aesthetic experience discussed earlier is itself emotional, but other elements of literature create emotional reactions as well. As with the expressive aspect, the degree to which literature is affective varies from author to author. Some writers try to make their works as unemotional and intellectual as possible. Alexander Pope's poetry, for example, appeals to our reasoning ability and to our interest in witty wordplay. Henry James's novels present moral problems that take on the quality of complicated puzzles. In contrast, other works are much in sentiment; they want us to feel deeply and sometimes to do something about the situations that evoke feelings in us, as in the case of reform fiction such as Charles Dickens's *Oliver Twist* and Harriet Beecher Stowe's *Uncle Tom's Cabin*. Some literary forms—tragedy, comedy, melodrama, the lament, the elegy—strive to elicit fairly specific emotional reactions from us.

The expressive and affective aspects of literature often work together. The author makes the reader feel what the author has felt. In *Native Son,* Richard Wright puts us in the shoes of a young African-American man living in an urban ghetto. He intends for us to be shocked by the violent crimes Bigger Thomas commits. But then he wants us to feel what it is like to be a victim of racism and, by feeling it, to see this victimization as a cause of Bigger's crimes. Wright is African-American, and his point is that the frustration and hatred Bigger Thomas feels are typical of the way many African-Americans feel, even though most have not committed violent crimes as Bigger has. Wright makes us aware of his feelings by causing us, through his novel, to feel what he has felt.

You can uncover the affective elements in works of literature in several ways. The most obvious is to ask, What emotions did the work raise in me? Another way is to ask, What emotional impact has the work had on others? Sometimes this impact is a matter of historical record, something you can read about, as in the case of the effect *Uncle Tom's Cabin* had on readers before the Civil War. You can also simply ask people questions: How did you like this book? How did it make you feel? Once you identify the emotional reactions the work typically draws from readers, you might ask, What reactions do you think the author was *trying* to create? Does the work achieve this effect?

## FOR FURTHER STUDY

Defining literature is an intriguing but prickly enterprise. Any definition raises objections and counterdefinitions. This chapter conforms largely to the view of literature in the opening section of René Wellek and Austin Warren's *Theory of Literature* (New York: Harcourt, 1942). Two works that take different and stimulating approaches are Terry Eagleton's *Literary Theory: An Introduction* (Minneapolis: University of Minnesota Press, 1983) and John M. Ellis's *The Theory of Literary Criticism: A Logical Analysis* (Berkeley: University of California Press, 1974).

# 3

# Analyzing Fiction

This chapter begins an analysis of the three major genres of literature: fiction, drama, and poetry. The word *genre* comes from French and means "type" or "kind." To identify literary genres is to classify literature into its kinds. Literary critics sometimes disagree about how to classify literature into genres. Some say the genres of literature are tragedy, comedy, lyric poetry, satire, the elegy, and so forth. But for our purpose, we will classify literature into three broad "kinds": fiction, drama, and poetry. This chapter begins with the most popular genre, fiction.

Although literary genres are interesting subjects in themselves, our purpose in this and the next two chapters is to identify things to think about that can help you interpret works of literature. To that end, we will look at many of the best known elements that characterize fiction, drama, and poetry. Your goal when you interpret elements of literature should not be to consider and comment on *every* element of a work. Although all the elements of a work contribute to its meanings, probably only several will stand out to you as the most important. Focusing on one or more of these is a fruitful strategy for discovering meaning in texts. The questions and "Thinking on Paper" exercises that follow the discussions of each element should help you do this. Furthermore, each of the sample essays in Chapter 14 illustrates how you can develop an interpretation by examining a single element of a work.

## THE NATURE OF FICTION

As a descriptive term, *fiction* is misleading, for although fiction does often include made-up or imaginary elements, it has the potential for being "true": true to the nature of reality, true to human experience. The intellectual activity that most resembles fiction is history. Writers of history and fiction attempt to create a world that resembles the multiplicity and complexity of the real world. Both attempt to speculate about the nature of the real world. But fiction is different from history in important ways, and these differences help reveal fiction's nature and uniqueness.

The most obvious difference is that writers of fiction can make up facts but that historians must take facts as they find them. In works of history, historians cannot manufacture facts to fill in the gaps of their knowledge. Consequently, the fictional world is potentially more complete and coherent than the historical world. Not only can writers of fiction produce facts at will, they can produce them to fit a coherent plan. If they have an optimistic view of reality, for example, writers can include only positive and affirming facts. Furthermore, they can know more about their worlds than historians (or anyone else) can know about the real world. They can enter their characters' minds, look into the heavens, create chains of cause and effect, and foresee the future. A second difference is that writers of fiction must establish some principle of order or coherence that underlies their work. They must establish at least an aesthetic order, and they may also impose a philosophical order upon their materials. Although historians often do both, they need do neither. Like newspaper reporters, historians need only record events as they occur, no matter how unrelated or senseless they may seem. A third difference is that writers of fiction must build conflict into their worlds, whereas historians need not. The events of history are not inevitably characterized by conflict, but the events of fiction always are.

All three of these differences point to qualities that make fiction enjoyable—its imaginative, orderly, and dramatic qualities. Two more differences reveal an equally important aspect of fiction—the kinds of reality it deals with and thus the kinds of truth it attempts to expose. The fourth difference, then, is that writers of fiction celebrate the separateness, distinctness, and importance of all individuals and all individual experiences. They assume that human experiences, whatever they are and wherever they occur, are intrinsically important and interesting. In contrast, historians record and celebrate human experiences that affect or represent large numbers of people—wars, rises and falls of civilizations, technological innovations, economic developments, political changes, and social tastes and mores. If historians discuss individuals at all, it is because they affect or illustrate these wider experiences. Henry Fleming, the protagonist of Stephen Crane's novel *The*

*Red Badge of Courage,* has no historical importance. As far as history is concerned, he is an anonymous participant in the Civil War battle of Chancellorsville, one soldier among thousands. Even his deeds, thoughts, and feelings do not necessarily represent those of the typical soldier at Chancellorsville. Yet, in the fictional world, they are important because they are *his* deeds, thoughts, and feelings. We are interested in him not for his connection with an important historical event but simply because he is a human being.

Finally, a fifth difference is that writers of fiction see reality as welded to psychological perception, as refracted through the minds of individuals. In contrast, historians present reality as external to individuals and thus as unaffected by human perception. Both historians and writers of fiction, for example, deal with time. But time for the historian is divisible into exact, measurable units—centuries, decades, years, months, weeks, days, hours, minutes, seconds. Time, for historians, is a river in which individuals float like so many pieces of driftwood. In contrast, writers of fiction present time as an experienced, emotional phenomenon, as a river flowing *inside* the mind. Its duration is not scientifically measurable but rather is determined by states of mind, the familiar when-I-am-happy-time-goes-fast, when-I-am-sad-time-goes-slowly phenomenon. Other aspects of reality take on a similar psychological dimension within works of fiction. A house may not be haunted, but the character perceives it as such out of fear and anxiety. A mountain may not be steep, but the character perceives it as such out of fatigue and aching muscles.

## THE ELEMENTS OF FICTION

The above explanation of the nature of fiction should help you know generally what to expect from it. But fiction, poetry, and drama all have more specific characteristics, and knowing what these are will help you identify and think about them as you read. The rest of this chapter includes definitions of the elements of fiction. Following each discussion are questions and "Thinking on Paper" exercises. Use these definitions, questions, and exercises to develop your ideas about works of fiction.

### Plot

Put simply, *plot* is what happens in a narrative. But this definition is too simple. A mere listing of events, even in the order in which they occur, is not plot. Rather, writers of fiction arrange fictional events into patterns. They select these events carefully, they establish causal relationships among events, and they enliven these events with conflict. A more complete and accurate definition, then, is that plot is a pattern of carefully selected, causally related events that contains conflict.

Although writers of fiction arrange events into many patterns, the most common is that represented by the *Freytag pyramid,* shown below, which was developed by the German critic Gustav Freytag in 1863. Although Freytag meant this diagram to describe a typical five-act tragedy, it may be adapted to apply to most works of fiction. At the beginning of this pattern is an *unstable situation,* a conflict that sets the plot in motion. The author's *exposition* here explains the nature of the conflict. He or she introduces the characters, describes the setting, and provides historical background. The author next introduces a series of *events,* all related by cause. One event may cause another event, which in turn causes another event, which causes the next event (husband gets angry with wife, who gets angry with kids, who get angry with dog, who sulks in the basement). Or several events may be linked to the same cause (a series of deaths at the beach, all caused by a monster killer shark). Whatever the causal relationship among events, each event intensifies the conflict so that the plot "rises" toward a *climax.*

The climax is the most intense event in the narrative. The rest of the story—the *falling action*—is usually brief. It contains events that are much less intense than the climax and that lead toward the resolution of the conflict and toward a *stable situation* at the end. Another term for falling action is *dénouement,* a French word meaning "unravelling."

An example of the Freytag pyramid is the stereotypical fairy tale in which the youngest son must seek his fortune (unstable situation: He has no source of income, no home). He goes into a far country whose king is offering a prize, the hand of his daughter for anyone who can ac-

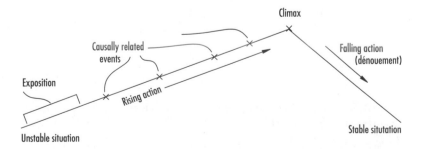

complish three tasks. The hero completes all three (rising action and climax: Each task is increasingly difficult, but the third is a humdinger). The king praises the hero but does not want his daughter to marry a commoner. The hero reveals that he is not, as he seems, a mere peasant but the son of a nobleman (falling action/dénouement: The conflicts now are minor and easily resolved). The hero marries the princess and lives happily ever after (stable situation: The hero has eliminated the initial conflict; he now has a wife, a source of income, and a home).

There are two general categories of conflict: external and internal. *Internal conflicts* take place within the minds of characters. An example is the good person who wrestles inwardly with temptation. *External conflicts* take place between individuals or between individuals and the world external to individuals (the forces of nature, human-created objects, and environments). The climactic shootout in an American western is an example of a physical, external conflict, but not all external conflicts are physical or violent. A verbal disagreement between two people is also an external conflict.

The forces in a conflict are usually embodied by characters, the most relevant being the protagonist and the antagonist. The term *protagonist* usually means "main character," but it might be helpful sometimes to think of the protagonist as someone who is fighting for something. The *antagonist* is the opponent of the protagonist; the antagonist is usually a person, but can also be a nonhuman force or even an aspect of the protagonist—his or her tendency toward evil and self-destruction, for example. Although a protagonist sometimes fights for evil—Macbeth, for example—we usually empathize with the protagonist and find the antagonist unsympathetic.

**Questions about plot**   Probably the most revealing question you can ask about a work of literature is, What conflicts does it dramatize? For fiction, this is a crucial question. You can break it down into subquestions, each of which might produce interesting ideas: What is the main conflict? What are the minor conflicts? How are all the conflicts related? What causes the conflicts? Which conflicts are external, which internal? Who is the protagonist? What qualities or values does the author associate with each side of the conflict? Where does the climax occur? Why? How is the main conflict resolved? Which conflicts go unresolved? Why?

An example of how you can use these questions to interpret fiction is Ernest Hemingway's story "Hills Like White Elephants." The story consists almost entirely of a dialogue between a young woman and man who are waiting for a train at a tiny station in the Spanish countryside. We learn that they have traveled widely, that they are intimate, that they are lovers—but they are in conflict. About what? The conflict they bring out into the open and discuss aloud concerns an abortion. The woman is pregnant, and the man urges her to have an abortion. He keeps telling her that the abortion will be "simple," "perfectly natural," and will make them "all right" and "happy." But she resists. She asks if after the abortion "things will be like they were and you'll love me." She says that they "could get along" without the abortion.

Gradually we realize that although the immediate conflict is over the abortion, there is a deeper, unspoken conflict. This more important conflict—the main conflict—is over the nature of their relationship. The man wants the abortion because it will allow him to continue the rootless and uncommitted relationship he has enjoyed with the woman up to now. The woman, however, wants a more stable relationship, one that having the child would affirm, one that she has apparently believed the man wanted too. Hemingway resolves the conflict by having the woman realize, in the face of the man's continued insistence on the abortion, that the relationship she wants with the man is impossible.

Examining the story's main conflict in this way helps to reveal several important things about the story. At first glance, it seems to have little "action," but examining the conflict reveals what its action is. Studying the conflict also helps to illuminate the characters: The man is selfish and obstinate; the woman is idealistic and somewhat innocent. Analyzing the conflict points to the meaning or theme of the story. Hemingway seems to support the woman's view of the way a loving relationship should be. He makes her the protagonist, the more sympathetic character of the two. Because examining conflict in works of literature is crucial to understanding them, such a study is a rich source of interpretations, perhaps the richest. This discussion of "Hills Like White Elephants" is but one of many examples of what an essay might do with conflict.

## ■ Thinking on Paper about Plot

1. On one side of a piece of paper, list the external conflicts of the work. On the other side, list the internal conflicts. Draw a line between the external and internal conflicts that seem related.

2. List the key conflicts. For each conflict, list the ways in which the conflict has been resolved, if it has.

3. Describe the turning point or climax. Explain what conflicts are resolved. List the conflicts that are left unresolved.

4. List the major structural units of the work (chapters, scenes, parts). Summarize what happens in each unit.

5. List the qualities of the protagonist and antagonist.

6. Describe the qualities that make the situation at the beginning unstable. Describe the qualities that make the conclusion stable.

7. List the causes of the unstable situations at the beginning and throughout the work.

## Characterization

Characters are the people in narratives, and *characterization* is the author's presentation and development of characters. Sometimes, as in fantasy fiction, the characters are not people. They may be animals, robots, or creatures from outer space, but the author gives them human abilities and human psychological traits. They really are people in all but outward form.

There are two broad categories of character development: simple and complex. The critic and fiction writer E. M. Forster coined alternate terms for these same categories: *flat* (simple) and *round* (complex) characters. Flat characters have only one or two personality traits and are easily recognizable as stereotypes—the shrewish wife, the lazy husband, the egomaniac, the stupid athlete, the shyster, the miser, the redneck, the bum, the dishonest used-car salesman, the prim aristocrat, the absent-minded professor. Round characters have multiple personality traits and therefore resemble real people. They are much harder to understand and describe than flat characters. No single description or interpretation can fully contain them. An example of a flat character is Washington Irving's Ichabod Crane, the vain and superstitious schoolmaster of "The Legend of Sleepy Hollow." An example of a round character is Shakespeare's Hamlet. To an extent, all literary characters are stereotypes. Even Hamlet is a type, the "melancholy man." But round characters have many more traits than just those associated with their general type. Because it takes time to develop round characters convincingly, they are more often found in longer works than in shorter ones.

Authors reveal what characters are like in two general ways: directly or indirectly. In the *direct* method, the author simply tells the reader what the character is like. Here, for example, is Jane Austen telling us very early in her novel *Pride and Prejudice* what Mrs. Bennet is like:

> She was a woman of mean understanding, little information, and uncertain temper. When she was discontented she fancied herself nervous. The business of her life was to get her daughters married; its solace was visiting and news.

When the method of revealing characters is *indirect,* however, the author shows us, rather than tells us, what the characters are like through what they say about one another, through external details (dress, bearing, looks), and through their thoughts, speech, and deeds.

Characters who remain the same throughout a work are called *static* characters. Those who change during the course of the work are called *dynamic* characters. Usually, round characters change and flat characters remain the same, but not always. Shakespeare's Sir John Falstaff (in *Henry IV, Part I* and *Part II* ), a round character, is nonetheless static. Dynamic characters, especially main characters, typically grow in understanding. The climax of this growth is an *epiphany,* a term that James Joyce used to describe a sudden revelation of truth experienced by a character. The term comes from the Bible and describes the Wise Men's first perception of Christ's divinity. Joyce applied it to fictional characters. His own characters, like Gabriel Conroy in "The Dead," perfectly illustrate the concept. Often, as in "The Dead," the epiphany occurs at the climax of the plot.

**Questions about characters**    You can ask many revealing questions about characters and the way they are portrayed: Are they flat, round, dynamic, or static? Do they change? How and why do they change? What steps do they go through to change? What events or moments of self-revelation produce these changes? What do they learn? Does what they learn help or hinder them? What problems do they have? How do they attempt to solve them? What types do they represent? If they are complex, what makes them complex? Do they have traits that contradict one another and therefore cause internal conflicts? Do they experience epiphanies? When, why, and what do their epiphanies reveal—to themselves and to us? How do they relate to one another? Do the characters have speech mannerisms, gestures, or modes of dress that reveal their inner selves? Is the character sad, happy, or in-between?

The overriding questions that any character analysis attempts to answer are simply, What is the character like? What are the character's traits? Consider the example of the woman in Hemingway's "Hills Like White Elephants," discussed earlier in this chapter. Hemingway drops hints that indicate something about her personality. She compares the Spanish hills to white elephants, a comparison that at first seems capricious but later suggests an imaginative, even artistic, quality that the man cannot comprehend. After she senses the man's true motivation for wanting the abortion, she looks out over the fields of ripe grain, the trees, the river, and the mountains beyond, and tells the man that "we could have all this" but that "every day we make it more impossible." She seems to connect the appreciation of nature—the sympathy they could feel for it—with the moral quality of their relationship. But because their relationship must remain superficial, she says that the landscape "isn't ours any more." Once again, the man lacks the imagination to make the connection, and he fails to grasp her moral point. Hemingway seems to admire the woman's ability to make these comparisons. It underscores her more obvious and admirable desire for a profound and lasting relationship. Another thing we learn about the woman is that she is a dynamic character. At the beginning of the story, she does not fully recognize the falseness of her relationship with the man. She seems genuinely to hope for something better. By the end of the story, however, she knows the truth and, from all appearances, has changed as a result. At the beginning she is innocent and dependent upon the man for her happiness; by the end she has lost her innocence and has become independent.

## ■ Thinking on Paper about Characterization

1. List the traits of the main characters in the story.

2. Describe the ways the author reveals the traits of a character.

3. Write a description of a complex character in which you try to account for every trait of the character.

4. Describe the emotional reaction a character has to an important event or events.

5. Write a paragraph explaining why a character changes.

6. Describe the scene in which a character has an epiphany. Explain what happens and what the character comes to see.

7. Mark the places in which the author or other characters make revealing statements about a character.

## Theme

Theme is perhaps the most obvious statement of the "truth" of a work. This discussion of theme, then, is a continuation of the discussion in Chapter 2 (on pages 20–24) of how literature is true. *Theme* is a central idea in the work—whether fiction, poetry, or drama. It is a comment the work makes on the human condition. It deals with four general areas of human experience: the nature of humanity, the nature of society, the nature of humankind's relationship to the world, and the nature of our ethical responsibilities. Theme answers questions such as these: Are human beings innately "sinful" or "good"? Does fate (environment, heredity, circumstance) control us, or do we control it? What does a particular social system or set of social practices (capitalism, socialism, feudalism, middle-class values and practices, genteel English country life, urban life, rural life, bureaucracy) do for—and to—its members? What is right conduct and wrong conduct, and how do we know?

For many readers, theme is an attractive element because it gives works meaning; it makes them relevant. But searching for theme has its pitfalls. To avoid them you should know several characteristics of theme. First, the theme of a work is *not* the same as the subject or topic of a work. Learn to distinguish between them. The *subject* is what the work is about. You can state the subject in a word or phrase. The subject of Shakespeare's Sonnet 116 (page 104) is love. In contrast, theme is what the work *says* about the subject. The statement of a work's theme requires a complete sentence, sometimes several sentences. The theme of Sonnet 116 is "Love remains constant whether assaulted by tempestuous events or by time."

Second, a work's theme must apply to people outside the work. For example, it is incorrect to say that the theme of "Rip Van Winkle" is "Rapid change in his environment threatens Rip's identity." This statement is true, but it is not the theme. You must state the theme in such a way as to include people in general, not just the characters in the story. A correctly stated theme for "Rip Van Winkle," then, would be "Rapid change in environment causes *many people* to feel their identity is threatened." Stating the theme in a work of literature means that you move from concrete situations within the work to generalizations about people outside the work. In this way, literature becomes a form of philosophy—universal wisdom about the nature of reality.

A third characteristic of theme is that there may be several, possibly even contradictory, themes in a work. This is especially true of complex works. A subject of Tolstoy's *Anna Karenina* is sacred versus profane love. But another, equally important subject is social entrapment. One theme of *Anna Karenina,* then, seems to be that people should not abandon "sacred" commitments, such as marriage and parenthood, for extramarital "loves," no matter how passionate and deeply felt they may be. This theme emerges from Anna's desertion of her husband and child for Count Vronsky. An alternate theme is that people, through little fault of their own, can become trapped in painful, long-lasting, and destructive relationships that they want desperately to escape. This theme emerges from Anna's marriage. When she was very young, Anna married an older man whom she now realizes is too petty, prim, and self-absorbed to satisfy her generous and passionate nature. So discordant is her relationship with her husband that it seems no less "immoral" than her affair with Vronsky. Tolstoy, in other words, draws complex, even contradictory lessons from Anna's adultery. She is not simply the sinful person; she is also the driven person. This combination of traits characterizes the condition of many people.

Fourth, some works may not have a subject or a theme. There may be so many contradictory or incompletely developed elements in a work that it seems impossible to say for sure what the work means. Examples of such works are Edgar Allan Poe's "The Raven" and "The Fall of the House of Usher."

Fifth, the subjects and themes of complex works can rarely be covered completely. Even when the author says what the work means, you cannot exclude other possibilities. To get at a work's theme, you must seek patterns in the concrete world that the author creates. You must extrapolate from the evidence. But you can rarely see all the evidence at once or see all the possible patterns that are inherent in the work. The best you can do is support your interpretations as logically and with as much evidence as you can. You may disagree with the author's conclusions about a given subject—with his or her theme. Your job is first to identify and understand the work's theme and then, if you are writing about it, to represent it fairly. To do this, however, is not necessarily to agree with the work. You are always free to disagree with an author's world view.

Sixth, theme may be a presentation of a problem rather than a moral or message that neatly solves the problem. Robert Penn Warren's novel *All the King's Men,* for example, raises the problem of morality in politics. A question the novel seems to ask is, How can political leaders in a democratic society do good when citizens are apathetic and easily misled? The character who embodies this question is a well-meaning and gifted politician who uses corrupt and violent means to attain good ends. By telling his story, Warren dramatizes the question. But he never really answers it. You cannot pull a neat moral out of the story of this character's rise and fall. Rather, to state the "theme" of this novel—or one theme—you need to summarize as accurately as you can the problem

Warren presents in the way he presents it. You could explain how the problem is worked out in this one character's life, but you could not necessarily generalize from that to all people's lives.

**Questions about theme**    The key questions for eliciting a work's theme are, What is the subject (that is, what is the work about)? Then, What is the theme (that is, what does the work say about the subject)? And, finally, In what direct and indirect ways does the work communicate its theme? In "Hills Like White Elephants," Hemingway does not state his subject and theme directly, but given his development of conflict and characterization, it seems fair to say that his subject is love (or loving relationships) and that one possible theme might be something like this: "Loving relationships are impossible without unselfish commitment from both partners."

We said that theme deals with four areas of human experience. A strategy for discovering a work's theme is to apply questions about these areas to the work. Here are some suggestions:

**The nature of humanity.** What image of humankind emerges from the work? From the way the author presents characters, can you tell if the author thinks people are "no damned good" (Mark Twain's phrase), or does the author show people as having redeeming traits? If people are good, what good things do they do? If they are flawed, how and to what extent are they so?

**The nature of society.** Does the author portray a particular society or social scheme as life-enhancing or life-destroying? Are characters we care about in conflict with their society? Do they want to escape from it? What causes and perpetuates this society? If the society is flawed, how is it flawed?

**The nature of humankind's relationship to the world.** What control over their lives do the characters have? Do they make choices in complete freedom? Are they driven by forces beyond their control? Does Providence or some grand scheme govern history, or is history simply random and arbitrary?

**The nature of our ethical responsibilities.** What are the moral conflicts in the work? Are they clear cut or ambiguous? That is, is it clear to us exactly what is right and exactly what is wrong? When moral conflicts are ambiguous in a work, right often opposes *right,* not wrong. What rights are in opposition to one another? If right opposes wrong, does right win in the end? To what extent are characters to blame for their actions?

Another strategy for discovering a work's theme is to answer this question: Who serves as *moral center* of the work? The moral center is the one person whom the author vests with right action and right thought (that is, what the *author* seems to think is right action and right thought), the one character who seems clearly "good" and who often serves to judge other characters. Not every work has a moral center; but in the works that do, its center can lead you to some of the work's themes. In Dickens's *Great Expectations,* for example, the moral center is Biddy, the girl who comes to Pip's sister's household as a servant. She is a touchstone of goodness for Pip, and when he strays from the good, his talks with Biddy and his remembrance of her help bring him back to it. *Great Expectations* is largely about morality (subject), and by studying Biddy we can uncover some of Dickens's ideas about morality (theme).

When identifying a work's moral center, answer questions such as these: What does the author do to identify this person as the moral center? (Part of your argument may simply be to show that a character is indeed the moral center.) What values does the moral center embody? Is the moral center flawed in any way that might diminish his or her authority? What effect does the moral center have on the other characters and on us?

## ■ Thinking on Paper about Theme

1. List the subject or subjects of the work. For each subject, see if you can state a theme. Put a check next to the ones that seem most important.

2. Explain how the title, subtitle, epigraph, and names of characters may be related to theme.

3. Describe the work's depiction of human behavior.

4. Describe the work's depiction of society. Explain the representation of social ills and how they might be corrected or addressed.

5. List the moral issues raised by the work.

6. Name the character who is the moral center of the work. List his or her traits.

7. Mark statements by the author or characters that seem to state themes.

## Setting

*Setting* includes several closely related aspects of a work of fiction. First, setting is the physical, sensuous world of the work. Second, it is the time in which the action of the work takes place. And third, it is the social environment of the characters: the manners, customs, and moral values that govern the characters' society. A fourth aspect—"atmosphere"—is largely, but not entirely, an effect of setting.

**Questions about place**   You should first get the details of the physical setting clear in your mind. Where does the action take place? On what planet, in what country or locale? What sensuous qualities does the author give to the setting? What does it look like, sound like, feel like? Do you receive a dominant impression about the setting? What impression, and why?

Once you have answered these questions, you can move on to a more interesting one: What relationship does place have to characterization and theme? In some fiction, geographical location seems to have no effect on characters. Indoors or out, in one locale or another, they behave the same. In other works, such as those by Thomas Hardy or Joseph Conrad, place affects the characters profoundly. In the story, "Among the Cornrows," Hamlin Garland depicts the relationship of environment to the process of making decisions:

> A cornfield in July is a hot place. The soil is hot and dry; the wind comes across the lazily murmuring leaves laden with a warm sickening smell drawn from the rapidly growing, broad-flung banners of the corn. The sun, nearly vertical, drops a flood of dazzling light and heat upon the field over which the cool shadows run, only to make the heat seem the more intense.
>
> Julia Peterson, faint with fatigue, was toiling back and forth between the corn rows, holding the handles of the double-shovel corn plow while her little brother Otto rode the steaming horse. Her heart was full of bitterness, and her face flushed with heat, and her muscles aching with fatigue. The heat grew terrible. The corn came to her shoulders, and not a breath seemed to reach her, while the sun, nearing the noon mark, lay pitilessly upon her shoulders, protected only by a calico dress. The dust rose under her feet, and as she was wet with perspiration it soiled her till, with a woman's instinctive cleanliness, she shuddered. Her head throbbed dangerously. What matter to her that the king bird pitched jovially from the maples to catch a wandering bluebottle fly, that the robin was feeding

its young, that the bobolink was singing? All these things, if she saw them, only threw her bondage to labor into greater relief.

Garland shows geographical environment pressuring Julia Peterson into a decision that will affect the rest of her life. Garland has already told us that Julia Peterson's parents treat her harshly and force her to work too hard. By emphasizing one sensuous quality, the heat, Garland makes us feel the hardship of her life. She has dreamed of a handsome suitor who will take her away from the farm and give her a life of ease, but the heat makes her feel that anything would be better than this misery. So when a young farmer happens along just after the incident described here and offers her a life of respect and only normal difficulty, she marries him. Garland shows that Julia's environment leads her to settle for less than what she really wants. She is not free to choose exactly as she would choose.

**Questions about time**   Three kinds of time occur in fiction, thus three types of questions about time are important. First, at what period in history does the action take place? Many stories occur during historical events that affect the characters and themes in important ways. Margaret Mitchell's *Gone with the Wind* and Tolstoy's *War and Peace* are examples. To answer this question, you may have to do background reading about the historical period. Tolstoy and Mitchell give you a great deal of historical information in their fiction, but many authors do not. In either case, you may need to supplement facts in the work with what you can find out elsewhere.

Second, how long does it take for the action to occur? That is, how many hours, days, weeks, years are involved? Authors often use the passage of time as a thematic and structuring device: the mere fact that some specific amount of time has passed may be important for understanding characters. Years go by in Alice Walker's *The Color Purple*, for example, allowing her characters to grow and change. But because of her method of telling the stories—through letters—we are not immediately aware of how much time passes until near the end of the book. Because we read the letters one after the other, we get the illusion of time passing quickly. In fact, the letters are written at long intervals, which means that we must consciously slow down the time of the novel to understand its effect on the characters. What clues, then, does the author give to indicate how much time is passing? Is the passage of time in the work relevant to characterization and theme? Is it important to the plausibility of the plot? If an author seems to obscure how much time is passing, why? Does the author use time as a structuring device?

Third, how is the passage of time perceived? Time may seem to move very slowly or very quickly, depending on a character's state of mind. Thus our recognition of how a character perceives time helps us understand the character's internal conflicts and attitudes.

In *Jane Eyre,* for example, Charlotte Brontë intertwines length of time and perception of time. Jane, the narrator, describes her stays at various "houses." She spends about the same amount of time at each house, but the length of her description of each stay is proportional to the value she places on it. She devotes 100 pages (in the Penguin edition) to her stays with the Reeds and at Lowood and 100 pages to her stay with the Rivers family. But she devotes 235 pages to her stay at Thornfield, where she falls in love with Mr. Rochester. The effect of these unequal proportions is to slow down the time spent at Thornfield and thus to emphasize Jane's emotional reaction to the experiences she has there.

Brontë uses this slowing-down method with specific events as well. In fact, the novel is a collection of highly charged, intensely felt moments in Jane's life that seem to last far longer than they actually do. The novel opens, for example, with Jane's imprisonment in the hated "red room" of the Reed mansion. As her anger subsides, she becomes aware that the room is "chill," "silent," and "solemn." She recalls that Mr. Reed died there. In a mirror she sees her "glittering eyes of fear moving where all else was still." Daylight "forsakes" the room. She feels "oppressed, suffocated" at thoughts of Mr. Reed's death and the possibility of her own. When she sees a light on the wall, she thinks it is a ghost. She screams. Mrs. Reed rushes to check on her. She thrusts Jane back into the room and locks the door. Jane faints from hysteria. The length of this description corresponds to Jane's perception of time, which in turn corresponds to her fear of the room. Each detail is like the tick of a loud clock.

What, then, is the relationship between the length of narrated events and the amount of time in which they occur? Is the author purposely slowing down or speeding up our perception of time? Why? What mental states or internal conflicts does a character's perception of time reveal?

**Questions about social environment**    Often the social environment represented in a work is of little importance. Sometimes, in fact, there is virtually no social environment. When it does seem important, an interpretation could emerge from these questions: What is the social environment portrayed in the work—the manners, mores, customs, rituals, and codes of conduct of a society? What does the author seem to think about them? (Approving? Ambivalent? Disapproving?) How do they affect the characters? Sinclair Lewis spends much of his novel *Babbitt* describing the social environment of his fictional midwestern city, Zenith. Then he shows that the pressure to conform to this environment is almost irresistible. His characters sometimes want to rebel against this pressure, but they are too weak to do so without extreme guilt or without threat to their economic and social security. Their social environment determines their behavior and entraps them.

**Questions about atmosphere**    *Atmosphere* refers to the emotional reaction that we and—usually—the characters have to the setting of a work. Sometimes the atmosphere is difficult to define, but it often is found or felt in the sensuous quality of the setting. Our emotional reaction to the Hamlin Garland passage above is pain, discomfort, weariness, and oppression, mainly because of his emphasis on the thermal sense, the sense of hot and cold. Your most fruitful questions about atmosphere will probably be, What methods does the author use to create the work's atmosphere? What does the author achieve by creating this atmosphere? Why does the author create this particular atmosphere? Sometimes, the author's purpose may simply be to play upon your emotions. Poe, for example, wants to scare us. Garland's purpose, however, is more meaningful. He seems to want to convince us of a philosophical point: Physical environment affects human behavior. Joseph Conrad in *Heart of Darkness* creates an atmosphere of mystery, foreboding, and imminent danger to reflect his hatred of colonialism and his belief that "civilized" people are capable of the worst barbarities.

## ■ Thinking on Paper about Setting

1. Mark the most extensive or important descriptions of physical place. Underline the most telling words and phrases.

2. Characterize physical locales, such as houses, rooms, and outdoor areas.

3. Explain the relationship to the physical place that one or more of the main characters has. Explain the influence that place exerts on the characters.

4. Arrange the main events in chronological order. Indicate when each event occurs.

5. Mark passages where a character's emotional state affects the way the passage of time is presented to us.

6. List the historical circumstances and characters that occur in the work. Explain their importance.

7. List the patterns of behavior that characterize the social environment of the work. For example, people drink heavily, go to church, have tea, gamble, throw parties, get in fights, marry, have children, cheat in business, wander restlessly, and so forth.

8. Mark scenes in which the author or characters express approval or disapproval of these patterns of behavior.

9. Explain the influence one or more of these patterns has on a character or characters.

10. Mark sections that contribute to atmosphere. Underline key words and phrases.

11. List the traits of the atmosphere.

## Point of View

*Point of view* is the author's relationship to his or her fictional world, especially to the minds of the characters. Put another way, point of view is the position from which the story is told. There are four common points of view, four positions the author can adopt in telling the story.

**Omniscient point of view**   In the omniscient position, the author—not one of the characters—tells the story, and the author assumes complete knowledge of the characters' actions and thoughts. The author can thus move at will from one place to another, one time to another, one character to another, and can even speak his or her own views directly to the reader as the work goes along. The author will tell us anything he or she chooses about the created world of the work. Many of the great eighteenth- and nineteenth-century novels use an omniscient point of view; examples are Hawthorne's *The Scarlet Letter,* Hardy's *Tess of the D'Urbervilles,* and Fielding's *Joseph Andrews.*

**Limited omniscient point of view**   When the limited omniscient position is used, the author still narrates the story but restricts (limits) his or her revelation—and therefore our knowledge—of the thoughts of all but one character. This character may be either a main or peripheral character. One name for this character is "central consciousness." A device of plot and characterization that often accompanies this point of view is the character's gradual discovery of himself or herself until the story climaxes in an epiphany (see pages 33–34). Examples of the limited omniscient point of view are Hawthorne's "Young Goodman Brown," Crane's "The Open Boat," and, for the most part, Austen's *Pride and Prejudice*. Sometimes the author restricts the point of view so severely that we see everything solely through the mind of a single character, like sunlight filtered through the leaves and branches of a tall tree. The later fiction of Henry James experiments with this severe restriction of the limited omniscient point of view. His story "The Beast in the Jungle" and his novel *The Ambassadors* are examples. Other writers, such as James Joyce, Virginia Woolf, and William Faulkner, carry James's experiments further with a "stream of consciousness" technique which puts the reader literally in the mind of a character. In the first section of Faulkner's *The Sound and the Fury* we experience the chaotic thoughts of a mentally retarded man, and we view the novel's world solely through his mind. A short story that uses a stream-of-consciousness technique is Katherine Anne Porter's "The Jilting of Granny Weatherall."

***First-person point of view*** In the first-person position, the author is even more restricted: One of the characters tells the story, eliminating the author as narrator. Whereas in the limited omniscient point of view the author can reveal anything about one character—even things the character may be dimly aware of—here, the narration is restricted to what one character *says* he or she observes. The character-narrator may be a major character who is at the center of events or a minor character who does not participate but simply observes the action. Examples of first-person narratives are Dickens's *Great Expectations,* Twain's *Huckleberry Finn,* Fitzgerald's *The Great Gatsby,* Poe's "The Cask of Amontillado," and Melville's "Bartleby the Scrivener." An unusual use of the first-person point of view is the epistolary narrative, which reveals action through letters. (An *epistle* is a letter and *epistolary* means "written in letters.") Samuel Richardson's *Pamela,* Henry James's "A Bundle of Letters," and Alice Walker's *The Color Purple* are all epistolary narratives.

***Objective (dramatic) point of view*** In the objective position, the author is more restricted than in any other. Though the author is the narrator, he or she refuses to enter the minds of any of the characters. The writer sees them (and lets us see them) as we would in real life. This point of view is sometimes called "dramatic" because we see the characters as we would the characters in a play. We learn about them from what they say and do, how they look, and what other characters say about them. But we do not learn what they think unless they tell us. This point of view is the least common of all. Examples are Ernest Hemingway's "Hills Like White Elephants" and "The Killers," Stephen Crane's "The Blue Hotel," and Shirley Jackson's "The Lottery."

**Tone**   *Tone* is also an aspect of point of view since it has a great deal to do with the narrator. Tone is the narrator's predominant attitude toward the subject, whether that subject is a particular setting, an event, a character, or an idea. The narrator conveys his or her attitude through the way narrative devices are handled, including choice of words. Sometimes the narrator will state point-blank how he or she feels about a subject; more often, the narrator's attitude is conveyed indirectly. Jack Burden, the narrator of Robert Penn Warren's *All the King's Men,* maintains a flippant and cynical tone through most of the narration. Jake Barnes, the narrator of Hemingway's *The Sun Also Rises,* maintains a stoical, hard-boiled tone. Dr. Watson, the narrator of the Sherlock Holmes stories, manifests a bemused, surprised tone.

**Questions about point of view**   Point of view is important to an understanding of a story in two main ways. First, the author may choose a particular point of view in order to emphasize one character's perception of things. Point of view also influences *our* perception of things. The omniscient narrator can tell us what a character thinks, but the limited omniscient and first-person points of view make us *experience* what the character thinks. To make the emphasis even more emphatic, an author may include several points of view in the same work. Dickens in *Bleak House* shuttles back and forth between a first-person narrative and an omniscient narrative. We see that the first-person narrator has a more limited view of things than the omniscient narrator. Point of view here becomes a means of developing character and of making a point about the limits of human perception.

Second, point of view is important when you suspect the trustworthiness of the narrator. A preliminary question is, Who tells the story? But a searching follow-up question is, Can you trust the narrator to tell you the truth about the events, characters, and setting of the story? You can almost always trust omniscient narrators. But you should be suspicious about first-person narrators and the "centers-of-consciousness" characters in limited omniscient stories. Sometimes these characters distort what they observe. Ask, then, if circumstances such as their age, education, social status, prejudices, or emotional states should make you question the accuracy or validity of what they say and think. Ask, also, if the author differentiates between his or her view of things and the characters' views.

Mark Twain makes such a distinction in *Huckleberry Finn*. When Huck sees the Grangerford house, he says, "It was a mighty nice family, and a mighty nice house, too. I hadn't seen no house out in the country before that was so nice and had so much style." He proceeds to describe the interior with awe and reverence. Although Huck is impressed with the furnishings, Twain clearly is not. We recognize Twain's attitude from the details Huck provides: the unread books, the reproductions of sentimental paintings, the damaged imitation fruit, the crockery animals, the broken clock, the painted hearth, the tablecloth "made out of beautiful oilcloth," the piano "that had tin pans in it." Huck also shows his admiration for Emmeline Grangerford's poetry by reproducing some of it to share with us. But we see, as Twain wants us to see, that the poetry is awful.

Finally, Huck is awestruck by the family's aristocratic bearing: "Col. Grangerford was a gentleman, you see. He was a gentleman all over; and so was his family. He was well born. . . . He didn't have to tell anybody to mind their manners—everybody was always good mannered where he was." Yet he fails to see, as Twain and we see, the ironic contrast between the family's good manners and its conduct of an irrational, murderous feud with another family. Twain's handling of point of view in this novel helps to develop both character and theme. By presenting Huck's credulous view of things, it develops Huck as an essentially innocent person. By ironically contrasting Twain's view to Huck's, it underscores the author's harsher and more pessimistic perception of "reality."

Once you have determined a work's point of view, ideas should emerge from two general questions: Why has the author chosen this point of view? What effects does it have on other elements of the story—theme, characterization, setting, language? Some follow-up questions are: What effect does the author's point of view have on us and the way we view the world of the work? For example, if the point of view is first person, we have a much more limited view than if it is omniscient. The omniscient point of view makes us feel as though we understand everything about the world of the work, as though everything revealed by the omniscient narrator is true. What perspective of the world, then, does the author want us to have? Also, what do we learn about the nature of human perception from the author's handling of first person and especially limited omniscience? Henry James's limited omniscience often shows people as blind to the needs and desires of other people and of themselves as well. If the point of view is first person, is the narrator telling the story to someone? If so, to whom? How do they react? What do we learn about the narrator from that fact? Try this question on Poe's "The Cask of Amontillado," for example, and see what you come up with. If the point of view is objective (dramatic), does it seem as though the narrator is emotionally uninvolved and rationally objective about the characters and events? What do we gain by not being able to enter the characters' minds?

## ■ Thinking on Paper about Point of View

1. Identify the point of view of the story. Describe how the story would change if it were told from each of the other points of view.

2. List the main characters in the story. Write a paragraph on one or more characters, explaining how the story would be different if that character were narrating it.

3. Mark places where the narrator or central consciousness differs from our view of reality or fails to see important truths that we or other characters see.

4. Mark places that are particularly expressive of the narrator's tone. List the characteristics of tone.

## Irony

Authors use irony pervasively to convey their ideas. But irony is a diverse and often complex intellectual phenomenon difficult to define in a sentence or two. Generally, *irony* makes visible a contrast between appearance and reality. More fully and specifically, it exposes and underscores a contrast between (1) what is and what **seems** to be, (2) between what is and what **ought** to be, (3) between what is and what one **wishes** to be, and (4) between what is and what one **expects** to be. Incongruity is the method of irony; opposites come suddenly together so that the disparity is obvious to discriminating readers. There are many kinds of irony, but four types are common in literature.

**Verbal irony**  Verbal irony is perhaps the most common form of irony. Most people use or hear verbal irony daily. In verbal irony, people say the opposite of what they mean. For example, if the day has been terrible, you might say, "Boy, this has been a great day!" The hearer knows that this statement is ironic because of the speaker's tone of voice and facial or bodily expressions or because the hearer is familiar with the situation and immediately sees the discrepancy between statement and actuality. Understatement and overstatement are two forms of verbal irony. In *understatement,* one minimizes the nature of something. "It was a pretty good game," one might say after seeing a no-hitter. Mark Twain's famous telegram is another example of understatement: "The reports of my death are greatly exaggerated." In *overstatement* one exaggerates the nature of something. After standing in a long line, you might say, "There were about a million people in that line!"

Why do people use verbal irony? The answer is that verbal irony is more emphatic than a point-blank statement of the truth. It achieves its effect by reminding the hearer or reader of what the opposite reality is and thus providing a scale by which to judge the present reality. Verbal irony often represents a mental agility—wit—that people find striking and, as with the Mark Twain retort, entertaining. Verbal irony in its most bitter and destructive form becomes *sarcasm,* in which the speaker condemns someone by pretending to praise him or her:

> Oh, you're a real angel. You're the noble and upright man who wouldn't think of dirtying his pure little hands with company business. But all along, behind our backs, you were just as greedy and ruthless as the rest of us.

**Situational irony**  In situational irony, the situation is different from what common sense indicates it is, will be, or ought to be. It is ironic, for example, that General George Patton should have lived through the thickest of tank battles during World War II and then, after the war, have been killed accidentally by one of his own men. It is ironic that someone we expect to be upright—a minister or judge—should be the most repulsive of scoundrels. Authors often use situational irony to expose hypocrisy and injustice. An example is Hawthorne's *The Scarlet Letter,* in which the townspeople regard the minister Arthur Dimmesdale as sanctified and angelic when in fact he shamefully hides his adultery with Hester Prynne, allowing her to take all the blame.

***Attitudinal irony***　Situational irony results from what *most* people expect, whereas attitudinal irony results from what one person expects. In attitudinal irony, an individual thinks that reality is one way when, in fact, it is a very different way. A frequent example in literature is the naïve character—Fielding's Parson Adams, Cervantes's Don Quixote, Dickens's Mr. Micawber, Voltaire's Candide—who thinks that everyone is upright and that everything will turn out for the best, when in fact the people he or she meets are consistently corrupt and the things that happen to him or her are destructive and painful.

***Dramatic irony***　Dramatic irony occurs in plays when characters state something that they believe to be true but that the audience knows to be false. An example is the play *Oedipus Rex*. Like all Greek tragedies, *Oedipus Rex* dramatizes a myth that its audiences know. Thus, when Oedipus at the beginning boasts that he will personally find and punish the reprobate who killed King Laius, the audience recognizes this boast as ironic. Oedipus does not know—but the audience does—that he himself is the unwitting murderer of Laius. Although dramatic irony gets its name from drama, it can occur in all forms of literature. The key to the existence of dramatic irony is the reader's foreknowledge of coming events. Many works become newly interesting when you reread them, because you now know what will happen while the characters do not; this dramatic irony intensifies characterization and makes you aware of tensions that you could not have known about during your initial reading.

***Questions about irony***　The first question to ask is, What are the most obvious ironies in the work? The second is, How are the ironies important? What, for example, are their implications? Shirley Jackson's "The Lottery" is layered with irony. An essay might deal with one of its ironies, such as the ironic contrast between the placid country-town setting and the horrible deeds done there. The setting is everyone's nostalgic image of the ideal American small town, with its central square, post office, country store, cranky old men, gossipy housewives, laconic farmers, mischievous children, settled routine, and friendly atmosphere. Is Jackson implying, then, that "normal" American communities conduct lotteries to decide which of their members is to be destroyed by the others? The answer is probably yes, she is suggesting just this. Americans are guilty of conducting "lotteries," perhaps not exactly in this manner, but with equal arbitrariness and cruelty. Instead of making this point directly, however, she implies it through the use of irony. And she achieves a much greater emphasis than if she were to state her accusation directly. She shocks us by associating something that we all agree is horrible with a way of life that up to now we had thought was "normal" and benign. The irony packs an emotional wallop that at least gets our attention and, she hopes, will get us thinking.

Other, more specific. questions about irony are these:

**Verbal irony:** If characters constantly use verbal irony, why? What do we learn about their attitudes toward the world? Does their verbal irony usually take the form of sarcasm? Are they, then, bitter, disappointed people or simply realistic?

**Situational irony:** What are the most obvious situational ironics? Arc the characters aware of the situational ironies? At what point do they become aware of them? Should we blame the characters for creating situational ironies or not understanding them? Does the author, for example, want *us* to do something about them—to reform society and ourselves?

**Attitudinal irony:** What attitudes do the characters have that contradict reality? Are we supposed to admire the characters who misconstrue the world, or are we to blame them for being naïve and deluded? What troubles do they encounter because of their attitudes?

**Dramatic irony:** What do you know about coming events or past events in the work that the characters do not know? When and what do they say that triggers this disparity? What does the author want us to think of them when they say these things? What effect does dramatic irony have on the plot? Does it, for example, make the plot suspenseful?

## ■ Thinking on Paper about Irony

1. Mark examples of verbal irony, either by the narrator or other characters. Explain how a character's verbal irony helps characterize him or her.

2. Mark episodes in which a character's beliefs and expectations are contradicted by reality. Explain the importance to characterization of these episodes.

3. List instances of situational irony; identify people, for example, whom we expect to behave in one way but who behave quite differently. Explain the importance to theme of these instances.

## Symbolism

In the broadest sense, a symbol is something that represents something else. Words, for example, are symbols. But in literature, a *symbol* is an object that has meaning beyond itself. The object is concrete and the meanings are abstract. Fire, for example, may symbolize general destruction (as in James Baldwin's title *The Fire Next Time*), or passion (the "flames of desire"), or hell (the "fiery furnace"). Symbols, however, are not metaphors; they are not analogies that clarify abstractions, such as the following metaphor from Shakespeare's Sonnet 116: love

is an ever-fixèd mark,
That looks on tempests and is never shaken.

Here, the abstract concept (the referent) is "love" and the clarifying concrete object is the stable mark (buoy, lighthouse, rock) that tempests cannot budge. A symbol, in contrast, is a concrete object with no clear referent and thus no fixed meaning. Instead, it merely suggests the meaning and, in an odd way, partly *is* the meaning. For this reason, the meaning of symbols is difficult to pin down. And the more inexhaustible their potential meaning, the richer they are.

There are two kinds of symbol: public and private. *Public* (conventional) *symbols* are those that most people in a particular culture or community would recognize as meaning something fairly definite. Examples of public symbols are the cross, the star of David, the American eagle, flags of countries, the colors red (for "stop") and green (for "go"), and the skull and crossbones.

*Private symbols* are unique to an individual or to a single work. Only from clues in the work itself can we learn the symbolic value of the object. There are many examples of private symbols in literature. In F. Scott Fitzgerald's *The Great Gatsby,* there is an area between the posh Long Island suburbs and New York City through which the major characters drive at various times and which Fitzgerald calls a "valley of ashes." It is a desolate, gray, sterile place, and over it all broods a partly obliterated billboard advertisement that features the enormous eyes of Doctor T. J. Eckleburg, an optometrist. Fitzgerald invests this area with symbolic meaning. He associates it with moral decay, urban blight, the oppression of the poor by the wealthy, meaninglessness, hell, and violent death. At one point he connects the eyes with failure of vision, at another with God, who sees all things. But we never know exactly what the valley of ashes represents; instead, it resonates with many possible meanings, and this resonance accounts for its powerful impact on readers.

**Questions about symbolism**  Not every work uses symbols, and not every character, incident, or object in a work has symbolic value. You should ask the fundamental question, What symbols does the work seem to have? You should, however, beware of finding "symbols" where none were intended. A second question, then, is necessary to the believability of any essay you might write on symbols: How do you know they are symbols? What does the author do that gives symbolic meaning to the elements you mention? Once you answer this question to your own—and your reader's—satisfaction, you can move on to a third and more interesting question: What does the symbol mean? You could, for example, write about the symbolic meaning of rain in Hemingway's *A Farewell to Arms.* The following dialogue between Frederic Henry and Catherine Barkley strongly suggests that Hemingway intended a symbolic meaning for rain; it also suggests what the symbol represents:

> "It's raining hard" [Frederic says]
> "And you'll always love me, won't you?" [Catherine replies]
> "Yes."
> "And the rain won't make any difference?"
> "No."
> "That's good. Because I'm afraid of the rain."
> "Why? . . . Tell me."
> "All right. I'm afraid of the rain because sometimes I see me dead in it."
> "No."
> "And sometimes I see you dead in it. . . . It's all nonsense. It's only nonsense. I'm not afraid of the rain. I'm not afraid of the rain. Oh, oh, God, I wish I wasn't." She was crying. I comforted her and she stopped crying. But outside it kept on raining.

Throughout the novel, Hemingway's recurrent association of rain with destruction of all kinds broadens its significance from a mere metaphor for death to other and more general qualities such as war, fate, alienation, foreboding, doom, and "reality." Because of these associations, the last sentence of the novel is more than just a description of the weather: "After a while I went out and left the hospital and walked back to the hotel in the rain." The sentence seems to suggest that Frederic is stoically and bravely facing the harsh realities—including Catherine's death, the war, the arbitrariness and cruelty of fate—represented by the rain.

## ■ Thinking on Paper about Symbolism

1. List the symbols in the work.

2. Mark the descriptions or episodes that give the symbols meaning.

3. List each symbol's possible meanings.

## OTHER ELEMENTS

In this chapter we have treated the elements most obviously identified with fiction. But other elements are also sometimes important in fiction: dialogue, description, metaphor, poetic use of language, diction. We will discuss these other elements in the next two chapters.

## FOR FURTHER STUDY

Booth, Wayne C. *The Rhetoric of Fiction.* 2nd ed. Chicago: University of Chicago Press, 1983.

Chatman, Seymour. *Story and Discourse: Narrative Structure in Fiction and Film.* Ithaca: Cornell University Press, 1978.

Cohan, Steven, and Linda M. Shires. *Telling Stories: Theoretical Analysis of Narrative Fiction.* New York, Routledge, 1988.

Forster, E. M. *Aspects of the Novel.* New York: Harcourt, 1954.

Fowler, Alistair. *Kinds of Literature: An Introduction to the Theory of Genres and Modes.* Cambridge: Harvard UP, 1982.

Poe, Edgar Allan. Reviews of Hawthorne's *Twice-Told Tales.* Published first in *Graham's Magazine,* April and May 1842; widely reprinted since.

Scholes, Robert. *Structuralism in Literature: An Introduction.* New Haven: Yale University Press, 1982.

Stevich, Philip, ed. *The Theory of the Novel.* New York: The Free Press, 1967.

Wellek, René, and Austin Warren. *Theory of Literature.* New York: Harcourt, 1956.

While in his review of Hawthorne's *Twice-Told Tales,* Poe declares on the one hand that Hawthorne is a "man of the truest genius" and on the other hand accuses him of "plagiarism," he also lays out the theoretical basis for the modern short story. He says, among other things, that the story should create a single impression with the greatest economy of means. His essay "The Philosophy of Composition" (1846) applies much the same principles to poetry. E. M. Forster was an important twentieth-century English novelist. In *Aspects of the Novel,* Forster coins and explains the terms "flat" and "round" characters, but he does much more. It is a beautifully written, compelling defense of what he thinks constitutes good fiction. Wayne C. Booth in *The Rhetoric of Fiction* makes many cogent comments about the nature of fiction at the same time that he argues a thesis. His thesis is that fiction is rhetorical—that it offers comments on the nature of reality and uses various devices to persuade us that these comments are valid. Stevich's *The Theory of the Novel* is a collection of essays and excerpts: it represents discussions of well known elements of fiction. Wellek and Warrens *Theory of Literature* is a cogent book about the nature of literature; it discusses all the genres but is especially good on fiction. Robert Scholes in *Structuralism in Literature* offers a lucid introduction to structuralism and explains how its critical methods have been applied to fiction. Steven Cohan and Linda Shires in *Telling Stories* and Seymour Chatman in *Story and Discourse* develop their own structuralist approach to fiction. Alistair Fowler's *Kinds of Literature* is a general study of literary genres.

# 4

# Analyzing Drama

rama contains many of the elements of fiction. Like fiction, drama contains plot, characters, theme, and setting. Like fiction, drama uses irony and symbolism. And indeed, you can read a play as you would a short novel, using your imagination to fill in all the "missing" material you typically find in fiction—character description, background information, vivid action scenes. Similarly, drama often contains many of the elements of poetry, and you can read the poetic passages in plays just as you read any poetry. Because of the great similarity of drama to fiction and poetry, the definitions, questions, and exercises stated in the preceding chapter on fiction and in the following chapter on poetry are all equally valid for drama. Use them to think about the plays as you read, to study specific plays systematically, and to generate your own interpretations of the plays.

## THE NATURE OF DRAMA

Drama is different from fiction and most poetry in one essential way: It is meant to be performed. Some theorists of drama argue that a play is incomplete *until* it is performed. According to the critic Bernard Beckerman in *Dynamics of Drama,* "a play is a mere skeleton; performance fleshes out the bones." When you read a play, you miss qualities the playwright intended as a part of the play. For one thing, you miss the audience, whose physical presence and reactions to the performance influence both the performance and your perception of the play. For another, you miss the set designers' vision of the atmosphere and physical world of the play. You miss the interpretive art of the actors and the illusion they can create of real life unfolding before your eyes. You miss the physical and emotional *experience* of drama that a production can give you.

This is not to say that reading a play carefully is not worth doing. Sometimes you miss aspects of plays during performance that most people can catch only when reading the play. This is especially true of plays written in poetry. Shakespeare, for example, not only has Romeo and Juliet, when they first meet, exchange comments that play upon a complex metaphor (a pilgrim coming to a shrine), but he also molds their exchange into a sonnet. It is unlikely that a playgoer, upon hearing this exchange, would think, "Aha! That was a sonnet!" Rather, you notice poetic devices such as rhyme scheme and complex patterns of imagery only by reading carefully. Even if your purpose is to produce the play, you must read carefully, because productions are based upon interpretations of the plays. "Literary" devices such as a sonnet may not be immediately recognizable by the audience, but they provide clues to how the playwright wanted the play performed. In fact, everything in the play is a clue to its possible performance and thus deserves studious attention.

To read a play with an eye to how the play might be produced, therefore, is to understand the play as the playwright conceived it. Since we examine the elements of fiction and poetry in Chapters 3 and 5, we will concentrate in this chapter on how you can use the possible performance of drama as a means of understanding its elements.

## THE ELEMENTS OF DRAMA

### Plot

Because the playwright has only a short time (two hours or so) to develop plot and because the playwright's audience experiences the play in one sitting, with little immediate opportunity to review it, the playwright must keep the plot simple and clear enough for an audience to grasp during the length of the performance. This means that the playwright cannot indulge in numerous subplots or in intricate plot complications; otherwise the playgoer would become confused. Playwrights, therefore, limit the number of characters in the play. (The fewer the characters, the simpler the plot can be.) Playwrights also emphasize conflict to keep the audience involved in the action and establish easily discernible patterns of cause and effect.

Although the playwright can present physical action without having to use words, the action (and the conflict implicit in the action) must be understandable to the audience. The most important and almost inevitable means for doing this is *dialogue*—people talking to people. Playwrights, then, strive to make every word of dialogue help move the plot forward. The near inevitability of dialogue also means that playwrights focus largely on conflicts between people rather than conflicts between people and nonhuman forces. In contrast, fiction need not represent characters' words or thoughts and so is freer to depict conflicts between people and nonhuman forces. Jack London's short story "To Build a Fire" does give the thoughts of the protagonist; but otherwise there is no "dialogue," just the author's record of the protagonist's conflict with the harsh Yukon landscape. It would be very difficult for a play to duplicate this kind of conflict. Plays sometimes do portray conflicts between people and nonhuman forces, but these conflicts are revealed through dialogue and usually through conflicts between the characters.

Because the time and space for a presentation is limited, certain kinds of action—battles and sports activities, for example—cannot be represented fully or literally on the stage. These activities must be concentrated or symbolized. A duel onstage, for example, might represent an entire battle; a plantation house that in act one is sparkling new but in act four is ramshackled might represent the activities that have brought a once-grand family to the brink of ruin. Sometimes the playwright has activities occur offstage. A character might describe events that have just taken place, but the audience does not see these events. It learns about them only through the dialogue.

The actions that take place during the presentation of the play— onstage or offstage actions—are usually only a part of a larger series of events. Bernard Beckerman helpfully distinguishes the two sets of actions by the terms *plot* (what occurs during the play) and *story* (what occurs before, during, and after the play). The "plot" of *Oedipus Rex,* for example, is Oedipus's attempt to rid Thebes of a blight and his resulting discovery of who he is and the nature of his crimes. The "story" of the play is Oedipus's entire history, starting with his parents' attempt to kill him when he was an infant and ending with his death at Colonus. Some plays feature a plot that is only a small part (but usually a very important and climactic part) of a story. Other plays feature a plot that is almost equivalent to the story. Shakespeare's *Macbeth,* for example, has almost no important past and future events; nearly all the action occurs within the play itself. Thus the plot and story of *Macbeth* are nearly equivalent. The events in *Hamlet,* however, occur after a murder and a marriage and, long before that, a war between Denmark and Norway, all of which profoundly affect the action within the play itself; the conclusion of the play, furthermore, suggests something of what the future of Denmark will be like under its new ruler, the Norwegian king Fortinbras.

The plotting in drama depends in part on establishing *audience expectations* of what will happen in the immediate future, as the play is unfolding. Both fiction and poetry, in contrast, focus more on what has already happened. The playwright, of course, predetermines the events in a play; but as we watch, we experience the illusion that the action is occurring in the present and that neither we nor the characters know what will happen next. This effect of expectation is heightened in drama, because as we watch the play we have little time to reflect on what has happened, whereas when we read a novel we at least have the choice of pausing and thinking about what we have read. Playwrights often rely heavily on what they predict our expectations will be, given certain kinds of action and certain kinds of characters. They may choose to fulfill our expectations or to surprise us by thwarting them.

The *structural divisions* of plays affect plot. Playwrights usually provide structural divisions to give playgoers physical relief—a few moments to stand up, walk about, stretch, or reflect (however briefly) on what they have seen. Structural divisions also serve to allow set changes. In addition to such performance considerations, structural divisions also mark off segments of the plot. *Formal structural divisions* are those specified in the play or the program—acts and scenes. *Informal structural divisions* can be smaller units within an act or scene, units not identified as such by the playwright but that nonetheless have a self-contained quality. In formal structural units, the playwright might call for the curtain to come down, the lights to go off, or the characters to leave the stage to signal the end of a unit. Shakespeare often ends his units with a couplet. In informal units, none of these things may happen; instead, the units may just flow together. Characteristic of all of them, however, is a rising action, a climax, and possibly a brief falling action. The climax of these units is usually a moment of revelation, either to the main characters, to other characters, or to the audience. An example is Hamlet's recognition at the climax of the play-within-a-play scene that King Claudius has murdered Hamlet's father, the former king. All of the units of a play contribute to the rising action of the entire play and lead finally to its main climax.

**Questions about plot**   We said that plot in drama needs to be relatively simple and clear. In the play you are studying, is it? If not, why would the playwright want to create confusion about the important conflicts and cause-and-effect relationships? Sometimes the playwright *tries* to make such confusion. Congreve in *The Way of the World,* for example, creates a pattern of relationships so confusing that an audience is hard put to figure out who has done what to whom, especially at the breakneck speed the play is usually performed. He probably does this on purpose to indicate the complicated texture of Restoration upper-class society and the difficulty of finding one's way through it safely and honorably. Basic questions are, What are the main conflicts? What has caused the conflicts existing at the beginning of the play? What causes the conflicts that emerge during the course of the play? Who is in conflict with whom? Why? Are any of the characters in conflict with forces larger than just individuals—society, for example, or fate? How are the conflicts resolved?

What actions occur offstage? Why does the author elect to place some actions offstage and other actions onstage? In *Macbeth,* for example, Shakespeare has the murder of King Duncan (at the beginning of the play) occur offstage, but later he has the murder of Banquo and, in another scene, the murder of Macduff's family (or part of it) occur onstage. Why, then, does he choose to put one murder offstage and other murders onstage? Questions that should lead to answers to this are, How do the characters react to the offstage events? Shakespeare probably places Duncan's murder offstage because he wants the audience to focus attention on Macbeth and Lady Macbeth's reaction to the murder. Related questions are, What does the playwright use to represent or symbolize action that occurs offstage? When Macbeth returns from killing Duncan, he carries the murder weapons, all covered with blood. His hands are covered with blood. When Lady Macbeth returns from smearing blood all over the sleeping guards, *her* hands are covered with blood. The more we see of this blood and the more they talk about it, the more grisly, and physical, and sticky the murder seems. Without actually describing the murder, Shakespeare uses a physical image, blood, and the characters' reaction to it to signal what the murder was like.

What is the "plot" of the play? What is the "story"? If the plot is only part of the story, why does the playwright choose this part? What has happened before the play begins? What will happen afterward? As Beckerman points out, if the plot is only part of a larger or continuing story, the characters are more likely to seem at the mercy of forces beyond their control; whereas, if the plot and story are roughly equivalent, the characters will seem more free to choose and mold their own fate. The plot of *Romeo and Juliet,* for example, is only one episode— the final episode, we hope—of a generations-long, murderous, and irrational family feud. Romeo and Juliet are, therefore, "star-crossed" and "death-marked"; try as they will, they cannot escape the undertow of their families' history. Even Prince Escalus, the only person in the play with both power and good sense, can do nothing to avert the concluding tragedy. Macbeth and Lady Macbeth, in contrast, choose to do evil at the beginning of the play and thus give rise to the forces that destroy them.

What expectations does the plot call up in the audience? Does the playwright fulfill those expectations? If not, how and why not? Most traditional comedy, for example, offers young lovers as staple characters. We expect the lovers, after suitable complications, to find happiness together, usually signaled at the end by betrothal or marriage. But sometimes the playwright introduces potential lovers, gives us something like a light comic tone, creates comic complications, but thwarts our expectations that they will marry. Examples are Etherege's *The Man of Mode,* Molière's *The Misanthrope,* and Shaw's *Mrs. Warren's Profession.* Another example is Chekhov's *The Cherry Orchard,* which he called a comedy, even though it is not always played as such. In this play, the main character, Lopakhin, and the adopted daughter of the family he is trying to rescue from economic disaster, seem meant for each other. There is much talk throughout the play of their marrying. Such a marriage would seem to be good for both of them. They agree to marry, and since they are sympathetic characters, the audience wants them to marry. Yet they never do. Why does Chekhov create the expectation and even hope of their marriage and then abort it? The answer to this question provides insight into Chekhov's purposes in *The Cherry Orchard;* and since he uses the same device in other plays—*Three Sisters,* for example—the answer throws light on his entire dramatic method.

What are the formal structural divisions of the plays? How many of them are there—three acts, four, five? How do the formal divisions reflect the playwright's purposes and materials? Oscar Wilde's *The Importance of Being Earnest,* for example, is divided into three acts. The first act takes place in London, the second and third in the country. This division reflects the double-identity motif in the plot, because the main character pretends to have two identities, a city identity and a country identity. The first two acts reflect these opposing identities. The third act, however, synthesizes the two. Events and revelations allow the main character to blend his city and country identities into one happy whole. The structure of the play, then, neatly reflects a "thesis, antithesis, synthesis" pattern of oppositions and resolution of oppositions.

What are the informal units of the play? For *all* the units, what are the climaxes of each? What is revealed in the climax—to the main character featured in the unit, to other characters, to the audience? How is a particular unit important to the whole play? What is the main climax of the play? What do you learn from it?

## ■ Thinking on Paper about Plot

1. List the conflicts revealed in each major section of the play (usually acts, but sometimes scenes).

2. Explain how one or more of these conflicts is first made evident. Pay close attention to dialogue.

3. Summarize how a conflict is developed through the whole play and how it is resolved.

4. Summarize the events, either in the past or present, that cause conflict. If there is one event that caused or causes all the conflicts, summarize it in detail and explain why and how it is so important.

5. List the external conflicts. How are they represented on stage? Through dialogue? Through physical action? Through symbolic stage props?

6. List the events that precede the action of the play. Explain the effect, if any, of these prior events on the action.

7. Summarize the events in each major structural unit of the play. Explain the relationship of the play's units to the plot's structure. Show how the action in each unit rises to a climax.

8. Mark some informal structural divisions in the play. Note the rising action and climax of these units.

9. Describe one important scene in detail. Explain how the characters' actions and dialogue reveal conflict. Explain the importance of the scene to the whole play.

10. Describe the climax of the play. Explain what conflicts are resolved.

11. List the main plot and the subplots. Explain the relationship of the subplots to the main plot.

12. List the events that occur offstage. Explain why the playwright has one or more of these occur offstage rather than onstage.

13. Summarize the situation at the beginning of the play and state what you expect to happen. Explain how the play does or does not fulfill those expectations.

## Characterization

As with plot, the playwright must keep character portrayal simple enough for an audience to understand during the course of a single performance. Therefore, the playwright must rely heavily on flat characters, especially stereotyped ("stock") characters, whose personalities and moral traits are easily caught and remembered by the audience. The playwright may even use unsubtle strategems of dress, dialect, physical movements, and names to communicate these traits. In Restoration and eighteenth-century comedy, for example, the names signal the traits of comic flat characters: Mrs. Loveit, Sir Fopling Flutter, Snake, Pert, Mr. Oldcastle, Lady Wishforit, Lady Sneerwell, Smirk, Handy. The playwright must also rely on static characters more heavily than dynamic characters, because restricted performance time limits the opportunity to make character changes plausible.

Edward Pixley has pointed out that when the play is dominated by flat characters, the excitement of the plot emerges from external conflicts; the focus is on action. When the play includes round characters, the excitement of the plot emerges from internal conflicts, or an interplay between external and internal conflicts; the focus is on characterization. In Wilde's *The Importance of Being Earnest,* for example, all the characters are flat; the charm of the play lies not in character development but in the witty language, in the mild satire rippling through the dialogue, and in the plot complications resulting from the confusion of identities. In contrast, Ibsen's *Hedda Gabler* presents a complex, round character, Hedda herself; and the interest of the play lies in what she will do next and why she will do it. Hedda does not change during the play, but her character traits intensify and become clearer to the audience. Round characters, therefore, hold the audience's attention by changing or, if they don't change, by becoming more intense. In either case, continual revelations about the characters grip the audience's interest.

Although the playwright may depend to an extent on exterior details to reveal character traits, the playwright's most important device for character development is dialogue—what the characters say and what they say about one another. But performance time is limited; the words of the dialogue cannot describe the character fully. Playwrights, therefore, rely heavily upon implication in the dialogue and upon "gaps"—information left out—to indicate what characters are like and what physical things they might be doing. Some critics mark this distinction with the terms *text* for the written dialogue and *subtext* for the implications and gaps. All literary genres make use of implication and gaps, but drama and poetry almost *must* rely on them because both genres are such compressed forms of communication.

A simple example of text and subtext is the scene near the beginning of *Hamlet* in which Hamlet, after a long absence, meets his university friends Horatio and Marcellus. The night before this meeting, Horatio and Marcellus have seen the ghost of Hamlet's father. But Hamlet doesn't know about the ghost; instead, he complains about his mother's marrying so soon after his father's death:

> HAMLET:   Would I had met my dearest foe in heaven
> Or ever I had seen that day [the wedding day], Horatio!
> My father—methinks I see my father.
> HORATIO:   Where, my lord?
> HAMLET:                          In my mind's eye, Horatio.
> HORATIO:   I saw him once. 'A was [he was] a goodly king.

If you were the actor playing Horatio, how would you say the line "Where, my lord?" The "gap" here is the nature of Horatio's response to Hamlet's statement, "My father—methinks I see my father." To fill the gap, you have to determine from the context how Horatio takes that statement (Shakespeare doesn't tell you how, as a novelist might), and you have to communicate his reaction to the audience by the way you say the line and by your physical demeanor. You might phrase the line as an incredulous question: "What? You see your father? But how could you, he's dead?" Or you might say it as a reflection of what you take to be Hamlet's witty mood: "I know you're joking, Hamlet. But tell me anyway. Where do you see your father?" Probably, however, you should say it in astonishment, as if you take it literally. After all, *you* have seen the ghost of Hamlet's father just a few hours before. You probably think Hamlet has now spotted the ghost, and so you say, "Good Lord, do you see it too? Where?" And you look fearfully around, trying to see the ghost too. When Hamlet indicates that he is only remembering his father, you calm down. At this point you might pause and make appropriate gestures to indicate your shift from fear and astonishment to calmness. The fact that you *have* made such a shift is indicated by your response to Hamlet. "Yes. Once, when the king was alive, I saw him too. He was an impressive-looking king." This last statement shows that Horatio has moved from thinking about a supernatural phenomenon (the ghost) to thinking about a natural one (Hamlet's father when he was alive).

This brief example illustrates the greatest value of understanding a play's subtext. By "reading" the implications and the gaps in the play, you uncover the inner states of the characters—what is going on in their minds and what their hidden nature is. You also establish a correspondence between the character's inner state and what the character says and does (the character's outer state). Interpretation of subtext is essential for actors, who must figure out how to say the dialogue and what to do onstage. But it is important for readers, too, even though a reader may not work out intonation and physical movements in as much detail as actors do. The reason is that a character's inner world is the key to the character's makeup and actions. Horatio, in the example above, is a flat character, and the problem of exposing his inner state is relatively uncomplicated. But doing so gives the performance—whether seen by an audience or imagined by a reader—vividness. Horatio springs to life. He is not just an automaton reading lines; he is a real person. As for round characters, the difficulty of uncovering their inner states is much greater, yet that is part of their fascination. Great characters like Oedipus, Macbeth, Hamlet, and Hedda Gabler grip our imaginations just because their inner states are complex and mysterious. The only way we can expose these inner states is by interpreting the subtext of the play.

Closely related to subtext in drama is *mask wearing*. Nearly every play employs the mask as a device for developing plot and characterization. Juliet wears a "mask"—pretends to be different from the way she really is—in order to fool her parents and run away with Romeo. Hamlet puts on a mask of madness to root out the murderer of his father. Hedda pretends to be the contented housewife in order to secure the wealth and social status she thinks she deserves. Macbeth and Lady Macbeth pretend to be the loyal servants and gracious hosts of King Duncan while plotting his murder. The audience may be fully aware of the mask and thus the disparity between appearance and reality, as, for example, in Juliet's case. Or the audience may be as unaware of the mask at first as are the other characters in the play, as in Hedda's case. And sometimes the mask wearers are themselves unaware or partially unaware of their masks; that is, they deceive themselves. Oedipus, for example, doesn't know that he is masking his true identity of king murderer. In all cases, both plot and characterization turn on revelation— the tearing away of the mask. At these moments of revelation, the audience and at least some of the characters see the reality behind the mask. Often the final unmasking comes at the climax of the plot. In *Othello,* for example, the climax occurs when Iago's mask is ripped away before Othello's shocked eyes.

**Questions about characterization and plot**   If the characters are flat, what are their dominant traits, and what is their function in the plot? How do they help establish the conflicts in the plot? If the characters are dynamic, how do they change—from what to what? If they are static, do their traits intensify or become clearer as the play moves on? If the characters are round, what can you learn from the subtext of the play about their inner states?

What "masks" are the characters wearing? Who is hiding what from whom? When are the masks removed? What causes their removal, and what are the results? In general, how would you play a particular character if you were the actor? What would your bearing—your physical appearance—be? Hedda Gabler, for example, is aristocratic, proud, and forceful; she seems strong but has an inner fragility. Her rival, Thea, is hesitant, unsophisticated, and afraid; she seems weak but has an inner strength. If you were acting these characters, how would you present yourself physically to convey these qualities? How would you show that Hedda seems strong but is in fact weak? You may not actually act Hedda, of course, but determining a physical presence for her forces you to analyze her and thus understand her better.

## ■ Thinking on Paper about Characterization

1. List the character traits of each major character.

2. List the devices, such as dress, names, and gestures, that help establish the traits of a character.

3. Describe in detail the traits of a complex character, especially contradictory and seemingly inexplicable traits.

4. Explain a character's motivations for doing the things he or she does. Focus especially on what the character seems to want. Explain the situations from which the character's motivations seem to emerge.

5. Describe the strategies a character devises for getting what he or she wants. Explain how effective those strategies are.

6. Describe the miscalculations a character makes and the effect they have.

7. Summarize how a character intensifies, changes, or comes into sharper focus for the audience. Trace the intensification, change, or focus through each major unit of the play. Explain what causes it.

8. Summarize a scene in which a major character faces a crisis. Explain what we learn about the character from the character's words and actions.

9. Summarize a scene in which a major character has a startling or affecting revelation. Explain what the revelation is, what causes it, and its effect on the character's future.

10. Explain how you would portray one of the characters in an important scene. Show how your performance would reveal the character's inner state.

11. Explain the relationship a major character has with the other major characters. Describe the alliances and conflicts the character has with the other characters. Describe the attitudes the character has toward the other characters and their attitudes toward him or her.

12. If there is one character who exerts control, intentionally or unintentionally, over other characters, describe the character in detail and explain the source and nature of that control. Describe the other characters' reactions to that control.

13. List the masks characters wear. Explain why a character wears a mask.

14. Trace one or more of these masks through the play. Explain how effectively the mask accomplishes the character's purpose.

15. Summarize the scene in which the mask is dropped. List the effects of the mask being dropped.

## Setting

Because of the limited time and space of dramatic productions, a play cannot create a "world" in the same detail and breadth a novel can. The worlds of novels like Tolstoy's *War and Peace* and Hugo's *Les Miserables,* with their multitude of characters, scenes, physical places, and battles, are impossible to show in drama. Rather, such worlds can be represented only fragmentarily. The playwright must use a shorthand method of presenting the setting so that the playgoer grasps enough information about it to understand whatever relationship it might have to characterization and theme. Sometimes the relationship is minimal, sometimes very close. *Setting* in drama is the same as in fiction: the social mores, values, and customs of the world in which the characters live; the physical world; and the time of the action, including historical circumstances.

The playwright has three main ways of communicating setting to an audience. First, we learn about setting from the characters' dialogue, dress, and behavior. In Sheridan's *School for Scandal,* we know immediately that the world of this play is leisured upper-class English society. We know this from the elaborately polite and mannered way in which the characters carry themselves and from the names they so freely drop—Sir Harry Bouquet, Lord Spindle, Captain Quinze, Lady Frizzle, the Dowager Lady Dundizzy. In *Hedda Gabler* the conversations between Hedda and Judge Brack let us know that they are aristocrats and that Hedda's husband and his family are middle class. Second, we learn about setting from the sets produced by the set designer. Sheridan doesn't tell us what the interiors for *School for Scandal* should look like. He says simply that throughout the play the setting is "London" and that in act one it is "Lady Sneerwell's house." A set designer, however, would do research on the interior design of fashionable homes in late eighteenth-century England and produce that image on stage. The set, in short, should "say" that these people are aristocrats.

Third, we learn about setting from the knowledge we *bring* to the performance. The playwright alludes to the nature of the setting and assumes we will fill in the details. As Americans, for example, we have relatively little trouble understanding the setting of Arthur Miller's *The Crucible,* even though it is set in seventeenth-century New England. Miller expects us to know something about the Salem witch trials and about the McCarthy "witch hunts" of the 1950s, and most Americans who see that play do know about them.

A problem surfaces, however, when the audience does not have the supplemental information to complete the setting of the play—audiences from other cultures or other time periods. Chekhov's plays are a case in point. *The Cherry Orchard,* for example, plays against a background of Russian history that Chekhov assumes we know: the reform acts of Czar Alexander II (1855–81), including the freeing of the serfs in 1861 and the establishing of the *zemstvo* system of local self-government; Alexander's assassination by anarchists in 1881; the rigid autocracy of the next czar, Alexander III (1881–94); and the ineffectual and repressive reign of his successor, Nicholas II (1894–1917), which revived revolutionary movements in the late 1890s. *The Cherry Orchard* focuses on the passing of a decrepit aristocratic order and the arising of a vigorous middle class and financial order. For us even to recognize this concern, it helps to know a little Russian history. Otherwise, we will be confused about why the aristocrats are so nostalgic, whimsical, and impractical in the face of imminent financial disaster. Chekhov wants us to see that their attitude is both a result of and a cause of this historical change.

A choice a playwright and set designer have in designing the sets is whether or not to give them symbolic value. Sets need not be symbolic. The sets in *School for Scandal* will usually be a literal suggestion of aristocratic drawing rooms and mean nothing more than that. To create the illusion of real rooms, the set designer can lavishly use physical detail—furniture, wallpaper, decorative doodads, architectural features, paintings, and clothes. But aspects of sets can take on symbolic or representational meaning. The simplest representational set is probably a bare stage, which can represent anything the playwright wants—a battlefield, a heath, a forest, or a gothic cathedral. The playwright can be blatantly symbolic, assigning obvious meanings to physical objects. Thornton Wilder does this in *Our Town* when he uses stepladders to represent houses. The playwright can also combine a realistic with a symbolic method. In *Hedda Gabler,* for example, Ibsen calls for solidly "real" things to be put in the two rooms we see of the Tesman house—an armchair, footstools, sofa, tables, French windows, and flowers in vases. Certain objects—Hedda's pistols, the portrait of General Gabler (Hedda's father), and the piano—become closely associated with her and her psychological disorders. Equally suggestive are the two rooms: one a large, elegant drawing room located in the front part of the stage and the other a smaller sitting room located in back. In act one Hedda's piano is in the drawing room, but in act two it is out of sight in the back room. In fact, as the play proceeds, the back room becomes more and more "Hedda's room" and the drawing room "Tesman's room." Even the portrait of General Gabler is in the back room. At the end of the play, Hedda retreats to the back room, pulls the curtains, frantically plays the piano, and shoots herself. It is as if the back room represents an increasingly restricted physical and emotional space for Hedda, until at last it becomes her prison and coffin.

**Questions about setting**   What do you learn about the setting from characters' behavior and dialogue? What kind of sets does the play seem to call for? What costumes would you have the actors wear? What costumes would best fit particular characters? Does the play seem to require background knowledge on your part to understand its setting? What are the symbolic possibilities in particular objects or in larger portions of the set? What relationships does the setting have to characterization? What emotional feel—atmosphere—

does the setting have? What relationships does the setting have to theme?

## ■ Thinking on Paper about Setting

1. For each major unit of the play, describe the place where the action occurs. If the playwright gives a description of the place, summarize the description. If the playwright does not give a description, use information from the dialogue to construct a description. Explain the relationship of place to action, characterization, and theme.

2. Identify the time of day of each unit of the play. Explain how the time of day is represented on stage and its effect on the characters and the action.

3. Identify the time of year of each unit of the play. Explain the relationship of time of year to action, characterization, and theme.

4. Identify the historical period of the play. Give any background information that would be useful for understanding the play. Explain the relationship of the historical period to action, characterization, and theme.

5. Describe the atmosphere of each major unit of the play.

6. Describe the costumes the characters wear. Explain the relationship between costumes, characterization, and theme.

7. Describe your design for the physical world—sets, costumes, sounds, lighting, the works—of one major unit of the play. Explain the reasons for your choices.

8. List the details of setting that have symbolic value. Explain what each symbolizes. Explain the relationship of symbolism to characterization and theme.

9. Explain each major character's attitude toward the setting.

## Theme

Playwrights build themes into their plays through the development and interrelationship of all the elements of drama, most of which are the same as for fiction. Three methods of developing theme, however, are particularly noteworthy: repetitions, symbols, and contrasts. All three lend themselves well to drama. Audiences can pick up on them easily during performances.

*Repetitions* can take many forms—a character's performing the same gesture over and over again, repeating the same phrase, stating the same idea, or appearing at regular intervals. But for repetitions to relate to theme, they must develop ideas. Shakespeare does just that in *Hamlet* by repeating and intertwining three concepts: Denmark as "rotten," human beings as sinful, and the king's role as crucial to the health of the state. He characterizes Denmark by repeatedly comparing it to a garden overrun with weeds and to a diseased body, analogies borne out by Hamlet's partial madness and Ophelia's complete madness and suicide. He has key characters dwell on the sinful nature of humankind. The queen says that her own soul is "sick," "as sin's true nature is." The king says that his "offense is rank, it smells to heaven" because it has "the primal eldest curse" upon it of Cain's murder of Abel. And Hamlet says that even the best people seem to have "some vicious mole of nature in them" that leads them from purity to corruption. (All three of these statements connect sin to sickness.) The corrupt state of Denmark, Shakespeare implies, is the result of the king's sin. For, as one character says, the king is like the hub of a wheel whose spokes connect to "ten thousand lesser things." Whatever the king does affects everyone in the state.

As we have said, *symbolism* can enrich setting; but, in fact, symbolism bears on both characterization and theme as well. It is often hard to separate the effect of symbolism on all three elements. In *Hedda Gabler,* for example, Ibsen contrasts Hedda's and Thea's hair to symbolize their different character traits. Hedda's hair is thin and dull; Thea's is thick and luxuriant. Hedda dates her long-standing rivalry with Thea from their school days, when, even then, Hedda threatened to "burn off" Thea's hair. Hedda seems at times to want to inspire people to create, but her efforts end up as destructive; whereas Thea has an innate and unconscious gift for inspiring creativity. This wellspring of inspiration and fertility is symbolized by Thea's hair, which helps explain Hedda's animosity toward it. It's hard to say just what Ibsen's themes in *Hedda Gabler* are; he may simply be trying to present, not explain, Hedda's mysterious perversities. But one implication of the hair symbolism may be that creativity is a mysterious quality existing even in someone as innocent and nonintellectual as Thea and that it may not have anything to do with the intellectual sharpness and forcefulness of people like Hedda. Whatever Ibsen's themes are, they are inextricably bound up with his characterization of Hedda and Thea.

A simpler—that is, easier to interpret—example of thematic symbolism occurs in Lorraine Hansberry's *A Raisin in the Sun.* Mrs. Younger, the main character, is the mother of a large extended family, but her environment—a stultifying, roach-infested, inner-city tenement—has kept her from giving the best of life to her children. The house she wants to buy in the suburbs becomes equivalent to new "earth" in which her children and grandchild can "grow," because, as she says, they are her "harvest." To emphasize the analogy between the house and a garden, Hansberry has Mrs. Younger constantly dreaming of working in the garden at the new house, and as a moving present, her children give her garden tools. The most visible symbol of Mrs. Younger's frustrations and aspirations, however, is a malnourished houseplant she has been trying for years to nurture. The audience sees the plant sitting in the window. Mrs. Younger fusses over it. Her children chide her for messing with it at all, but she persists. The last thing we see her do is say goodbye to the oppressive apartment and carry the plant out the door. At the new house, it will revive in the sunshine and clean air of a better world. The message seems clear: People are like plants; they become healthy—mentally, morally, and physically—only in hospitable environments.

Like symbolism, *contrast* is a device for developing not just theme but characterization and plot as well, and contrast usually bears on all three. We have already seen many examples of contrast in the plays we have discussed so far: romantic love (Romeo and Juliet) versus social requirements (the Montagues and the Capulets), Thea versus Hedda, Macbeth versus Duncan, old Russia versus new Russia, Hamlet's father versus the new king. Often, playwrights repeat scenes and circumstances but vary them in such ways that the similarities and differences create aesthetic and thematic effects. *Macbeth* illustrates the aesthetic device of "framing" the work by putting nearly identical events at the beginning and end. At the beginning, Scotland has just defeated Norway. The traitorous Thane of Cawdor is executed, and Macbeth triumphantly displays the head of another rebel by putting it on a stake. As a reward for valor, the king designates Macbeth the new Thane of Cawdor. At the end of the play, another battle is fought; Macbeth is killed as a "usurper," and his head is cut off and held aloft as a sign of revenge and victory. Ironically, Macbeth has changed places with the first Thane of Cawdor in both name and nature, and the circumstances of their deaths are almost identical.

A more far reaching example of contrast is the Surface brothers in Sheridan's *School for Scandal.* Joseph Surface pretends to be good, but he is in fact selfish and destructive. Charles Surface leads a carefree and careless life; he seems to be a wastrel, but he is in fact generous and honest. Their uncle and benefactor, Sir Oliver Surface, a brusque but warmhearted man, has just returned to England after a long absence and wants to ferret out the true nature of his two potential heirs. To do this he visits each brother separately, disguised as someone else. Both scenes are so similar that an audience cannot fail to notice the similarity; Sheridan uses the similarity to contrast the brothers. The first scene, with Charles, does indeed expose his good qualities. The audience now knows how the scene will go and gleefully awaits the second scene, in which the despicable Joseph will almost certainly be exposed. This contrast not only develops plot and character, it also points a moral—that the appearance of goodness is worthless without the practice of goodness.

**Questions about theme**   What repetitions occur in the play? What patterns of meaning can you make out of these repetitions? What symbols does the author deliberately establish? How do you know they are symbols? What do the symbols seem to mean?

What contrasts does the playwright establish? Which are the obvious contrasts and which are the not-so-obvious contrasts? In *Romeo and Juliet,* for example, we easily spot the contrast between the lovers and the parents, but other contrasts are suggestive: Romeo is different from Juliet and is perhaps partly to blame for their deaths; Prince Escalus is different from the parents; the nurse's attitude toward love contrasts starkly with Juliet's; the friar's attitude toward love is different from Romeo's. Any one or a combination of these contrasts would make a good focus for an interpretation. How is contrast related to the conflicts in the plot? Hedda and Thea are not only different from each other, they are in conflict. What values, then, do the contrasting sides of a conflict manifest?

## ■ Thinking on Paper about Theme

1. List the subjects of the play (the issues or problems the play seems to be about). State themes for each of these subjects (what the play seems to be saying about these issues and problems).

2. Mark speeches and sections of dialogue that help develop a particular theme. Look especially for "the big speech," which will typically be longer than most and will forcefully state a theme. Hamlet's "To be or not to be" speech is an example. There may be more than one "big speech." Summarize them and explain how the actions of the play develop their ideas.

3. Explain in detail how an important scene helps develop themes.

4. Trace the development of one theme through the play. Mark all the passages that help develop this theme. Summarize the plot as it relates to this theme.

5. List the images (sensuous images, metaphors) that recur in the play. Explain what ideas they seem to develop.

6. List other repetitions (characters' actions and words, characters' obsessions, scenes, details of setting). Explain their relationship to characterization and theme.

7. List the symbols in the play. For each symbol, list its meanings.

8. Describe the important contrasts in the play (of characters, scenes, values, actions, physical objects). Explain how these contrasts help expose character traits and develop theme.

## Irony

The presence of an audience at performances of plays affects profoundly the way plays are written and the way productions are conceived. The actors, of course, pretend to be real people involved in real human relationships. But unlike real life, these fictional activities are witnessed by an audience of total strangers. It is as if the front wall of your neighbor's house were taken away and the whole neighborhood were standing outside watching everything your neighbors were doing, hearing everything they were saying. The playwright or producer must decide whether to exclude or include the audience as participants in the play. If the choice is to exclude the audience, the production assumes that no one is watching. The production establishes a physical and psychological distance between the performance and the audience (the performance lighted, the auditorium dark; the performance up on stage, the audience down and away from the stage), and the actors pretend the audience is not there. If the choice is to include the audience, then measures are taken to bring the audience "into" the play. The physical distance between performance and audience may be reduced (by building the stage out into the auditorium or by having the actors circulate among the audience). The actors may look at the audience, gesture to it, or talk to it as if the audience were another person. Shakespeare's drama includes these possibilities with its numerous asides and soliloquies.

One prominent device that relies entirely on the presence of an audience, and on what the audience is thinking, is dramatic irony. *Dramatic irony* in effect does acknowledge the presence of the audience, because it gives the audience the privilege of knowing things the characters do not know but almost certainly will soon know. Dramatic irony occurs when characters say or do something that has meaning the audience recognizes but the characters do not. The concept of dramatic irony can be extended to all situations in which characters are blind to facts the audience knows. Sometimes only the audience is aware of the ironic contrast between the character's words or actions and the truth; sometimes the audience shares this knowledge with other characters onstage.

In the two parallel scenes in *School for Scandal,* for example, the audience knows that Sir Oliver Surface is wearing a mask to test his nephews—and of course Sir Oliver knows—but the nephews do not. So the audience recognizes as ironic everything the nephews do and say that works for or against their self-interest, particularly in the case of Joseph, who would treat Sir Oliver with meticulous courtesy if only he knew who he was. In another scene from this play, Lady Teazle hides behind a screen while her husband, unaware of her presence, talks about her. When he says that he wants to leave her a lot of money upon his death, but that he does not want her to know about it yet, we recognize his statement as ironic, because we know—and he doesn't— that Lady Teazle has heard everything.

A powerful example of dramatic irony occurs in the last scenes of Shakespeare's *Othello.* Before Desdemona goes to bed, she sings a song about a man who accuses his love of being promiscuous. She asks Emilia, her lady-in-waiting, if any woman could so treat her husband. Emilia says that some might for the right "price," but Desdemona says that she could not do so "for the whole world." The audience recognizes her comments as ironic, because Othello, unbeknownst to Desdemona, is nearly insane with the belief that she is a "whore" and plans to kill her for it. Later, when Othello is strangling Desdemona, he boasts that even if he is "cruel" he is at least "merciful," because he will kill her quickly without allowing her to "linger in : . . pain." But his "mercy" contrasts horribly with our knowledge of her innocence and the quality of mercy she justly deserves. When he defends his murder to Emilia, he says,

> Cassio did top her. Ask thy husband [Iago] else.
> O, I were damned beneath all depth in hell

But that I did proceed upon just grounds
To this extremity. Thy husband knew it all.

We know, and poor Othello is about to find out, that Iago has betrayed
him and that he has in truth had no "just grounds" for the "extremity"
of his deed.

**Questions about irony**   To what extent does the playwright
seem to want the audience involved in the action? How would you perform such audience-involving devices as soliloquies and asides? To
whom, for example, would you have the actors make asides? What advantages are there in performing the play as if the audience is not there?

Like fiction and poetry, drama uses all kinds of irony. Verbal irony
is very prevalent simply because drama relies so heavily on dialogue.
Sometimes the director and actors themselves must decide whether
particular lines are ironic. When Thea, for example, tells Hedda about
inspiring Loevborg to write his book, Hedda interjects comments such
as "Poor, pretty little Thea"; "But my dear Thea! How brave of you!";
"Clever little Thea!" It is almost certain that Hedda means these statements ironically. The actress would probably say them, then, with
enough sarcasm to let the audience know how Hedda really feels about
Thea's successes, but with not enough bite to let the slow-witted Thea
pick up on the irony.

What are the ironies, then, in the play you are studying? How do
they relate to characterization and theme? Most importantly, what dramatic ironies does the playwright build into the play? Do the dramatic
ironies—such as Othello's repeated description of Iago as "honest"—
create a pattern of revelation or meaning? Why do the dramatic ironies
appear where they do in the play?

### ■ Thinking on Paper about Irony

1. Explain the extent to which the play seems to invite audience par-
   ticipation.

2. Mark the instances in the play of dramatic irony. Explain what the
   dramatic irony reveals about characterization and theme.

3. Mark the instances of verbal irony. Explain what the verbal irony reveals about the characters who use it.

4. List the instances of situational irony. Explain the importance of situational irony to characterization and theme. (For a definition of situational irony, see Chapter 3.)

5. List the instances of attitudinal irony. Explain the importance of attitudinal irony to characterization and theme. (For a definition of attitudinal irony, see Chapter 3.)

## Subgenres

The best-known subgenres of drama are tragedy and comedy, but there are many others: melodrama, theater of the absurd, allegory, comedy of manners, the spectacle, the masque, modern drama, farce, and tragicomedy. Some, like musicals, opera, and ballet, shade into other art forms. Although defining subgenres is not a purpose of this book, you may find fruitful interpretations by means of such definitions.

Definitions of *tragedy,* for example, usually begin with the first and most famous definition, that in Aristotle's *Poetics.* Aristotle based his definition on an inductive examination of Greek tragedy, and he seems in particular to have had Sophocles's plays in mind. His definition focuses primarily on the effect of the play on the audience and on the nature of the tragic hero. The hero, he says, inspires "pity" and "fear" in the audience: pity because the hero doesn't deserve his fate and fear because the hero's fate could be anyone's. The audience, in other words, identifies deeply with the tragic hero. The hero is noble but flawed. He has one principal flaw—in Sophocles, usually the flaw of pride. This flaw Aristotle called a *hamartia,* literally a "miscalculation." Because of the hero's flaw, he suffers emotionally and experiences a reversal of fortune, moving abruptly from a high place (high social position, wealth, responsibility, purity) to a low place. Before this reversal occurs, the hero understands for the first time his flawed state and his error-filled ways. This moment is the "recognition" and usually occurs at the climax of the play. The hero recognizes that he is responsible for his deeds and that they contradict a moral order inherent in the entire cosmos. The effect of the play on the audience is to induce a *catharsis,* a feeling of emotional release and exuberance.

Aristotle planned to write as comprehensively on *comedy* as on tragedy, but either that part of the *Poetics* was lost, or he never got around to it. It is hard to see, however, how he could have made comedy any less enigmatic than it still appears to us, for the nature of comedy is difficult to pin down, both artistically and psychologically. Numerous essays have been written trying to explain why people laugh, and all are speculative. Laughter is only one of the puzzling aspects or products of comedy. Most people would agree on some of the aspects of comedy. Comedy is the depiction of the ludicrous; that is, a gross departure from the serious. Therefore, in order to see something as comic, you must first understand what is "serious." Drama communicates to a community of playgoers, so the comic in drama is closely related to what the community *thinks* is serious. If the community thinks that proper attire for men is a business suit, tie, and polished shoes, then a gross distortion of that dress—by a clown in a circus, for example—would be comic. The basic methods of signaling the ludicrous are incongruity and exaggeration. It is incongruous for a haughty, spiffily dressed man, walking nose in the air, to slip and fall face first into a mud hole or to be hit in the face with a cream pie. Furthermore, comedy must cause no pain to the audience. This means that the audience cannot identify as deeply with comic figures as it does with tragic figures and that the method of presentation—language, acting, setting—must communicate an air of "fantasy." Through its methods and style, the production constantly says, "This isn't true. It's only a joke." The fantasy element in comedies helps explain why they almost always end happily, whereas tragedies end unhappily. Finally, the characters in comedy are more "realistic" than in tragedy. They are more like us, whereas in tragedy they are, even in their flawed state (sometimes *because* of their flawed state), far nobler than we are.

**Questions about subgenres** Definitions of genres and subgenres are useful only if they help you understand specific works. Aristotle was trying to understand Greek tragedy, so it does non-Greek tragedies an injustice to apply his definition to them rigidly. The same goes, really, for anyone's definition of a subgenre, because literature is too varied and complex a phenomenon to fit neatly into categories. You should use definitions like Aristotle's as insights into the probable nature of a work and base your questions on those insights. You can take every part of these definitions of tragedy and comedy and turn each into a probing question aimed at a specific work: What is the character's major flaw? Does he or she have more than one flaw? When does the recognition scene occur? What does the character recognize? What incongruities cause the comedy? What do the incongruities reveal about the playwright's attitude toward the characters and setting?

Are there hints of satire in these incongruities? How does the playwright establish the detachment necessary for us to laugh?

You might also apply definitions like these to works that do not quite fit the categories and see what you come up with. Some people regard *Hedda Gabler* as something like a "tragedy" but not exactly an Aristotelian tragedy. Will any parts of Aristotle's definition apply to *Hedda Gabler?* Which fit well, which do not? Does Hedda have a "tragic flaw"? Is she responsible for her actions? Is she to blame for the harm she does? Does she have a moment or moments of recognition? Is she nobler than we are? Does she experience a "reversal"? How does the audience feel after seeing or reading the play? Does the audience experience pity and fear for Hedda?

Some of the most interesting questions about subgenres emerge from plays that mix subgenres. Why, for example, are there comic elements in Shakespeare's tragedies? What is *The Cherry Orchard*—a comedy, a tragedy, or both? Are we supposed to laugh or cry at the fate of Chekhov's ineffectual aristocrats? If Aristotle's definition or someone else's has no explanation for a particular feature of a play, can you invent an explanation of your own?

## ■ Thinking on Paper about Subgenres

1. If you know the category the play belongs to (tragedy, comedy, farce, and so forth), find a good definition of the category. List the characteristics of the category.

2. Take one item from the list and explain how well it applies to the play. If Hamlet is a tragic character, for example, what might be his tragic flaw? What constitutes his reversal? When does he experience a recognition? How does the audience respond to him?

## FOR FURTHER STUDY

Aristotle. *The Poetics.* Various editions.

Beckerman, Bernard. *Dynamics of Drama: Theory and Method of Analysis.* New York: Drama Book Specialists, 1979.

Bentley, Eric. *The Playwright as Thinker: A Study of Drama in Modern Times.* New York: Harcourt, 1967.

Corrigan, Robert W., ed. *Tragedy: Vision and Form.* San Francisco: Chandler, 1965.

————. *Comedy: Meaning and Form.* New York: Harper, 1981.

Esslin, Martin. *An Anatomy of Drama.* New York: Hill and Wang, 1976.

————. *The Theatre of the Absurd.* Garden City: Doubleday, 1969.

Hartnoll, Phyllis, ed. *The Oxford Companion to the Theatre.* 4th ed. Oxford: Oxford University Press, 1983.

———— and Peter Found, eds. *The Concise Oxford Companion to the Theatre.* Oxford: Oxford University Press, 1993.

Kernodle, George, Portia Kernodle, and Edward Pixley. *Invitation to the Theatre.* 3rd ed. San Diego: Harcourt, 1985.

Styan, J. L. *The Elements of Drama,* Cambridge: Cambridge University Press, 1969.

Kernodle, Kernodle, and Pixley's *Invitation to the Theatre* and Esslin's *An Anatomy of Drama* are both general introductions to the elements of drama. Beckerman's *Dynamics of Drama* and Styan's *The Elements of Drama* concentrate on the performance aspects of drama. Beckerman attempts to establish a critical vocabulary and a system for analyzing drama as a performed art. Aristotle's *Poetics* is perhaps the most famous book ever written on literature. It contains his analysis of tragedy, with a few glances at comedy. Corrigan's books on comedy and tragedy anthologize essays and excerpts about these two complex subgenres. They deal with elements such as form, character types, language, and world view. Bentley's *The Playwright as Thinker* deals with the emergence of "modern" drama at the end of the nineteenth century and discusses the importance of playwrights such as Shaw, Ibsen, Strindberg, Brecht, and Sartre. Esslin's *The Theatre of the Absurd* defines and exemplifies post–World War II theatre by covering playwrights such as Samuel Beckett, Eugène Ionesco, Jean Genet, Harold Pinter, Edward Albee, and Arthur Kopit. Hartnoll's *Oxford Companion to the Theatre* describes subgenres and elements of drama as well as such things as actors, actresses, literary movements, famous productions, and national drama. Hartnoll and Found's *Concise Oxford Companion to the Theatre* updates some entries from the *Oxford Companion* and excludes entries about people under age forty.

# 5

# Analyzing Poetry

Poetry shares many elements with its sister genres, drama and fiction. And indeed, many works of drama and fiction are written in the form of poetry. Plays by Shakespeare, Goethe, Molière, Marlowe, Maxwell Anderson, and T. S. Eliot; narrative works by Homer, Chaucer, Dante, Longfellow, Whittier, Jeffers, Milton, Spenser, Tennyson, and Browning are examples. But poetry is usually different from prose drama and fiction in several key ways. In general, it is more concentrated— that is, poetry says more in fewer words. Poets achieve this concentration by selecting details more carefully, by relying more heavily on implication (through figurative language, connotation, and sensuous imagery), and by more carefully organizing the form of their poetry (through rhythmic speech patterns and "musical" qualities such as rhyme). Because of the relative shortness of poetry and because of its greater concentration, it demands a more complete unity than prose fiction; nearly every word, sound, and image contributes to a single effect.

Poetry is a complex subject. The following is a *brief* survey of its elements, with questions and exercises that should lead you to analyze and generate ideas about individual poems.

## THE ELEMENTS OF POETRY

### Characterization, Point of View, Plot, Setting, and Theme

Some poems—"narrative" poems—are very similar to prose fiction and drama in their handling of characterization, point of view, plot, and setting. Thus many of the same questions that one asks about a short story, novel, or play are relevant to these poems. Most poems,

however, do not offer a "story" in the conventional sense. They are usually brief and apparently devoid of "action." Even so, a plot of sorts may
be implied, a place and time may be important, a specific point of view
may be operating, and characters may be dramatizing the key issues of
the poem. In any poem there is always one "character" of the utmost
importance, even if he or she is the only character. This character is the
speaker, the "I" of the poem. Often the speaker is a fictional personage,
not at all equivalent to the poet, who may not be speaking to the reader
but to another character, as is the case in Marvell's "To His Coy Mistress" and Browning's "My Last Duchess." The poem might even be a dialogue between two or more people, as in ballads such as "Edward" and
"Lord Randal" and in Frost's "The Death of the Hired Man." Thus the
poem can be a little drama or story, in which one or more fictional characters participate. But more typically, one character, the "I," speaks of
something that concerns him or her deeply and personally. Such poems
are called "lyric" poems because of their subjective, musical, highly
emotional, and imaginative qualities. They are songlike utterances by
one person, the "I."

**Questions about characterization, point of view, plot,
setting, and theme**   In analyzing poetry, your first step should be
to come to grips with the "I" of the poem, the speaker. You should answer questions such as these: Who is speaking? What characterizes the
speaker? To whom is he or she speaking? What is the speaker's tone?
What is the speaker's emotional state? Why is he or she speaking? What
situation is being described? What are the conflicts or tensions in this
situation? How is setting—social situation, physical place, and time—
important to the speaker? What ideas is the speaker communicating?

Matthew Arnold's "Dover Beach" provides an example of how you
can use most of these questions to get at the meanings of a poem.

### DOVER BEACH

MATTHEW ARNOLD

The sea is calm to-night.
The tide is full, the moon lies fair
Upon the straits; on the French coast the light
Gleams and is gone; the cliffs of England stand,
Glimmering and vast, out in the tranquil bay.
Come to the window, sweet is the night-air!
Only, from the long line of spray

Where the sea meets the moon-blanched land,
Listen! you hear the grating roar
Of pebbles which the waves draw back, and fling,
At their return, up the high strand,
Begin, and cease, and then again begin,
With tremulous cadence slow, and bring
The eternal note of sadness in.

Sophocles long ago
Heard it on the Aegean, and it brought
Into his mind the turbid ebb and flow
Of human misery; we
Find also in the sound a thought,
Hearing it by this distant northern sea.

The Sea of Faith
Was once, too, at the full, and round earth's shore
Lay like the folds of a bright girdle furled.
But now I only hear
Its melancholy, long, withdrawing roar,
Retreating, to the breath
Of the night-wind, down the vast edges drear
And naked shingles° of the world.

Ah, love, let us be true
To one another! for the world, which seems
To lie before us like a land of dreams,
So various, so beautiful, so new,
Hath really neither joy, nor love, nor light,
Nor certitude, nor peace, nor help for pain;
And we are here as on a darkling plain
Swept with confused alarms of struggle and flight,
Where ignorant armies clash by night.

°beaches covered with pebbles

Because Dover is an English port city, one of several points of departure for the European continent, the speaker has apparently stopped for the night on his way to Europe. As he looks out of his hotel window, he speaks to another person in the room, his "love" (last stanza). Arnold traces the speaker's train of thought in four stanzas. In the first stanza, the speaker describes what he sees, and his tone is contented, even joyous. He sees the lights on the French coast and the high white cliffs of Dover "glimmering" in the moonlight. He invites his companion to share the glorious view. As he describes the sound of the surf to her, his tone alters slightly; the sound reminds him of "the eternal note of sadness." This melancholy tone deepens in the second stanza. There the speaker connects the sea sound with a passage in Sophocles, probably the third chorus of *Antigone,* which compares the misery of living under a family curse to the incessant roar of a stormy sea beating against the land.

In the third stanza, the remembrance of Sophocles's comparison leads the speaker to make a more disturbing comparison of his own. He likens the sea to faith—apparently religious faith, both his own and that of his age. He says that at one time the "Sea of Faith" was full but now has withdrawn, leaving a "vast," "drear," and coarse world. By the fourth stanza, the speaker has fallen into despair. He says that what merely looks beautiful—the panorama seen from his window—is only a false image of the world, which in reality is absurd and chaotic. He has only one hope, his companion, whom he now urges to be true to him as he is true to her. The speaker, in short, is an erudite, thoughtful, but deeply troubled person. The poem takes him from momentary contentedness to near hopelessness. The stimulus for his train of thought is the place of the poem—Dover Beach—and the companion to whom he addresses his remarks. All these elements—thoughts, place, and companion—are interrelated.

## ■ Thinking on Paper about Characterization, Point of View, Plot, Setting, and Theme

Many of the exercises one does on poetry consist of marking the poem itself. You might, then, photocopy the poem and write on the photocopy rather than the book. Some photocopy machines will enlarge images. Since poems are often published in small print, taking advantage of this feature would allow you to see the poem better and have more space to write. You might want to make more than one copy of the poem. Use different copies for marking different aspects of the poem.

1. Find the subject, verb, and object of every sentence in the poem. Sometimes this will be easy; reading poetry will be like reading clear prose. But sometimes it will not. Because poetry often conforms to structural requirements and because it is a condensed form of communication, sentence structures are sometimes distorted and words are left out. In such cases, you will have to put the sentence in normal order and insert missing words.

2. Paraphrase the poem. This is one way to make sure you understand every sentence.

3. Identify the speaker of the poem. Underline the words and phrases that help characterize the speaker and bring out the speaker's concerns. Describe in detail the traits of the speaker and of any other characters in the poem.

4. Describe the situation of the poem: where the speaker is, what time of day it is, what season of the year, what historical occasion, to whom the speaker is speaking, why. List the external and internal conflicts of the poem.

5. State the issues that concern the speaker (what the poem is about). Explain the speaker's ideas (the themes of the poem). Note any changes in the speaker's mood or ideas as the poem moves from unit to unit. Explain what the speaker is trying to accomplish.

6. Describe the speaker's tone (angry, lyrical, hopeful, bitter, nostalgic, sarcastic, compassionate, admiring, sorrowful, amused, and so forth). Note any changes of tone.

7. If the speaker is not the poet, describe the poet's attitude toward the speaker and to the issues raised by the poem. Indicate any differences between the poet's attitude and the speaker's.

8. Describe important contrasts made in the poem. Explain their relationships to characterization and theme.

9. Relate the poem's title to its themes.

10. Explain any allusions in the poem. An *allusion* is a reference to historical events and people, to mythological and biblical figures, and to works of literature. Allusions always invite comparison between the work at hand and the items referred to. An example of an allusion is Arnold's reference to Sophocles in "Dover Beach." Arnold invites us to bring the weight of Sophocles's tragedies to bear on the subject matter of his poem. An allusion is a compact way of adding meaning to the work. Explain, then, the implications of the allusions.

## Diction

Basically, *diction* refers to the poet's choice of words. Poets are sensitive to the subtle shades of meanings of words, to the possible double meanings of words, and to the denotative and connotative meanings of words. As we say in Chapter 2, *denotation* is the object or idea—the referent—that a word represents. The denotation of a word is its core meaning, its dictionary meaning. *Connotation* is the subjective, emotional association that a word has for one person or a group of people. Poets often choose words that contribute to the poem's meaning on both a denotational and a connotational level.

**Questions about diction**   Examine the words in a poem for all their possible shades and levels of meaning. Then ask how these meanings combine to create an overall effect. Note, for example, the effect that connotation creates in William Wordsworth's "A Slumber Did My Spirit Seal."

### A SLUMBER DID MY SPIRIT SEAL

WILLIAM WORDSWORTH

A slumber did my spirit seal;
 I had no human fears—
She seemed a thing that could not feel
 The touch of earthly years.

No motion has she now, no force;
 She neither hears nor sees;
Rolled round in earth's diurnal course,
 With rocks, and stones, and trees.

In order to create the stark contrast between the active, airy girl of the first stanza with the inert, dead girl of the second, Wordsworth relies partly on the connotative effect of the last line. We know the denotative meaning of "rocks, and stones, and trees," but in this context the emotional or connotative meaning is unpleasant and grating. Rocks and stones are inanimate, cold, cutting, impersonal. And although we usually think of trees as beautiful and majestic, here the association of trees with rocks and stones makes us think of tree roots, of dirt, and thus of the girl's burial. The rocks and stones and trees are not only non-human, they confine and smother the girl. Another example of connotation is the word *diurnal,* which means "daily." But the Latinate *diurnal* has a slightly more formal connotation than the prosaic *daily.*

The effect of the word is to make the processes of nature—death, the revolving of the earth, the existence of rocks and stones and trees—seem remote, remorseless, and inevitable.

Be alert for wordplay—double meanings and puns. The speaker in Andrew Marvell's "To His Coy Mistress," for example, tries to persuade a reluctant woman to make love with him. His argument is that time is running out, and unless we take opportunities when they appear, we will lose them. He concludes his speech with a pun:

> Thus, though we cannot make our sun
> Stand still, yet we will make him run.

That is, we cannot stop time (make the sun stop), but we can bring about new life (a child: "son"), which is one way of defeating decay and death. Some poets, such as e. e. cummings, make imaginative wordplay a dominant trait of their poetry. In "anyone lived in a pretty how town," cummings uses pronouns on two levels of meaning. The words *anyone* and *noone* mean, on the one hand, what we expect them to mean ("anybody" and "nobody"); but on the other hand they refer to two people, male and female, who fall in love, marry, and die.

## ■ Thinking on Paper about Diction

1. Circle all the words you do not know. Look them up in the dictionary.

2. Underline words that seem especially meaningful or well chosen. For each word, explain denotations and connotations.

3. Underline any wordplay such as double meanings and puns. Explain what the wordplay adds to the sense of the poem.

4. Underline any uses of unusual words—slang, profanity, archaisms, foreign language words, made-up words. Explain what qualities and meanings these words add to the poem. Discuss how the poem would be different without them.

5. Identify the level of diction in the poem (formal, informal, colloquial, slangy, dialect). Explain what the poem gains from the use of this level. Explain what it would lose by changing to a different level.

6. Explain how the choice of words contributes to the speaker's tone.

## Imagery: Descriptive Language

When applied to poetry, the term *imagery* has two meanings. First, imagery represents the descriptive passages of a poem. Although the word *imagery* calls to mind the visual sense, poetic imagery appeals to all the senses. Sensuous imagery is pleasurable for its own sake, but it also provides concreteness and immediacy. Imagery causes the reader to become personally, experientially involved in the subject matter of the poem. Furthermore, the poet often uses descriptive imagery to underscore other elements in a poem. The selection of detail and the vividness imparted to images help create tone, meaning, and characterization.

An example of descriptive imagery is the first stanza of John Keats's narrative poem "The Eve of St. Agnes":

> St. Agnes' Eve—Ah, bitter chill it was!
> The owl, for all his feathers, was a-cold;
> The hare limped trembling through the frozen grass,
> And silent was the flock in woolly fold;
> Numb were the Beadsman's fingers, while he told
> His rosary, and while his frosted breath,
> Like pious incense from a censer old,
> Seemed taking flight for heaven, without a death,
> Past the sweet Virgin's picture, while his prayer he saith.

This stanza appeals to the thermal sense (the chill of the evening, the frozen grass), the sense of touch (the beadsman's numb fingers), the visual sense (the beadsman saying his rosary before the picture of the Virgin), the sense of motion (the hare trembling and limping through the grass, the beadsman's frosted breath taking flight toward heaven), and the sense of sound (the silent flock, the sound of the beadsman's monotonous prayer). The dominant sensuous appeal, however, is to the thermal sense. Keats uses every sensuous image in the stanza to make us feel how cold the night is.

## Imagery: Figurative Language

Critics today use *imagery* in a second sense. They use it to mean figurative language, especially metaphor. *Figurative language* is the conscious departure from normal or conventional ways of saying things. This could mean merely a rearrangement of the normal word order of a sentence, such as the following: "Sir Gawain the dragon slew" or "This do in remembrance of me." Such unusual rearrangements are called "rhetorical" figures of speech. But much more common and important to poetry is a second category of figurative language: tropes. *Tropes* (literally, "turns") extend the meaning of words beyond their literal meaning, and the most common form of trope is metaphor. *Metaphor* has both a general and a specific meaning. Generally, it means any analogy. An *analogy* is a similarity between things that are basically different. Specifically, metaphor means a particular kind of analogy and is contrasted with the simile. A *simile* uses *like* or *as* to claim similarities between things that are essentially different; for example, "Her tears were like falling rain." The following stanza from Shakespeare's "Fair Is My Love" contains several similes (indicated by the added italics):

> Fair is my love, but not so fair as fickle;
> *Mild as a dove*, but neither true nor trusty;
> Brighter than glass, and yet, *as glass is, brittle;*
> Softer than wax, and yet, *as iron, rusty;*
> A lily pale, with damask dye to grace her;
> None fairer, nor none falser to deface her.

A metaphor also claims similarities between things that are essentially unlike, but it eliminates the comparative words and thus equates the compared items. For example, "My heart was a tornado of passion." The poem "Love Is a Sickness" by Samuel Daniel contains several metaphors (indicated here by the italics):

### LOVE IS A SICKNESS

SAMUEL DANIEL

> *Love is a sickness* full of woes,
>   All remedies refusing.
> A *plant* that with most cutting grows,
>   Most barren with best using
>             Why so?
>
> More we enjoy it, more it dies,
> If not enjoyed it sighing cries,
>             Hey ho.

Love *is* a torment of the mind,
 A *tempest* everlasting,
And Jove hath made it of a kind
 Not well, nor full, nor fasting.
                    Why so?

More we enjoy it, more it dies,
If not enjoyed it sighing cries,
                    Hey ho.

Analogies can be directly stated or implied. The similes and metaphors in the above poems by Shakespeare and Daniel are directly stated analogies; but when Daniel in the last lines of each stanza says that love "sighs," he implies a kind of analogy called *personification;* he pretends that love has the attributes of a person. When the poet develops just one analogy throughout the whole poem, the analogy is called an *extended metaphor.* Thomas Campion's "There Is a Garden in Her Face" contains an extended metaphor comparing the features of a woman's face to the features of a garden:

## THERE IS A GARDEN IN HER FACE

### THOMAS CAMPION

There is a garden in her face,
Where roses and white lilies grow,
A heavenly paradise is that place,
Wherein all pleasant fruits do flow.
There cherries grow, which none may buy
Till "Cherry ripe!"° themselves do cry.

Those cherries fairly do enclose
Of orient pearl a double row;
Which when her lovely laughter shows,
They look like rosebuds filled with snow.
Yet them nor peer nor prince can buy,
Till "Cherry ripe!" themselves do cry.
Her eyes like angels watch them still;
Her brows like bended bows do stand,
Threatening with piercing frowns to kill

°A familiar cry of London street vendors

All that attempt with eye or hand
Those sacred cherries to come nigh,
Till "Cherry ripe!" themselves do cry.

**Questions about imagery**  Imagery is an important—
some would argue the most important—characteristic of poetry. You
should try to identify the imagery of a poem. Ask, then, what senses
the poet appeals to and what analogies he or she implies or states directly. Ask, *Why* does the poet use these particular images and analogies? In "Dover Beach," for example, Arnold meaningfully uses both
descriptive and metaphorical imagery. He emphasizes two senses, the
visual and the aural. He begins with the visual—the moon, the lights
of France across the water, the cliffs, the tranquil bay—and throughout the poem he associates hope and beauty with what the speaker
sees. But the poet soon introduces the aural sense—the grating roar
of the sea—which serves as an antithesis to the visual sense. These
two senses create a tension that mirrors the conflict in the speaker's
mind. The first two stanzas show the speaker merely drifting into a
perception of this conflict, connecting sight with hope and sound
with sadness. By the third stanza, he has become intellectually alert to
the full implications of the conflict. He signals this alertness with a
carefully worked out analogy, his comparison of the sea with faith. In
the fourth stanza, he sums up his despairing conclusion with a stun-
ning and famous simile:

And we are here as on a darkling plain
Swept with confused alarms of struggle and flight,
Where ignorant armies clash by night.

This final analogy achieves several purposes. First, it brings the
implication of the descriptive imagery to a logical conclusion. No
longer can the speaker draw hope from visual beauty; in this image, he
cannot see at all—it is night, the plain is dark. He can only hear, but the
sound now is more chaotic and directly threatening than the mere ebb
and flow of the sea. Second, the analogy provides an abrupt change of
setting. Whereas before, the speaker visualized an unpeopled plain,
now he imagines human beings as agents of destruction. He implies
that a world without faith must seem and be arbitrary and violent. Finally, the analogy allows the speaker to identify his own place in this

new world order. Only loyalty is pure and good, so he and his companion must cling to each other and maneuver throughout the world's battlefields as best they can.

## ■ Thinking on Paper about Descriptive Language

1. Mark the descriptive images. For each image, name the sense appealed to. Characterize the dominant impression these images make.

2. Explain the relationship of descriptive images to the speaker's state of mind.

3. Describe how the descriptive images create a sense of the time of day and season of the year.

4. Note any progression in the descriptive images; for example, from day to night, hot to cold, soft to loud, color to color, slow to fast.

5. Explain how the descriptive images help create atmosphere and mood. Slow movements, for example, are conducive to melancholy; speed to exuberance and excitement.

## ■ Thinking on Paper about Figurative Language

1. Mark the similes in the poem. Underline or circle the words that signal the comparisons (words such as *like, as, similar to, resembles*). Explain the implications of the analogies (that is, what they contribute to the meaning of the poem).

2. Mark the metaphors in the poem. Explain the implications of the analogies.

3. Mark any personification in the poem. Underline the words and phrases that make the personification clear.

4. Poets often use analogies to help make an abstract quality, such as "love" or "my love's beauty" or "my current predicament" or "the destructive effect of time" or "God's grandeur," concrete and knowable. They do so by comparing the abstract quality to something the reader knows well. Almost always this "something" is a physical object or reality. Name the abstract quality the poet wants to clarify and the object the poet is comparing it to. List the qualities of the object. Explain how the comparison has clarified the abstraction.

5. List the senses appealed to in each analogy. Describe the dominant sensuous impression created by the analogies.

## Rhythm

All human speech has rhythm, but poetry regularizes that rhythm into recognizable patterns. These patterns are called *meters*. Metrical patterns vary depending on the sequence in which one arranges the accented (á) and unaccented (ă) syllables of an utterance. The unit that determines that arrangement is the foot. A *foot* is one unit of rhythm in a verse. Probably the most natural foot in English is the iambic, which has an unaccented syllable followed by an accented syllable (ăá). Here are the most common metrical feet:

| | |
|---|---|
| iamb (iambic) ăá | ăbóve |
| trochee (trochaic) áă | lóvelў |
| anapest (anapestic) ăăá | ŏvĕrwhélm |
| dactyl (dactylic) áăă | róyăltў |
| spondee (spondaic) áá | bréak, bréak |

Poets further determine the arrangement of metrical patterns by the number of feet in each line. The following names apply to the lengths of poetic lines:

monometer (one foot)

dimeter (two feet)

trimeter (three feet)

tetrameter (four feet)

pentameter (five feet)

hexameter (six feet)

heptameter (seven feet)

octameter (eight feet)

A very common line in English poetry is iambic pentameter; it contains five iambic feet. Shakespeare wrote his plays in iambic pentameter, and the sonnet is traditionally composed in iambic pentameter (see pages 104–105 for some examples).

Another feature of line length is that each line may have a fixed number of syllables. When people speak of iambic pentameter, they usually think of a line containing five accented syllables and ten syllables in all. Even if the poet substitutes other feet for iambs, the number of syllables in the line comes out the same—ten for iambic pentameter, eight for iambic tetrameter, six for iambic trimeter, and so forth. When a line of poetry is measured by both accents and syllables, it is called *accentual-syllabic*. Most English poetry is accentual-syllabic, as in these iambic tetrameter lines from "To His Coy Mistress":

> Hăd wé bŭt wórld ĕnoúgh, ănd tíme,
> Thĭs cóyneš, ládў, weré nŏ críme.

Each line has four iambic feet—four accented syllables, eight syllables in all. But not all English poetry is accentual-syllabic. Sometimes it is just accentual. Traditional ballads, for example, often count the number of accents per line but not the number of syllables:

> "O whére hae ye beén, Lord Rańdal, my són?
> O wheŕe hae ye beén, my hańdsome young mán?"
> "I hae beén to the wíld woód; móther, máke my bed soón,
> For I'm weáry wi huńting, and fáin wald lie doẃn."

The third line of this stanza contains six accented syllables but thirteen (not twelve) syllables. The first two lines contain four accents but ten (not eight) syllables. And the last line contains four accents but twelve (not eight) syllables. The important factor in purely accentual lines is where the accent falls; the poet can freely use the accents to emphasize meaning. One of the accents in line three, for example, falls on *wild*, which expresses the treacherous place from which Lord Randal has returned.

Because individuals hear and speak a language in different ways, *scanning* a poem (using symbols to mark accented and unaccented syllables and thus identify its metrical pattern) is not an exact science. Some poets establish easily recognizable—often strongly rhythmical— metrical patterns, and scanning their poems is easy. Other poets use more subtle rhythms that make the poetic lines less artificial and more like colloquial language. The best poets often deliberately depart from the metrical pattern they establish at the beginning of the poem. When you scan a poem, therefore, you need not force phrases unnaturally into the established metrical pattern. Always put the accents where you and most speakers would normally say them. The poet probably intends for them to go there.

When you scan a poem, be alert for caesuras. A *caesura* is a strong pause somewhere in the line. You mark a caesura with two vertical lines: ‖. Consider the caesuras in this jump-rope rhyme:

> Cinderella, dressed in yellow,
> Went upstairs ‖ to kiss a fellow.
> Made a mistake; ‖ kissed a snake.
> How many doctors did it take?
> One, two, three, four . . .

A likely place for a caesura is in the middle of the line, and if the meter of the poem is tetrameter, then a caesura in the middle neatly divides the line in half. Such is the case in lines 2 and 3 of this poem. A caesura may also occur near the beginning of a line or near the end. Or there may be no caesuras in a line, as is probably the case in lines 4, 5, and possibly 1 of this poem. Caesuras often emphasize meaning. Caesuras in the middle of lines, for example, can emphasize strong contrasts or close relationships between ideas. In line 3, both the caesura and the rhyme of "mistake" with "snake" link the abstraction (the mistake) with the action (kissing the snake).

A profound example of the relationship between meaning and caesura—indeed, between meaning and all the qualities of poetic sound—is Shakespeare's Sonnet 129:

### SONNET 129

WILLIAM SHAKESPEARE

> Th' expense of spirit ‖ in a waste of shame
> Is lust in action; ‖ and, till action, lust
> Is perjured, murderous, bloody, full of blame,
> Savage, extreme, rude, cruel, not to trust;
> Enjoyed no sooner ‖ but despisèd straight;                5
> Past reason hunted; ‖ and no sooner had,
> Past reason hated, ‖ as a swallowed bait,
> On purpose laid ‖ to make the taker mad;

Mad in pursuit, ‖ and in possession so;
Had, having, and in quest to have, extreme;                    10
A bliss in proof; ‖ and proved, a very woe;
Before, a joy proposed; ‖ behind, a dream.
All this the world well knows; ‖ yet none knows well
To shun the heaven ‖ that leads men to this hell.

Here Shakespeare establishes a pattern of contrasts and similarities, and he uses caesura and other sound devices to establish them. One of these devices is the accentual pattern. Like most sonnets, this one has ten syllables per line and is supposed to be iambic pentameter. But for many of these lines, Shakespeare has only four accents per line, not five. This allows him to make some of his comparisons equal in weight. Line 5, for example, has a strong caesura and four accented syllables:

Enjóyed no soóner ‖ but despiśèd straíght.

The effect is to contrast strongly the two emotional states, pleasure and guilt; and since Shakespeare puts guilt last, he gives it more weight. Lines 11 and 12, however, contain caesuras and five accents each, making the two-part divisions within the lines unequal. Note how this relates to the meaning of the lines:

A bliśs in próof; ‖ and próved, a véry wóe;
Befóre, a jóy propósed; ‖ behińd, a dréam.

The "weaker" sides of the lines contain the pleasure part of the equation and emphasize the brevity and insubstantial quality of pleasure; the "strong" sides emphasize either naïve expectation or guilt.

**Questions about rhythm**    Metrics has many uses in poetry. It provides a method of ordering material. It creates a hypnotic effect that rivets attention on the poem. Like the rhythmic qualities of music, it is enjoyable in itself. Children, for example, take naturally to the strongly rhythmic qualities of nursery rhymes and jump-rope rhymes; jump-rope rhymes, in fact, are that rare form of literature that children teach each other. But probably the greatest importance of metrics is that it establishes a pattern from which the poet can depart. Good poets rarely stick to the metrical pattern they establish at the beginning of the poem or that is inherent in a fixed form like the sonnet. Sonnet 129, on pages 97–98, is a striking example. Sometimes they depart from the established pattern to make the language sound more colloquial. Such is partly the case in "Dover Beach" and Browning's "My Last Duchess," both of which are spoken by fictional characters. Sometimes poets depart from the pattern to emphasize specific parts of the poem's content. This is why you should be sensitive to the natural rhythms of the language when you scan a poem. Take, for example, these lines from Sonnet 129: Lust is like

| | |
|---|---|
| a swallowed bait, | 7 |
| On purpose laid to make the taker mad: | 8 |
| Mád iñ pŭrsúit, añd iñ pŏsséssiŏn só; | 9 |
| Hád, háviñğ, añd iñ quést tŏ háve, eẍtréme; | 10 |
| A bliss in proof; and proved, a very woe; | 11 |
| Before, a joy proposed; behind, a dream. | 12 |

All of these lines fit the iambic scheme except lines 9 and 10. Why? The reason is that Shakespeare wants to emphasize certain words in these two lines, particularly the first words in each. The accents in line 10 are especially emphatic, for the accents emphasize the past ("had"), the present ("having"), the future ("quest" and "have"), and the psychological and moral nature of all three ("extreme").

Questions to ask about rhythm in poetry, then, are these: What metrical pattern does the poem use? What is appealing about the pattern? How closely does the poet stick to the established pattern? If closely, why and what effect is the poet striving for? For example, does the poem have a singsong quality? If so, why does the poet do this? Where does the poem vary from the established pattern? Why? How does the poet use pauses, especially caesuras, within each line? Why?

## ■ Thinking on Paper about Rhythm

1. Count the number of syllables for each line. Write the number at the end of the line.

2. Read the poem aloud, then mark the accented and unaccented syllables of each line.

3. Draw a vertical line between each foot in the line.

4. Identify the metrical pattern (iambic, trochaic, and so forth) and the length of the lines (pentameter, hexameter, and so forth).

5. Use two vertical lines to mark the caesuras in the poem. Explain how the caesuras relate to the sense of each line.

6. Underline the places where the poet departs from the established metrical pattern of the poem. Explain how these departures relate to the sense of each line. Show which words are emphasized by the departures.

7. Explain the appropriateness of the metrical pattern to the poem's meaning.

8. Describe how easy or difficult it is to read the poem aloud. Does the metrical pattern slow you down? Or does it allow you to read smoothly? Explain how the difficulty or ease of reading the metrical pattern relates to the poem's meaning and purpose.

## Sound

Poets delight in the sound of language and consciously present sounds to be enjoyed for themselves. They also use them to emphasize meaning, action, and emotion, and especially to call the reader's attention to the relationship of certain words. Rhyme, for example, has the effect of linking words together. Among the most common sound devices are the following:

**onomatopoeia**—the use of words that sound like what they mean ("buzz," "boom," "hiss," "fizz").

**alliteration**—the repetition of consonant sounds at the beginning of words or at the beginning of accented syllables ("the *w*oeful *w*oman *w*ent *w*ading *W*ednesday").

**assonance**—the repetition of vowel sounds followed by different consonant sounds (*O*, the gr*o*ans that *o*pened to his ears").

**consonance** (or *half-rhyme*)—the repetition of final consonant sounds that are preceded by different vowel sounds (the beas*t* climbed fas*t* to the cres*t*").

**rhyme**—the repetition of accented vowels and the sounds that follow. There are subcategories of rhyme:

*masculine rhyme* (the rhymed sounds have only one syllable: "ma*n*-ra*n*," "dete*ct*-corre*ct*").

*feminine rhyme* (the rhymed sounds have two or more syllables: "s*ubtle*-re*buttal*," "de*ceptively*-per*ceptively*").

*internal rhyme* (the rhymed sounds are within the line).

*end rhyme* (the rhymed sounds appear at the ends of lines).

*approximate rhyme* (the words are close to rhyming: "book-buck," "watch-match," "man-in").

Edgar Allan Poe's "To Helen" illustrates many of these sound devices:

## TO HELEN

EDGAR ALLAN POE

Helen, thy beauty is to me — masculine rhyme/ end rhyme
Like those Nicean barks of yore,
That gently, o'er a perfumed sea,
alliteration     The weary, way-worn wanderer bore
To his own native shore.                                5

consonance     On desperate seas long wont to roam       6
Thy hyacinth hair, thy classic face
Thy Naiad airs have brought me home    approximate rhyme   8
To the glory that was Greece
And the grandeur that was Rome.

assonance     Lo! in yon brilliant window-nich           11
How statue-like I see thee stand!    internal rhyme
The agate lamp within thy hand,
Ah! Psyche, from the regions which
Are Holy Land!

**Questions about sound**     It's easy to lose yourself in an analysis of the mechanical intricacies of a poem's sound structure and forget why you are making the analysis in the first place. You want to ask, What sound devices does the poet use? You also should ask, Why does the poet use them? How do they help establish the poem's tone, atmosphere, theme, setting, characterization, and emotional qualities? In Poe's "To Helen," for example, the alliteration in the fourth line ("*w*eary, *w*ay-*w*orn *w*anderer") underscores the fatigued state of the wanderer. The consonance of "seas" and "airs" in lines 6 and 8 emphasizes the contrast between them; one is "desperate" but the other assuages despair. And the assonance in line 11 ("*in* yon br*i*lliant w*i*ndow-n*i*ch"), with its emphasis on high, tight, "i" sounds, helps to characterize the luminousness of the place where Helen, statuelike, stands.

Be especially alert to the relationships between ideas established by rhyme, most notably by internal rhyme and end rhyme. Rhyme, of course, is a musical device that makes the sound of the poem attractive to the ear, but it can be used meaningfully as well. Turn back to Sonnet 129 and examine the complex sound associations Shakespeare creates there. The words sound rough, almost painful, with their harsh consonants, all of which illustrate the frustrated and frenetic emotional state Shakespeare ascribes to lust. Note the variation on "s" sounds in the first line.

> Th' expense of spirit in a waste of shame

Line 3 begins a list of qualities, and Shakespeare divides and associates them through assonance and alliteration: Lust

> Is perjured, murderous, bloody, full of blame.

The words *perjured* and *murderous* are linked by assonance (the "er" sounds), and they focus on evil deeds (falsehood, murder), leading to the second half of the line. The words *bloody* and *blame* are linked by alliteration, and they focus on the results of evil deeds, especially murder: blood and guilt. The linkages signaled by the poem's end rhyme are also meaningful: shame/blame, lust/not to trust, no sooner had/ make the taker mad, extreme/dream, yet none knows well/leads men to this hell.

In the poem you are analyzing, what linkages of meaning are there to *all* the sound qualities of the words—especially to the obvious ones, such as alliteration, internal rhyme, and end rhyme? What light do these linkages throw on the themes of the entire poem?

## ■ Thinking on Paper about Sound

1. Underline instances of alliteration, assonance, and consonance in the poem. Explain the relationship between these devices and the sense of the lines where they occur.

2. Circle rhymed words. Explain what similarities and contrasts the rhymed words call attention to.

3. Circle words that have meaningful or attractive sound qualities, such as onomatopoetic words. Explain how these words add to the poem's sense.

4. When the sounds of a poem are harsh and grating, the effect is called *cacophony.* When they are pleasing and harmonious, the effect is called *euphony.* Underline instances of cacophony or euphony. Explain how they relate to the poem's sense.

5. Describe any sound devices in the poem that catch you by surprise. Explain how and why the poet uses such surprises.

## Structure

Poets give structure to their poems in two overlapping ways: by organizing ideas according to a logical plan and by creating a pattern of sounds. Arnold arranges "Dover Beach" in both ways, as do most poets. He divides the poem into four units, each of which has a pattern of end rhyme, and he arranges the whole poem rhetorically—that is, by ideas. Each unit elaborates a single point, and each point follows logically from the preceding one.

Perhaps the most common sound device by which poets create structure is end rhyme, and any pattern of end rhyme is called a *rhyme scheme.* Rhyme scheme helps to establish another structural device, the *stanza,* which is physically separated from other stanzas by extra spaces and usually represents one idea.

Stanzas typically have the same structure: the same number of lines, length of lines, metrical patterns, and rhyme schemes. Poets, of course, can create any rhyme scheme or stanza form they choose, but they often work instead within the confines of already established poetic structures. These are called *fixed forms.* Stanzas that conform to no traditional limits, such as those in "Dover Beach," are called *nonce forms.* The most famous fixed form in English is the *sonnet.* Like other fixed forms, the sonnet provides ready-made structural divisions by which a poet can organize ideas. But it also challenges poets to mold unwieldy material into an unyielding structure. The result is a tension between material and form that is pleasing both to poet and reader.

All sonnets have fourteen lines of iambic pentameter. The two best known kinds of sonnets are named for their most famous practitioners. A *Shakespearean sonnet* rhymes abab/cdcd/efef/gg and has a structural division of three quatrains (each containing four lines) and a couplet. A *Petrarchan sonnet* rhymes abbaabba in the octave (the first eight lines) and cdecde in the sestet (the last six lines). Poets often vary the pattern of end rhyme in these kinds of sonnets; this is especially true of the sestet in the Petrarchan sonnet. Note, for example, the following sonnet by Wordsworth. Each kind of sonnet has a *turn,* a point in the poem at which the poet shifts from one meaning or mood to another. The turn in the Shakespearean sonnet occurs between lines 12 and 13 (just before the couplet). The turn in the Petrarchan sonnet occurs between the octave and the sestet. In both forms, the part of the poem before the turn delineates a problem or tension; the part after the turn offers some resolution to or comment on the problem, and it releases the tension.

## SONNET 116

### WILLIAM SHAKESPEARE

| | | |
|---|---|---|
| Let me not to the marriage of true minds | a | |
| Admit impediments. Love is not love | b | |
| Which alters when it alteration finds, | a | |
| Or bends with the remover to remove: | b | 4 |
| Oh, no! it is an ever-fixèd mark, | c | |
| That looks on tempests and is never shaken; | d | |
| It is the star to every wandering bark, | c | |
| Whose worth's unknown, although his height be taken, | d | 8 |
| Love's not Time's fool, though rosey lips and cheeks | e | |
| Within his bending sickle's compass come; | f | |
| Love alters not with his brief hours and weeks, | e | |
| But bears it out even to the edge of doom. | f | 12 |
| If this be error and upon me proved, | g | |
| I never writ, nor no man ever loved. | g | 14 |

three quatrains

turn → couplet

Shakespeare molds the ideas and images of this poem to fit its form perfectly. He states the theme—that love remains constant no matter what—in the first quatrain. In the second, he says that cataclysmic events cannot destroy love. In the third, he says that time cannot destroy love. Finally, in the couplet, he affirms the truth of his theme.

## THE WORLD IS TOO MUCH WITH US

### WILLIAM WORDSWORTH

|  | | |
|---|---|---|
| The world is too much with us; late and soon, | a | |
| Getting and spending, we lay waste our powers; | b | |
| Little we see in nature that is ours; | b | |
| We have given our hearts away, a sordid boon! | a | 4 |
| This Sea that bares her bosom to the moon, | a | |
| The winds that will be howling at all hours, | b | |
| And are up-gathered now like sleeping flowers, | b | |
| For this, for everything, we are out of tune; | a | 8 |
| It moves us not.—Great God! I'd rather be | c | |
| A Pagan suckled in a creed outworn; | d | |
| So might I, standing on this pleasant lea, | c | |
| Have glimpses that would make me less forlorn; | d | |
| Have sight of Proteus rising from the sea; | c | |
| Or hear old Triton blow his wreathèd horn. | d | 14 |

octave — (first 8 lines), turn → (at line 9), sestet — (last 6 lines)

Wordsworth uses the structure of the Petrarchan sonnet to shape his ideas. In the octave he states his general theme—that materialistic values and activities dull our sensitivity to nature. But he divides the octave into two quatrains. In the first he states his theme; in the second he exemplifies it. He then uses the sestet to suggest an alternate attitude, one that might produce a greater appreciation of nature's mystery and majesty.

**Questions about structure**   You can find definitions of many fixed forms—ballad, ode, heroic couplet, Alexandrine stanza, rhyme royal stanza, Spenserian stanza, and so forth—by looking them up in handbooks of literature (see the reading list at the end of this chapter). However, since poets do not always use fixed forms, and since there are many ways to give poetry structure, you should try to answer this question: What devices does the poet use to give the poem structure? Does the poet use rhyme scheme, stanzas, double spaces, indentations, repetition of words and images, line lengths, rhetorical organization? As with rhythm and sound, a follow-up question is of equal consequence: How does the poem's structure emphasize or relate to its meaning? An example of such a relationship is the final stanza of "Dover Beach," in which Arnold uses end rhyme to emphasize opposing worldviews:

| | |
|---|---|
| Ah, love, let us be true | a |
| To one another! for the world, which seems | b |
| To lie before us like a land of dreams, | b |
| So various, so beautiful, so new, | a |
| Hath really neither joy, nor love, nor light, | c |
| Nor certitude, nor peace, nor help for pain; | d |
| And we are here as on a darkling plain | d |
| Swept with confused alarms of struggle and flight, | c |
| Where ignorant armies clash by night. | c |

The rhyme scheme of the first four lines is almost the same as the next five lines; the only difference is the addition of the fifth line. This similarity divides the stanza in half, and the difference in rhymes corresponds to the difference of the ideas in the two halves.

## ■ Thinking on Paper about Structure

1. Mark the rhyme scheme of the poem or stanza. (Use the three examples on pages 104, 105, and above as models for doing this.)

2. Draw horizontal lines between each division of the poem or unit of the poem. In a sonnet, for example, mark divisions between quatrains, couplets, octaves, and sestets. (Use the poems mentioned in the above assignments.)

3. Summarize the meaning of each division of the poem. In a Shakespearean sonnet, for example, summarize the meaning of each quatrain and the couplet. In a Petrarchan sonnet, summarize the meaning of the octave (and the quatrains within the octave) and the sestet. For both kinds of sonnet, indicate how the meaning changes after the turn.

4. Within the poem or stanza, summarize the relationships between ideas suggested by the end rhyme. A couplet, for example, wherever it may appear in the poem or stanza, almost always states one idea or indicates a close connection between the sense of the two lines.

5. If one or more lines are shorter or longer than most of the others, describe the effect of that different length on the sense and impact of the poem or stanza.

6. Account for variations from the established rhyme scheme. Explain how the variations relate to the sense of the poem or stanza.

7. Describe and explain the significance of subtle differences between sections or stanzas in a poem. Ballads, for example, often rely on *incremental repetition,* the repeating of phrases and lines from stanza to stanza but with slight changes. The changes enhance suspense by altering the meaning of each stanza.

8. Outline the units of meaning in the poem. That is, indicate where the poet moves from one idea to another. Show how the units of meaning relate to visual structural divisions (such as stanzas), if they do.

9. Describe the imagery of each unit. Show what images dominate each unit. Show differences in imagery from unit to unit. Explain how the images help create the sense of the unit.

10. Some poems, for instance ballads, the songs in Shakespeare's plays, and popular songs, were meant to be sung. For one of these poems, explain the effect of this intention on the poem (choice of words, metrical pattern, rhyme, other sound devices, stanzaic form). If you can, listen to a recording of the song.

11. Some poems, such as George Herbert's "Easter Wings" and many of the poems by e. e. cummings, create an effect by the way they look on the page. Choose one such poem and explain the relationship between how it looks and other elements of the poem, including rhyme scheme, metrical pattern, line length, word choice, and meaning.

## Free Verse

One sometimes puzzling form of poetry is *free verse.* It is puzzling because it is hard to see obvious structural elements in it. The first practitioner of free verse in modern times was Walt Whitman (beginning with the 1855 edition of *Leaves of Grass*). Many people, when they saw Whitman's poetry for the first time, wondered if it was really poetry. They asked why any "prose" writings could not be arranged into lines of varying lengths and be called poetry. Since Whitman's time, many poets have written in free verse, and there is one very well-known antecedent to Whitman's free verse: the Bible. Hebrew poetry has its own complicated system of rhythms and sound associations, but when it is translated into English it comes out as free verse. Here is a well-known example (from the 1611 King James translation):

> The Lord is my shepherd; I shall not want.
> He maketh me to lie down in green pastures; he leadeth me
>    beside the still waters.
> He restoreth my soul; he leadeth me in the paths of righteousness
>    for his name's sake.
> Yea, though I walk through the valley of the shadow of death, I
>    will fear no evil, for thou art with me; thy rod and thy staff they
>    comfort me.
> Thou preparest a table before me in the presence of mine
>    enemies; thou anointest my head with oil; my cup runneth
>    over.
> Surely goodness and mercy shall follow me all the days of my life,
>    and I will dwell in the house of the Lord for ever.

Free verse is "free" in certain ways. It avoids strict adherence to metrical patterns and to fixed line lengths. But it is not entirely "free," for it uses other ways of creating rhythm and sound patterns. First, it often uses the sound qualities of words to create associations within words—assonance, alliteration, internal rhyme, and so forth. Second, it creates rhythm by repeating phrases that have the same syntactical structure. See the Twenty-third Psalm, for example: "He maketh me," "he leadeth me," "he restoreth my soul," "he leadeth me." A more blatant example appears in the "out of" phrases in the first section of Whitman's "Out of the Cradle Endlessly Rocking":

> Out of the cradle endlessly rocking,
> Out of the mocking-bird's throat, the musical shuttle,
> Out of the Ninth-month midnight . . .

Third, free verse can establish rhythms within lines by creating phrases of about equal length. Finally, free verse can vary lines meaningfully. Whitman, for example, will sometimes have a series of long lines and then one very short line that comments pertly on the preceding lines or resolves a tension within them.

**Questions about free verse** Questions about free-verse poetry, then, should be similar to questions about any poetry. What structural devices—divisions within the poem, line length, repeated syntactical units—does the poet use, and how do they complement the poet's meaning? What patterns of imagery—descriptive and figurative—does the poet use? What sound devices does the poet weave into the poem? Why does the poet choose the words he or she does? Who is the speaker, and to what situation is the speaker responding?

## ■ Thinking on Paper about Free Verse

1. Read the poem aloud. Note the phrases that create the rhythm of the poem.

2. Underline repeated phrases in the poem, as with the "out of the cradle" phrase in Whitman's poem.

3. Mark with double vertical lines the caesuras in each line of the poem.

4. Mark the accents in each line of the poem.

5. Explain why the lines end where they do.

6. Note any variation between short phrases and long phrases. Explain how these variations relate to the sense of the poem.

7. Explain the relationship between the rhythms of the poem and its meaning and purpose.

8. Mark and account for all of the sound qualities of the poem: alliteration, assonance, cacophony, euphony, internal rhyme, and so forth.

## Symbolism

Poets frequently use symbolism because, among other reasons, symbols are highly suggestive yet can be established in just a few words. As we say in Chapter 4, a symbol is an object—usually a physical object—that represents an abstract idea or ideas. The most powerful symbols are those that do not exactly specify the ideas they represent. An example of a symbol in poetry occurs in the Twenty-third

Psalm, printed on page 108. The poem begins with a metaphor: God is like a shepherd and I (the speaker) am like one of his sheep; just as a shepherd takes care of his sheep, so will God take care of me. But the poem shifts from metaphor to symbol with phrases such as "green pastures," "still waters," and particularly "the valley of the shadow of death." The meanings of "green pastures" (nourishment, security, ease) and "still waters" (peace, sustenance, calm) are fairly easy to ascertain. But the meaning of "the valley of the shadow of death" is more difficult. It does not seem to mean just death, but a life experience—perhaps psychological or spiritual—that is somehow related to death (the "shadow" of death) and that we must journey through (through the "valley"). Perhaps the indefiniteness of this phrase, combined with its ominous overtones, explains the grip it has had on people's imaginations for generations.

Another example of a symbol in poetry is William Blake's "The Sick Rose" (1794):

### THE SICK ROSE

WILLIAM BLAKE

O Rose, thou art sick.
The invisible worm
That flies in the night
In the howling storm

Has found out thy bed
Of crimson joy,
And his dark secret love
Does thy life destroy.

This poem can possibly be read as a literal treatment of a real rose beset by some real insect that preys on roses. But Blake probably means for the rose, the worm, and the action of the worm to be taken symbolically. For one thing, the poem occurs in Blake's collection of poems *Songs of Experience,* suggesting that it represents the ominous aspects of life, particularly human life. For another, much of the poem makes little sense unless it can be taken symbolically: the "howling storm," the bed of "crimson joy," the worm's "dark secret love," for example. What, then, do these things represent? One interpretive approach would be to consider word meanings that Blake, who read widely in symbolic Christian literature, may have had in mind. The archaic meaning of "worm" is dragon, which in Christian romance represented evil and harks back to the devil's appearance to Eve as a snake. Also in Christian romance, the rose represented female beauty and purity and sometimes represented the Virgin Mary. Blake seems, then, to be symbolizing the destruction of purity by evil. The poem probably also has sexual implications, since, for example, the worm (a phallic image) comes at "night" to the rose's "bed." In general, the poem may represent the destruction of all earthly health, innocence, and beauty by mysterious forces. The point is that although we get the drift of Blake's meaning, we do not know precisely what the symbolic equivalents are. Yet the symbols are presented so sensuously and the action so dramatically that the poem grips us with a mesmerizing power.

When you read poetry, be alert for symbols, but persuade yourself—and certainly your reader—that the objects you claim to be symbols were intended as such by the author. Remember that not *every* object in a poem is a symbol. What, then, are the symbols in the poem you are reading? Why do you think they are symbols? What do they mean? In answers to this last question, offer reasonable and carefully thought out explanations for your interpretations. Stay close to what the author seems to have intended for the symbols to mean.

## ■ Thinking on Paper about Symbolism

1. Circle the symbols in the poem.

2. List the possible meanings of each symbol. Explain what evidence suggests these meanings.

3. Explain what each symbol contributes to the overall meaning of the poem.

## FOR FURTHER STUDY

Boulton, Marjorie. *The Anatomy of Poetry.* London: Routledge, 1953.

Fussell, Paul, Jr. *Poetic Meter and Poetic Form.* New York: Random, 1967.

Harmon, William, and C. Hugh Holman. *A Handbook to Literature.* 7th ed. Englewood Cliffs: Prentice Hall, 1995.

MacLeish, Archibald. *Poetry and Experience.* Boston: Houghton, 1961.

Preminger, Alex, and T. V. F. Brogan, eds. *The New Princeton Encyclopedia of Poetry and Poetics.* Princeton: Princeton University Press, 1993.

Reeves, James. *Understanding Poetry.* New York: Barnes, 1965.

Marjorie Boulton's *The Anatomy of Poetry* and James Reeves's *Understanding Poetry* offer thorough explanations of the elements of poetry. Both attempt the difficult task of defining poetry. Paul Fussell, Jr., provides a lucid explanation of metrical patterns and poetic structures and how one uses them to analyze poetry. His book concludes with an inviting bibliography. Archibald MacLeish is a fine American poet who, in *Poetry and Experience,* offers his own view of poetry. Holman and Harmon's *Handbook to Literature* is an encyclopedia of literary terms. Preminger and Brogan's *The New Princeton Encyclopedia of Poetry and Poetics* is a superb resource that covers not only the elements and genres of poetry but such things as movements (Romanticism, Renaissance, Classicism), national poetry (Chinese, Mexican, Korean, Latin American), and theory. Entries such as "Structuralism," "Russian Formalism," "Poetry, Theories of," "Deconstruction" provide pithy introductions to recent theoretical approaches to poetry.

# 6

# *Evaluating the Quality of Literature*

D
o you like the literary works you read? When you read literature, you probably cannot avoid answering that question. We all spontaneously evaluate the works read: We like a work, we feel neutral about it, we dislike it. Furthermore, most of us feel uneasy when we hear other people evaluate works we have strong feelings about. We read a work we love only to have somebody tell us they thought it was terrible. Or we read a supposedly wonderful work only to feel let down and disappointed by it. How can you decide for yourself which works are "good" and which ones are "bad"? An easy way is to let other people tell you: your friends, teachers, book reviewers, respected literary critics. Without question, we learn and grow by opening our minds to the opinions of such people. But sometimes the wisdom of tradition can be wrong about literary quality. Even when we think critical judgment may be right, we still must decide matters of quality for ourselves: *Which* great works do *I* like the best? Although critics disagree about the best ways to evaluate literature, this chapter offers some guidelines that may be helpful to you. Evaluation is worth doing for itself, but it can also generate interpretations. Our evaluations of works almost always link to what we think they mean. We think they are good because we like their ideas; we think they are bad because we dislike their ideas. Evaluation and interpretation, then, go hand in hand. As we evaluate, we also interpret.

## DO YOU LIKE THE WORK?

The best place to begin is with yourself. You have a right to decide whether the work is "good" for you. Does the work speak clearly and forcefully to your needs and interests? Does it give you pleasure? If so, then for you it is "good"; if not, for you it is "bad." You may, of course, change your mind when you read the work again. Perhaps the first time you read it you were too young or inexperienced to appreciate its themes and formal devices. Or perhaps a work that once seemed brilliant, now, years later, seems flat and superficial. All kinds of things—your age, circumstances, depth of knowledge, breadth of experience, time constraints, emotional state—affect your evaluation of the works you read.

As you analyze your personal evaluation of a work, keep these questions in mind:

1. If you like the work, why do you? Is it the characters, the setting, the mood, the humor, the ideas, the action, the sentiment, the language? Why does it please you?

2. Does the work move you emotionally? Do you care about its ideas, characters, events? If so, why?

3. If you dislike the work, where specifically does it fail for you? Even if you think highly of a work, what flaws do you think it has?

4. If your acquaintances like or dislike the work, do you agree with their reasons?

In addition to assessing your own evaluation of a work, you may want to judge it "objectively," using principles of evaluation that apply to many readers, not just yourself. People who write book reviews attempt to do this. Reviewers may talk personally about a work, but they also try to give reasons why other people should or should not read it. What are some of the principles that guide their decisions?

Literary critics over the ages have developed principles for evaluating literature. They do not always agree, and their standards of excellence vary from age to age and person to person, but their ideas should help you think about the quality of the works you read. The following questions focus on some of the components of "good" literature. Even if you do not especially like a work, these questions may help you see why other people like it, and they may enhance your own appreciation of it.

## IS THE WORK UNIFIED AND COHERENT?

Many critics claim that unity and coherence are a work's most important aesthetic qualities. If a work is unified and coherent, it is "good."

If not, it is "bad." A *unified* work creates a single effect and has a single aim or purpose; a *coherent* work uses all its elements to attain that effect, to contribute to that aim or purpose.

Critics who value unity in works feel that seemingly superfluous elements mar the quality of works. Sir Walter Scott's novel *Ivanhoe*, for example, begins with a heavy emphasis on Ivanhoe's relationship with the Saxon heroine Rowena, as if it and she are to be important parts of the novel. The story then inexplicably changes its emphasis from their relationship to concentrate on Ivanhoe's troubled relationship with the more exotic and more interesting Rebecca. Another example in *Ivanhoe* would be the character who "dies" in battle, is mourned at length, and then suddenly sits up and proclaims himself recovered. Scott gives no reason for this remarkable reversal; he just puts it in. In fact, Scott often seems to be writing to please the momentary interests of his readers. He wants to tell a good story, not to create a unified work of art. Consequently, some critics downgrade the quality of *Ivanhoe*. They admit that it is a good "read" the first time through, but conclude that it does not reward more careful attention. O. Henry is another writer whom some critics deride, in this case for his contrived endings. In his short stories, he creates a set of circumstances only to produce endings that don't follow logically from these circumstances. These endings may pleasantly surprise us by their happy turn of events, but they seem inconsistent with what precedes them and thus are ultimately unsatisfying.

It may be that critics overemphasize the importance of unity and coherence in literature. Some forms of literature, namely novels, long narrative poems, and plays, lend themselves to disparateness. Shakespeare and Dickens include extraneous elements in their works, and yet their works are unquestionably "great." Works that benefit most from the demand for unity and coherence are short works like stories and poems, in which practically every word can count toward a total effect and in which coherence is recognizable almost at a glance. But most good works, including long ones, seem to have an *overall* sense of consistency and order, even if a few elements may not seem to fit the pattern. Careful analysis of the texts should reveal such patterns.

## DOES THE WORK GIVE CONTINUAL PLEASURE?

Does the work give pleasure the first time through? Does it give pleasure on subsequent readings? Answers to these questions are obviously subjective and vary from person to person. One way to answer them is to examine a work's history. If a work has survived several generations of readers, the answer to both questions might be yes. If a work was very popular with one generation but with no others, the answer to the first question might be yes and to the second no. Such historical evidence is inadequate, however. A work might be rediscovered, or it might never have been popular but nonetheless have been read and reread by an elite group. Or it might be too new to have become popular.

The pleasure-giving quality of literature is mysterious. Two criteria for evaluating it may be helpful. First, some critics hold that novelty and surprise are major causes of pleasure. Thus many novels give pleasure by using exotic settings, unusual characters, and suspenseful plots. Publishers call such novels "page turners" because they compel the reader to keep turning the page to find out what will happen next. The novels of Robert Louis Stevenson, Jack London, James Fenimore Cooper, Alexander Dumas, Rafael Sabatini, James Michener, Agatha Christie, Leon Uris, Herman Wouk, Allen Drury, Victoria Holt, and a host of other best-selling writers are examples of page turners. The novelty of the material makes our first-time experience with the work exciting and fun, but good works of art should give pleasure beyond a first-time reading. You should be able to reread them and *continue* to find novelty and to be surprised. The limitation of a suspenseful plot is that once you know "what happens," its chief interest is dissipated. If a work continues to be new to you, then it is "good."

A second criterion for evaluating the pleasure a work provides is the distinction critics make between easy and difficult beauty. Difficult beauty, they maintain, is preferable to easy beauty. Elements that give immediate pleasure, such as dramatic plots, simple ideas, heroic characters, euphonious language, glamorous settings, and happy endings do not give as lasting satisfaction as materials that seem at first to discourage enjoyment, such as tragic events, plain and troubled characters, dissonant language, threatening landscapes, undramatic happenings, and pessimistic ideas. The reason may be that the difficult materials emerge from aspects of life that deeply affect us emotionally and intellectually, and we take longer-lasting satisfaction in seeing works of art put them in order. The easy materials, in other words, give superficial pleasure; the difficult materials give profound pleasure.

## IS THE WORK TRUE?

Critics are divided about the importance of "truth" in literature. Some contend that even though a work may represent great ideas, it still may not be good. Others argue that a work can be very skillfully assembled, but if it has no relation to the real world, then it is not as good as works that do. Each reader must resolve this controversy to his or her own satisfaction. Probably, however, the works that people read again and again are those that offer some insight into the nature of the real world. In this section we will discuss some questions that should help you to determine the quality of the "truth" offered in literary works.

## Is the Work Meaningful?

Although it is possible to have meaningless works in other media—dance, music, painting, sculpture—it is probably impossible to create a totally meaningless work of literature. The reason is that literature uses an inherently meaningful medium: language. Words are symbols. At least on a practical level, they connect with aspects of reality, and the stringing of words together into phrases makes them coherent. Words become ideas. Also, literature represents real life, at least superficially, or else we could not understand it. If it did not, it would be another art form, either visual (a kind of "painting") or aural (a kind of "music"), but not literature.

However, literature can *avoid* meaning by creating imaginary worlds that have little practical relation to the real world. Usually this literature is "escapist" because it emphasizes the ideal—characters, settings, and events that rarely exist in the real world. In the dissolute court of Charles II (king of England, 1660–85), the most popular works of literature were long French romances depicting impossibly honorable courtiers and impossibly beautiful and chaste heroines interacting in an impossibly just court. A modern example would be Ian Fleming's James Bond thrillers, whose protagonist possesses incredible skills and tolerances, meets an endless sequence of willing, shapely females, gets caught up in bizarre conspiracies (like voodoo on the Southern Railroad), and clashes with supervillains who gain immense power and yet who stupidly tell Bond all their secrets. Usually such works are enjoyable for a single reading, or they are important for what they reflect of the values and tastes of their reading public. But because they have little relation to the real world, they are quickly forgotten. They are not "good" literature.

## Does Your Perception of the Real World Square with the Author's?

One way to assess the meaningfulness of a work is to compare its presentation and interpretation of reality with your own perceptions and experience. Of course, your experience is not the totality of experience. You also should consider other readers' experiences and reactions to the work. But we are all limited by time and space. We must base decisions about truth on what we know now, not on what other people know or on what we will know later. Such decisions are valid and important.

## Does the Work Present the Probable and the Typical?

Since authors best communicate their interpretations of reality by presenting the probable and typical, your assessment of their ability to do so is crucial to determining a work's meaningfulness. Examples of atypical characters are the flat characters of melodrama: the unmotivated villain, the pure-as-the-driven-snow heroine, the square-jawed hero. Examples of improbable events are the hero's arrival just in time to rescue the heroine from being sawed in half or run over by a train, the corrupt politician's sudden conversion to righteousness, the spendthrift father's avoidance of financial rain by inheriting a fortune or winning the state lottery.

## Does the Work Present a Mature Vision of Reality?

Any work can offer an interpretation of reality, but some interpretations are immature and simpleminded. More valuable are those that reflect qualities that serious, thoughtful people would accept. These include a recognition of the world's potential for injustice and tragedy, of the ambiguity inherent in moral choices and judgments, of the complexity of human events and decisions, of the three-dimensionality of human nature. The world is filled, for example, with people who do both evil and good. A mature view recognizes that such people are equal to more than just a limited set of actions. The death-row murderer has some admirable (or at least sympathetic) traits. The philanthropist is capable of destructive acts and of cruelty. All people are flawed and all people have redeeming traits.

## Does the Work's Interpretation
## of Reality Deserve Serious Reflection?

Sometimes we may find ourselves in disagreement with a work's world view. Sinclair Lewis's *Babbitt,* James Joyce's *Ulysses,* Arthur

Miller's *The Crucible,* Allen Ginsberg's *Howl,* and D. H. Lawrence's *Lady Chatterley's Lover* present views of the world that have been extremely controversial and that many people still find objectionable. If you object to a work's ideas, you can test their quality by asking if the author has rendered them vividly, has represented his or her position fairly (that is, has kept opposing positions in sight), and has focused on ideas that are worth thinking about. One value of literature is that it compels us, through the force and logic of its imagined worlds, to give serious consideration to important concepts with which we are unfamiliar or with which we disagree. If the artist renders his or her ideas compellingly and if they are important, then that is all he or she can be expected to do. The author's ideas are "good." But just because a work has artistic integrity does not mean we have to agree with the author's world view.

## Is the Work Universal?

Does the work transcend the ideology of the author? Does it transcend the narrow concerns, obsessions, and prejudices of one reader, one group, one society, one nation, one generation, one century?

These questions represent one test of a work's quality. The better a work can "live" beyond the interests of a few readers, the better the work is. This does not mean that everyone will like the works of Chaucer, Dante, Shakespeare, Spenser, Milton, Wordsworth, Racine, Goethe, Molière, Emily Brontë, Homer, Ovid, Dickens, Emily Dickinson, or George Eliot. It means that their works have touched an ever-increasing number of people, that they have universal appeal. It also means that the *ideas* represented in their works are in accord with most people's perception of reality, even though those ideas might emerge from narrow ideological concerns. John Bunyan, for example, was a radical, nonconformist English minister living in a time famous for its fierce struggles between religious groups. He was a mentally wracked, obsessive Calvinist whose narrative *The Pilgrim's Progress* reflects anguish over his immediate condition—he was in jail—and over his state of grace. He meant it as a guide for members of his own sect. Yet even though its protagonist, "Christian," must travel the straight and narrow Puritan road to the "Celestial City," somehow Christian becomes more than a seventeenth-century Puritan. His struggles, temptations, emotions, and interests are those that we all feel as we make our way through life. His companions may have allegorical names—Obstinate, Hopeful, Faithful, Pliable, Mr. Worldly Wiseman, Talkative, Giant Despair—but they embody people that any of us might meet. His places—Vanity Fair, the Slough of Despond, Doubting Castle, the Valley of the Shadow of Death—have a psychological and even a physical reality that has meaning for all readers. The basic theme of the book—that life threatens and tests our emotional and moral integrity with ambiguous situations—is one that we all recognize as true. Christian could as well be called "Everyman," for his pilgrimage is real to many people, no matter of what faith, nationality, or century.

### Are the Ideas of the Work Consistent with One Another and with the Form of the Work?

A work's ideas must emerge convincingly from its form, not be imposed on that form. One should be able to induce the work's ideas from its materials. No one, including the author, should have to tell us what a work means. Furthermore, if all the elements of a work are logically related to one another and to an overriding purpose, then the work's ideas will also be consistent with one another. A work should not, for example, show us that one thing is true in one part and that a contradictory thing is true in another part. Henry David Thoreau seems to do this in *Walden,* where throughout he praises the "indescribable innocence and beneficence of Nature" and then in the chapter called "Higher Laws" says that "Nature" (the "animal" part of humanity) is evil and must be suppressed; nature is "hard to be overcome, but she must be overcome."

## IS THE LANGUAGE OF THE WORK APPEALING?

The appeal of an author's use of language, especially if it is prose rather than poetry, may be hard to define. The writer may be especially adept at imitating the rhythms of spoken speech, at using internal rhyme, at choosing apt and delightful words, at building suspenseful sentences, at making witty or striking analogies. Emerson and Thoreau are famous, for example, for their pithy, rhetorical phrasing. We expect the language of poetry to be appealing, but one test of the quality of any work is the ability of its language to grip us. The stories and novels of F. Scott Fitzgerald may sometimes seem trivial but they are wonderfully, charmingly written. The attractiveness of a work's language helps make it "good."

## DOES THE AUTHOR PRESENT HIS OR HER WORLD VIVIDLY AND INTENSELY?

This quality, like compelling language, is difficult to define, but some authors have the ability to imprint their worlds so vividly on our imaginations that no matter how ridiculous those worlds may be, we delight in the mere rendering of them. Poe and Dickens describe scenes that are utter nonsense (Dickens has one of his villains, whose name is "Krook," die of spontaneous combustion) but are so graphic that we enjoy them nonetheless. The energy and virtuosity of a work may give pleasure no matter what the materials.

## HOW WELL DOES THE WORK USE GENERIC ELEMENTS?

Are the characters believable? Is the plot plausible? Are the symbols appropriate? These are but a few questions dealing with specific elements in a work. For more detailed discussions of these questions, see Chapters 3, 4, and 5.

# 7

# *Specialized Approaches to Analyzing Literature*

The preceding chapters describe strategies for interpreting literature, that draw mainly upon information in the works themselves. Other interpretive methods, however, often require specialized knowledge, knowledge that comes from disciplines such as linguistics, philosophy, anthropology, and psychology. Some of these approaches are more accessible than others, but all of them are based on principles that are provocative and that might help you interpret works as you read and study them. These approaches not only contain theories of what literature is and how one should study it, but they also state or imply concepts whose implications extend well beyond the study of literature. This chapter describes some of the best known of these specialized approaches and places them in a historical framework. If you are interested in following up on any of these approaches, each discussion includes a brief list of sources for further reading. An overview of these and other theoretical approaches to literature is *A Handbook of Critical Approaches to Literature,* third edition, edited by Wilfred L. Guerin, et al. (New York: Oxford University Press, 1992). K. M. Newton's *Interpreting the Text: A Critical Introduction to the Theory and Practice of Literary Interpretation* (New York: St. Martin's, 1990) thoughtfully probes how twentieth-century critical approaches help readers interpret literature. Gerald Graff's *Professing Literature: An Institutional History* (Chicago: University of Chicago Press, 1987) is a readable history of how critical approaches have affected the teaching of literature in the United States. Wendell V. Harris's *Dictionary of Concepts in Literary Criticism and Theory* (New York: Greenwood, 1992) and Frank Lentricchia's *Critical Terms for Literary Study* (Chicago: University of Chicago Press, 1995) provide definitions and brief discussions of theoretical concepts.

## HISTORICAL CRITICISM

Two specialized approaches, historical and biographical criticism, emerged in the nineteenth century as a result of the widespread faith in science. Critics felt that they could understand literature best by studying the factual causes of the work: the social and cultural environment from which it came, the author's life, the author's intentions, the sources on which the work was based. They believed that their approach was "scientific" because they were dealing with objective reality—historically verifiable facts—and were using a scientific method for collecting such facts.

*Historical criticism* attempts to study literature by period and movement. This approach recognizes that literary phenomena—methods of composition, subject matter, and philosophical outlook—characterize various historical periods. Thus, the use of blank verse in plays characterizes the Shakespearean era; the use of heroic couplets, the Neoclassical era. An emphasis on free will characterizes the Romantic movement; a philosophy of determinism, the Realistic and Naturalistic movements. A focus on hedonistic self-indulgence distinguishes the 1920s; an attention to social conflict, the 1930s. The historical approach also assumes that literary periods and movements are dynamic. As one period reaches exhaustion, another period begins.

The historical approach has several goals: to study a work's relationship to its own and other periods, to learn more about a writers culture, to place the work within an evolving tradition (such as the novel, Christian literature, allegory, political fiction, the epic), to compare it with the literature of other countries. The most important goal of historical criticism, however, is to illuminate the work. We know, for example, that Jack London read the most influential thinkers of his day, Darwin and Spencer; by studying their ideas, we understand better the philosophical implications of London's fiction. T. S. Eliot, like other poets of the early twentieth century, read the French Symbolist poets; by studying their poetry, we understand Eliot's methods better. John Steinbeck depicted the social dislocations of poor people in the 1930s, and by studying their problems and the social theories prominent then, we understand his themes better.

Undergraduate survey courses typically use a historical approach. They present a country's literature chronologically or thematically and show how authors exemplify their periods. The papers you write for survey courses will often focus on the relationship between a work and its historical context. One way to generate interpretations for these courses is to apply definitions of social, intellectual, and literary trends to individual works—definitions of concepts such as romanticism, realism, neoclassicism, symbolism, the Renaissance, modernism, surrealism, Darwinism, imagism, and naturalism. The most obvious source of these definitions is your instructor, but you can also find good definitions in dictionaries of literary terms, literary histories, encyclopedias, history books, and other sources of background information. Another source of interpretations is comparisons—comparisons of works from different movements, comparisons of works from the same period. A third source is the cultural traits authors describe or draw upon for their themes. William Faulkner, for example, used the "Southern Myth" in his fiction—a nostalgic, glorified concept of Southern ideals and history that evolved before the Civil War and received acute enlargement afterward. Faulkner never says directly that he focuses on this myth, but by studying Southern history and observing the myth in other works, we can see that he does so, and thus we can understand better the unspoken, implied tensions in his work.

Two comprehensive examples of historical criticism are the *Columbia Literary History of the United States* (New York: Columbia UP, 1988) edited by Emory Elliott and others, and *The Literary History of England*, second edition (New York: Appleton, 1967), edited by Albert C. Baugh and others. Two venerable works that attempt to establish the "spirit of the age" as background for understanding literature are E. M. W. Tillyard's *The Elizabethan World Picture* (New York: Random House, 1943) and M. I. Finley's *The World of Odysseus* (New York: Penguin, 1954). E. D. Hirsch, Jr., in *Validity in Interpretation* (New Haven: Yale University Press, 1967) argues that the best interpretation of works of literature must rest on ascertaining the authors' intentions. One does this by historical and biographical investigation. A fine historical treatment of a genre is Walter Allen's *The English Novel: A Short Critical History* (New York: Dutton, 1954).

# BIOGRAPHICAL CRITICISM

The *biographical approach* relates the author's life and thought to his or her works. Usually the author's life and thought are reflections of his or her time and are thus important aspects of the historical approach. Sometimes a writer may have been ahead of his or her time, or may even be unclassifiable. Or the writer may have been the predominant figure of the time. Or the writer's life may have been the major source of his or her literary material. For whatever reason, a writer's life may shed light on his or her literature and the literature of the era.

The biographical approach has two major advantages. First, it helps to illuminate elements within a work—words, allusions to local and historical events, conflicts, themes, characters, and setting. Learning, for example, that F. Scott Fitzgerald had an ambivalent attitude toward people with great wealth prompts us to look for a similar ambivalence in his works. Second, works often take on an added significance when we see them as expressions of authors' deep concerns and conflicts. The more we empathize with a writer's problems, the more meaningful his or her works may seem to us. The more we know about the full historical and biographical context of a work's themes, the more relevant they may seem to all human experience.

Third, we can discover more about a work's meaning and importance by trying to understand the author's intentions and audience. Authors don't always state their intentions; even when they do, we may not interpret their works the way they intended. Knowing something about their intentions and the reactions they wanted to draw from their original audiences gives us at least a starting point for understanding their works, and sometimes we recover understandings of works that time has otherwise erased.

If you use the biographical approach, avoid two mistakes. First, avoid equating the work's contents with the author's life. They are not necessarily the same. No matter what the source of a work's material may be, it is a *recreation* of life, a stylization and alteration of it. Literature is "fictional." Some scholars argue that even nonfictional writings such as memoirs and autobiographies have a fictional quality. Second, avoid using unsound sources of information. Many biographies are highly speculative or contain erroneous information. Not until the twentieth century, for example, did we have a biography of Edgar Allan Poe that did not distort, sometimes grossly, the facts about his life.

Three fine and enjoyable examples of biographical criticism are K. J. Fielding's *Charles Dickens: A Critical Introduction* (Boston: Houghton, 1964), F. W. Dupee's *Henry James: His Life and Writings* (Garden City: Doubleday, 1956), and Arthur Mizener's *The Far Side of Paradise: A Biography of F. Scott Fitzgerald* (Boston: Houghton, 1965).

## SOCIAL CRITICISM

The economic theories of Karl Marx and the psychological theories of Sigmund Freud gave birth early in the twentieth century to three critical approaches that were influential before World War II and that, with modifications, continue to be practiced today. They are social criticism, psychological criticism, and archetypal criticism.

*Social criticism* is similar to historical criticism in recognizing literature as a reflection of its environment. It would focus, for example, on the ways in which Jane Austen's novels depict the emphasis on decorum and etiquette by the English country gentry at the end of the eighteenth century. In recent times, especially between World War I and World War II, social criticism has described a particular kind of social reality and sometimes a particular economic and social theory. Social critics were most active in the 1930s during the Great Depression. They applauded literature that depicted the struggles of the poor and downtrodden, especially when they engaged in strikes against oppressive capitalist bosses. Examples of literature with such strong "proletarian" elements are the works of Carl Sandburg, Émile Zola, Maxim Gorky, Nikolai Gogol, Frank Norris, Charles Dickens, Richard Wright, John Steinbeck, Theodore Dreiser, John Dos Passos, and James T. Farrell. The social critics usually approved of a socialist solution to the problems of the oppressed, and they sometimes judged the quality of works solely on the basis of their Marxist orientation. Partly because of this narrowness of focus and rigidity of standards, the social approach, as it was applied in the 1930s, has lost some of its appeal. It showed, however, that many works do reflect society in great detail, that they sometimes attempt to reform society, and that understanding them means, in part, grappling with the social issues they reflect. A well-known and thorough work of social criticism is Granville Hicks's *The Great Tradition: An Interpretation of American Literature Since the Civil War* (New York: Macmillan, 1935).

If the social approach seems relevant to works you want to write about, you should first define the social situations the works describe and identify the authors' attitudes toward them. Do the authors, for example, seem to have solutions in mind? Do they feel that society has to be the way they describe it? If you suspect that the authors depict a historical situation and you want to compare their treatment with the actual events, then you will need to seek reliable secondary sources. (Primary and secondary sources are discussed in Chapter 11.) If you want to argue that particular economic or social theories help to explain an author's social concerns in a work, you will need reliable explanations of those theories.

Since World War II, a new generation of Marxist critics has infused social criticism with renewed vigor. An example is the Hungarian critic Georg Lukacs, who argues that literature should reflect the real world.

Lukacs does not mean that literature should be a mirror image of society by, for example, giving detailed descriptions of its physical contents or its patterns of behavior. Rather, literature should represent the economic tensions in society as described in Marx's writings. Ironically, for Lukacs, works that give an accurate description of the real world may be less "real" than works that emphasize themes (ideas) over description. Lukacs believes that literature might even have to distort reality in order to represent the "truth" about society. To show the economic struggles caused by capitalism, for example, an author might have to create character types one would never meet in real life. Lukacs, therefore, prefers the novels of Balzac to those of Flaubert, because even though Balzac's plots and characters are less plausible than Flaubert's, Balzac reveals the economic pitfalls of capitalism as Marx saw them.

A general introduction to Marxist literary criticism is Peter Demetz's *Marx, Engels, and the Poets: Origins of Marxist Literary Criticism* (Chicago: University of Chicago Press, 1959). For a brief overview of contemporary Marxist criticism, see David Forgacs's "Marxist Literary Theories" in *Modern Literary Theory: A Comparative Introduction*, edited by Ann Jefferson and David Robey (Totowa, NJ: Barnes and Noble, 1982). A defense of the Marxist approach is Terry Eagleton's *Marxism and Literary Criticism* (Berkeley: University of California Press, 1976). Eagleton's *Literary Theory: An Introduction* (Minneapolis: University of Minnesota Press, 1983) surveys modern critical theory from a Marxist point of view.

# PSYCHOLOGICAL CRITICISM

*Psychological criticism* attempts to apply modern psychological theories to authors and their works. Because of Sigmund Freud's predominance in the field of psychology in the twentieth century, psychological criticism usually relies upon the complex and multiple theories of his. Although not all of Freud's ideas relate to literature, many literary critics find three of them very attractive: the dominance of the unconscious mind over the conscious, the expression of the unconscious mind through symbols (most notably in dreams), and the primacy of sexuality as a motivating force in human behavior. These three ideas are related. Freud believed that sexual drives reside in the unconscious, that the conscious mind represses them, and that unconscious symbols usually represent this repressed sexual energy.

The earliest Freudian critics saw literature as a kind of "dream" and thus a source of insight into the authors themselves. Using works of literature as symbolic representations of an author's subconscious, Freudian critics would create a psychological portrait of the author. An example of this kind of psychobiography is Marie Bonaparte's *The Life and Works of Edgar Allan Poe: A Psychoanalytic Interpretation* (London: Imago Press, 1949). Early Freudian critics also used psychoanalytic principles to analyze characters in works of literature. They looked upon characters as having motivations, conflicts, desires, and inclinations similar to those of real people. They sought psychological clues to the makeup of literary characters, especially the unconscious symbolic expressions found in dreams and repeated patterns of behavior and speech. In Eugene O'Neill's *Long Day's Journey into Night*, for example, whenever Mary Tyrone raises her hands to her hair, she unconsciously expresses anxiety about her wrecked youth, health, and innocence. Many authors purposely incorporated psychological theories into their works. Eugene O'Neill, D. H. Lawrence, Sherwood Anderson, and Tennessee Williams, for example, were familiar with Freudian psychology. Some writers employed structural devices drawn from psychological theories. Examples are the *stream of consciousness* technique, which conforms to William James's ideas about the workings of the conscious mind; and the surrealistic technique, which conforms to Freud's ideas about the undisciplined unconscious. Examples of stream-of-consciousness narration are James Joyce's *Portrait of the Artist as a Young Man* and *Ulysses,* William Faulkner's *The Sound and the Fury,* T. S. Eliot's "The Love Song of J. Alfred Prufrock," Virginia Woolf's *To the Lighthouse,* and O'Neill's *Strange Interlude.* Examples of surrealism are Joyce's *Finnegans Wake* and the fiction of Franz Kafka.

Many other works of literature were also rich fields for early psychological criticism, even though they may not have been directly influenced by psychological theories. Freudian critics were interested in any works that are themselves dreamlike, such as Lewis Carroll's *Alice in Wonderland,* or that contain accounts of characters' dreams, as do some of Dostoevsky's novels. Other works have appealed to psychological critics because of their heavy emphasis on complex or unusual characters.

Recent psychological critics continue to find in Freud's theories a rich source of ideas about literature, but whereas earlier critics focused on author and characters, recent critics have turned their attention to the relationship between text and reader. The critic Norman Holland, for example, argues that the text contains a secret expression of what the reader wants to hear. The reader is not consciously aware of this urge, but it is nonetheless the cause of his enjoyment of the work. The French critic Jacques Lacan holds that the structure and devices of literature make it similar to the unconscious, which Lacan claims is a product of language and is structured like language.

One of the most influential works of early psychological criticism is Ernest Jones's *Hamlet and Oedipus* (New York: Norton, 1949), in which Jones, a psychiatrist, argues that Hamlet's problems stem from Oedipal conflicts. An anthology of psychological criticism is *Literature and Psychoanalysis* (New York: Columbia UP, 1983), edited by Edith Kurzweil and William Phillips. This collection opens with writings by Freud, includes a sampling of Freudian critics from early to recent times, and gives examples of Freudian approaches to individual works of literature such as *Alice in Wonderland* and Kafka's fiction. *The Purloined Poe: Lacan, Derrida, and Psychoanalytic Reading* (Baltimore: Johns Hopkins UP, 1988), edited by John P. Muller and William J. Richardson, features psychoanalytic readings of Edgar Allan Poe's detective story "The Purloined Letter." It includes an influential essay by Jacques Lacan as well as responses to Lacan's approach by other critics.

# ARCHETYPAL CRITICISM

*Archetypal criticism* emerged from the theories of the Swiss psychologist Carl Jung. Jung accepted Freud's concept of the unconscious mind, but whereas Freud held that each person's unconscious is unique, Jung argued that a part of the unconscious is linked by historical associations and communal "memories" to the unconscious minds of all people. To represent this phenomenon, he coined the phrase "collective unconscious." He believed that certain human products and activities—myth, symbols, ritual, literature—reproduced these memories in the form of "archetypes." Jung defined an *archetype* as any figure or pattern that recurred in works of the imagination from generation to generation. Although there are many possible archetypes, they fall into three broad categories.

## Archetypal Characters

The first category, characters, contains such figures as the hero, the rake, the scapegoat, the outcast, the hypersensitive youth, the earth mother, the martyr, the *femme fatale,* the rebel, the cruel stepmother, the saint, the "spiritual" woman, the tyrannical father, star-crossed lovers, and the ruler. The following are examples of literary treatments of some of these archetypes: the *femme fatale* (Shakespeare's *Antony* and *Cleopatra*, Mérimee's *Carmen*, Keats's "La Belle Dame sans Merci," Zola's *Nana*); the tyrannical father (Besier's *The Barretts of Wimpole Street*, Shakespeare's *King Lear*, Longfellow's *Hiawatha*); the hero (Hemingway's *For Whom the Bell Tolls*, Cooper's *The Last of the Mohicans*, Malory's *Morte d'Arthur*, the anonymous *Sir Gawain and the Green Knight*, Homer's *The Iliad*); the scapegoat (Jackson's "The Lottery," Melville's *Billy Budd*); the outcast (Dickens's *Great Expectations*, Hugo's *The Hunchback of Notre Dame*, the Book of Job, Coleridge's "The Rime of the Ancient Mariner," Tennyson's "The Lady of Shalott"); the rake (Byron's *Don Juan*, Richardson's *Clarissa*, Etheridge's *The Man of Mode*, Goldsmith's *She Stoops to Conquer*, Marvell's "To His Coy Mistress," Wycherley's *The Country Wife*); and star-crossed lovers (Marlowe's "Hero and Leander," Shakespeare's *Romeo and Juliet*, Hawthorne's *The Scarlet Letter*).

## Archetypal Situations

The second category, situations, includes the quest, the initiation, the journey, the fall, death and rebirth, and the task. Some works, like *Oedipus Rex*, contain more than one archetypal situation. Oedipus makes a "quest" for the truth about King Laius's murderer. He has already performed a task—solving the riddle of the Sphinx's—that saved the kingdom. When he achieves his quest, he suffers a catastrophic fall (from highest in the land to lowest). The quest is usually combined with a journey, as in the search for the Holy Grail of Arthurian legend, and often results in the initiation of a naïve, inexperienced protagonist into the hardship and complexity of life. Examples of works dealing with initiation are Hawthorne's "Young Goodman Brown," Joyce's "Araby," Dickens's *Great Expectations*, Fitzgerald's *The Great Gatsby*, Crane's *The Red Badge of Courage*, and Hardy's *Jude the Obscure*. The death–rebirth archetype appears in myth and fantasy as the literal death and rebirth of a character—Snow White and Sleeping Beauty, for example—but in more realistic literature it often appears in connection with seasonal changes: fall (old age), winter (death), spring (rebirth), summer (life and fruition). In such works, seasonal changes emphasize the metaphorical death and rebirth of a character or place. For example, Émile Zola's *Germinal* concludes with spring, and the renewal of plant and animal life coincides with the end of the workers' strike. The mining town has "died" as an economic entity, but with the end of the strike it is reborn. Spring also represents the germination and growth of ideas that will lead to a better life for the workers. Often allied with the death–rebirth situation is a descent into hell. In some works, such as Homer's *The Odyssey,* Virgil's *The Aeneid,* and Dante's *The Divine Comedy,* the protagonist literally descends into hell. But in works that shun fantasy, the journey is metaphorical and equivalent to a traversal of hell-like places (T. S. Eliot's *The Waste Land*) or to psychological states of deep despair. Dostoevsky's Raskolnikov in *Crime and Punishment* emerges, at the end, from a psychological hell brought on by his cold-blooded murder of an innocent person. Tennessee Williams's play *Orpheus Descending* and Jean Cocteau's film *Orphée* are conscious metaphorical uses of the journey-into-hell archetype.

## Archetypal Symbols and Associations

The third category of archetypes is symbols and associations, many of which suggest polarities. Examples are light–darkness (light equals knowledge, hope, purity, spirituality; dark equals ignorance, despair, evil, bestiality), water–desert (water equals rebirth, life, creativity; desert equals spiritual and intellectual sterility, death), heights–depths (heights equal achievement, sublimity, heaven, revelation, purity; depths equal dejection, mystery, entrapment, hell, death), and the already mentioned spring–winter. One critic argues that the novels of Hemingway use the height–depth polarity: When Hemingway's characters occupy high places, things go well for them; when they descend to the lowlands, the fragile order of their world falls apart.

## The Appeal of Archetypal Criticism

Jung's theories are controversial among psychologists, but they have attracted literary critics for several reasons. One is that remarkably similar patterns do exist from culture to culture. Early Christian missionaries, for example, encountered myths celebrating a martyred, resurrected hero who promised to return and bring a new, golden age. Such was the case when the Aztecs mistook Cortez for the god Quetzalcoatl. Another reason is Jung's contention that archetypes have a profound emotional and intellectual impact on people, that people unconsciously recognize them as being somehow profoundly meaningful. This theory helps critics explain, apart from aesthetics, the long-lasting appeal of such works as *Oedipus Rex,* the *Odyssey,* portions of the Bible, the Greek myths, and fairy tales. The archetypal approach also helps explain the appeal of art forms that lack high aesthetic quality—

but that are nonetheless very popular—such as American westerns, detective and spy stories, and soap operas. In fact, critics often use the archetypal approach to understand not just the literature of a culture but the culture itself. A culture's recurring emphasis on extensive travel, for example, might suggest restlessness and rootlessness. Patterns featuring strong, dominant females might suggest a diminished masculine role. Recurrent violence might indicate a lack of patience to solve complex problems peacefully and lastingly. Archetypal critics have made all of these points about American society.

Perhaps the most practical attraction of archetypal criticism is simply the recognition that patterns in literature do exist and recur, that they often give structure to a work, that many artists have used them in one way or another, and that, for whatever reason, they often deal with profound aspects of human experience. You don't have to believe in Jung's theories to use the archetypal approach to literature. You need only be alert to the possibility of recurring patterns and write about them if you find them meaningful.

Norman Friedman in Chapter 16 of *Form and Meaning in Fiction* (Athens: U of Georgia P, 1975) provides thought-provoking descriptions of frequently used archetypal patterns. A work that thoroughly explores one archetype is Joseph Campbell's *The Hero with a Thousand Faces* (New York: Pantheon, 1949). Two controversial, but enjoyable, works of archetypal literary criticism by Leslie A. Fiedler are *Love and Death in the American Novel*, revised edition (New York: Stein, 1966) and *No! In Thunder: Essays on Myth and Literature* (New York: Stein, 1972). The most important spokesperson for archetypal criticism is Northrop Frye; see especially *The Educated Imagination* (Bloomington: Indiana UP, 1964) and *Anatomy of Criticism* (Princeton: Princeton UP, 1957).

## NEW CRITICISM

In the United States perhaps the most influential movement in literary criticism since World War II has been New Criticism. Although New Criticism began well before World War II, with the criticism of T. S. Eliot and I. A. Richards, it received its fullest expression after the war by such critics as John Crowe Ransom, W. K. Wimsatt, Allen Tate, Cleanth Brooks, and Robert Penn Warren. These and other New Critics published best-selling textbooks that established practical and easily understood ways of teaching and studying literature. These ways continue to influence the study of literature in American higher education.

The term "New Criticism" comes from the title of a book published by John Crowe Ransom in 1941, *The New Criticism* (Norfolk, CT: New Directions). Ransom surveyed the work of recent ("new") critics and thereby made clear some of his own critical principles. Other critics who agreed with Ransom came to be called the New Critics. The New Critics break dramatically with the nineteenth-century emphasis on historical and biographical background. They hold that understanding and appreciating a work of literature need have little or no connection with the author's intention, with the author's life, or with the social and historical circumstances that may have influenced the author. Everything the reader needs to understand and appreciate a work is contained within the work itself.

The New Critics see their method as "scientific." The work is a self-contained phenomenon made up of "physical" qualities—language and literary conventions (rhyme, meter, alliteration, plot, point of view, and so forth). These qualities can be studied in the same way a geologist studies a rock formation or a physicist the fragmentation of light particles.

Some New Critics, like Cleanth Brooks, claim that the meaning contained in works of literature cannot be paraphrased, cannot be stated in a straightforward, "scientific" way. One can state what a work is "about" or summarize a work's themes, but a work's meaning is much more complex than such statements alone. Brooks argues that a work's complexity lies in its "irony" or paradoxes. A *paradox* is a statement that seems contradictory but is nonetheless true. Statements such as "the first shall be last" or "you must lose your life to gain it" are paradoxes. Brooks claims that good works of literature are filled with paradoxes, with apparently contradictory meanings. In William Wordsworth's poem "It Is a Beauteous Evening," for example, a child seems oblivious to the beauty of nature but is, paradoxically, more aware of it than anyone else. The young lovers in John Donne's poem "The Canonization" paradoxically discover that by rejecting life they capture the intensity of life.

The New Critics use their theories about literature to judge the quality of works of literature. A "good" work, they believe, should contain a network of paradoxes so complex that no mere summary of the work can do them justice; yet, a good work should also have unity. The author achieves this unity by balancing and harmonizing the conflicting ideas in the work. Everything in the work is meaningfully linked together. Because the New Critics favor complex—yet unified—works, they downgrade works that seem simple or seem to lack unity. They prefer "difficult" works that contain apparently illogical and troubling material. They prefer works that stay away from social and historical subject matter and that deal rather with private, personal, and emotional experience. They prefer indirect representation—symbolism, metaphor, connotation—to realistic representation.

For an overview of New Criticism, see *Modern Literary Theory: A Comparative Introduction* (Totowa, NJ: Barnes and Noble, 1982), edited by Ann Jefferson and David Robey. Two influential New Critical essays are "The Intentional Fallacy" and "The Affective Fallacy," both by W. K. Wimsatt and Monroe Beardsley, contained in Wimsatt's *The Verbal Icon: Studies in the Meaning of Poetry* (Lexington: U of Kentucky P, 1954). A readable and stimulating work of New Criticism is Cleanth Brooks's *The Well Wrought Urn: Studies in the Structure of Poetry* (New York: Harcourt, 1947). See especially Chapter 1 ("The language of Paradox") and Chapter 11 ("The Heresy of Paraphrase").

# STRUCTURALISM AND POST-STRUCTURALISM

## Structuralism

Like New Criticism, *structuralism* denies the value of historical, social, and biographical information and concentrates on identifiable elements in works of literature. Unlike New Criticism, its theory and methodology are grounded in linguistics. Although some nineteenth-century thinkers anticipated structuralist principles, structuralism originated from the work of the Swiss linguist Ferdinand de Saussure (1857–1913). Early in the twentieth century, Saussure gave three innovative courses in linguistics. Because he left no notes on the content of these courses, his students pooled their notes and published a reconstruction of the courses called *Course in General Linguistics* (LaSalle, IL: Open Court, 1986; published originally in 1916). This work is the basis of Saussure's fame and provides the theoretical underpinning of both structuralism and post-structuralism.

Saussure made several points about the nature of language that have provided new pathways for studying literature. First, a language is a complete, self-contained system and deserves to be studied as such. Before Saussure, linguists studied the history of languages (how languages evolved and changed through time) and the differences among languages; for this kind of study, Saussure coined the word *diachronic* (literally "through time"). Saussure argued that, instead of its history, linguists should study how a language functions in the present, how its parts interrelate to make up a whole system of communication. This kind of study Saussure called *synchronic* ("at the same time"). Second, Saussure claimed that a language is a system of signs. He defined a *sign* as consisting of a sound plus the thing the sound represents. He called the sound the *signifier* and the thing represented the *signified*. Third, Saussure said that the sounds that make up a language system are arbitrary. Any sound, it doesn't matter which one, could represent a given thing. The sound for the concept "tree" varies from language to language, yet users of each language know that the sound represents "tree." Fourth, any given language is self-contained. The signs that make up a language have no meaning outside the system of that language. Finally, Saussure distinguished between the whole system, which he called *langue* (French for "language"), and one person's use of the system, which he called *parole* (French for "word" or "speech"). Langue consists of everything that makes the system work, such as words, grammatical structures, and inflections. Parole consists of these same elements but with variations from user to user. Each speaker of a language uses the same system but does so in a slightly different way.

In the 1930s and 1940s, literary critics began applying Saussure's ideas and methods to the study of literature. This application has taken two different but often merging paths, literary criticism and cultural criticism. A term that describes both kinds of criticism is *semiotics,* the systematic study of signs. For most practical purposes, the terms *structuralism* and *semiotics* are synonymous.

Structuralist literary critics attempt to show that literature is a form of language or that it functions like language. These critics see the individual work of literature as similar to parole, and literary genres or literature in general as similar to langue. Just as linguists study instances of parole in order to understand langue, literary critics study works of literature in order to understand the system of signs that make up a genre or literature as a whole. They might study a Sherlock Holmes story in order to understand detective fiction, a specific poem in order to understand lyric poetry, a short story in order to understand narrative, a Shakespeare play in order to understand drama, a Louis L'Amour novel in order to understand westerns, or a James Bond novel in order to understand spy fiction.

One kind of structuralist literary criticism is *stylistics,* the study of the linguistic form of texts. Stylistics can deal with both prose and poetry, but it has dealt mainly with poetry, particularly with the qualities of language that distinguish poetry from prose. Some stylistic critics claim that it is *only* qualities of language that distinguish poetry from prose. By analyzing individual poems, these critics attempt to identify those qualities.

Structuralists who study whole cultures attempt to understand a culture's sign systems. The most prominent practitioner of this kind of criticism is the French anthropologist Claude Lévi-Strauss. Lévi-Strauss claims that a culture is bound together by systems of signs and that these systems are like language. He uses Saussurian linguistics as a way of describing the "grammar" of these systems. All aspects of a culture—technology, religion, tools, industry, food, ornaments, rituals—form sign systems. The people of the culture are unaware of these systems, so the structural anthropologist's task is to bring them to light. Lévi-Strauss is perhaps best known for his study of myth. He examines multiple versions of single myths in order to isolate their essential structural units. Although Lévi-Strauss applies his theories to the study of tribal cultures, other critics, like the Frenchman Roland Barthes, use Lévi-Strauss's approach to "psychoanalyze" modern society. They look for the unconscious sign systems that underlie all aspects of Western culture, including foods, furniture, cars, buildings, clothing fashions, business, advertising, and popular entertainment.

Structuralist analysis of culture and literature often merge, because literature can be considered an artifact of culture. Literature is a system of signs that can be studied for itself or for its place in a given culture. As a result, structuralist critics often shy away from complex and classic works and focus instead on popular literature. The Italian critic Umberto Eco writes essays on spy thrillers and the comic book story of Superman. He has even written a "semiotic" detective novel, *The Name of the Rose* (San Diego: Harcourt, 1983). Structuralist critics also are usually more interested in fitting a work within a culture or a tradition than in understanding the work itself.

For an introduction to structuralism, see Leonard Orr's *Semiotic and Structuralist Analyses of Fiction: An Introduction and a Survey of Applications* (Troy, NY: Whitston, 1987). Orr describes structuralist theory, then provides an annotated bibliography of important works of structuralist criticism. A clear and readable book-length treatment is Robert Scholes's *Structuralism in Literature: An Introduction* (New Haven: Yale UP, 1974). Tzvetan Todorov's "The Grammar of Narrative" in *The Poetics of Prose* (Ithaca: Cornell UP, 1977) equates narrative structure to sentence structure. Umberto Eco's *The Role of the Reader: Explorations in the Semiotics of Texts* (Bloomington: Indiana UP, 1979) includes essays on Superman and James Bond. A collection of stylistic studies is *Linguistics and Literary Style,* edited by Donald C. Freeman

(New York: Holt, Rinehart and Winston, 1970); see, for example, J. M. Sinclair's "Taking a Poem to Pieces."

## Post-Structuralism

*Post-structuralism* evolved from Saussure's theories of language. It accepts Saussure's analysis of language and uses his methodology to examine the language of literary works, but it concerns itself with the relationship between language and meaning. Post-structuralism, in fact, offers a radical theory of reading that rejects the certainty of meaning altogether. The most influential post-structuralist critic is the Frenchman Jacques Derrida.

The basis of Derrida's radical skepticism is Saussure's distinction between signifier and signified. Theorists of language have long maintained that words (signifiers) represent identifiable objects (the signified). The word "tree" represents the object "tree." But Saussure questioned the pervasiveness of such one-to-one correspondences. Words, he said, usually refer not to objects but to "concepts," which are expressed by other words. It seems possible, then, that language, or at least parts of language, may not refer to anything in the sensuously apprehendable world. Saussure said that language is a self-contained system and that in order to function it does not need to reflect reality, it needs only to reflect itself. Signs gain meaning from other signs in the system, not necessarily from the real world.

Derrida and other post-structuralist critics conclude from Saussure's theories that there is a "gap" between signifier and signified. This gap blurs the meaning of the signifier so that we cannot know exactly what it refers to. The resulting ambiguity is multiplied by the connection of signifier to signifier in an endless chain, no part of which touches the real world. A literary text is equivalent to just such a chain. It is a self-contained system that exists independently of the real world. As we read, we absorb this system with our consciousness, which Derrida maintains is itself made up of language. Reading is the confrontation of one language system (our consciousness) with another (the text). Recovering meaning from texts, then, is impossible, because interpretations of a text never point to the real world but only to more language. Our interaction with the text makes us *think* we are moving toward meaning, but we never get there.

The purpose of post-structuralist criticism is to expose the meaninglessness of texts. Derrida calls his critical method *deconstruction*. To "deconstruct" a work, the critic analyzes the text, especially its language, to show that whatever connection may seem to exist between the text and the real world is an illusion created by the author's clever manipulation of language. The critic attempts to show that whatever the author may intend for the work to mean or whatever a reader may think it means is always undercut by the ambiguity of the work's language. The gap between signifier and signified is symptomatic of a "space" of emptiness, nothingness, non-meaning that lies at the heart of every text. The presence of this space, the critic tries to show, makes the text an "abyss" of limitless and contradictory meanings.

Post-structuralist criticism is not very reassuring for someone who wants to understand a work better. However, it does reveal, through the application of a rigorous and sophisticated method of analysis, the complexity of literature; and post-structuralist skepticism about meaning points to the mysteriousness of art—the inexplicable something in art that grips our imagination.

A brief explanation of both structuralism and post-structuralism is Ann Jefferson's "Structuralism and Post-Structuralism," in *Modern Literary Theory: A Comparative Introduction* (Totowa, NJ: Barnes and Noble, 1982). More thorough are several chapters on post-structuralism in Art Berman's *From the New Criticism to Deconstruction* (Urbana: U of Illinois P. 1988). A clearly written book-length study is Christopher Norris's *Deconstruction: Theory and Practice* (New York: Methuen, 1982). Norris discusses structuralism, New Criticism, Marxist and psychoanalytic criticism, and philosophical influences on post-structuralism.

# READER-RESPONSE CRITICISM

*Reader-response criticism* studies the interaction of reader with text. Reader-response critics hold that the text is incomplete until it is read. Each reader brings something to the text that completes it and that makes each reading different. Reader-response critics vary on what that "something" is. Recent psychoanalytic critics, such as Jacques Lacan and Norman Holland, say that the something is the unconscious. Post-structuralist critics say that it is the "language" that makes up the conscious mind. Marxist critics say that it is the economic ideology of the dominant culture. Critics interested in the relationship of culture and literature say that it is a whole way of looking at the world, absorbed from the reader's cultural environment. Whatever readers bring to the text, the text has no life of its own without the reader.

Of all the post–World War II movements in literary criticism, reader-response criticism perhaps most successfully challenges the dominance of New Criticism in the university classroom. It borrows methodology from New Criticism, structuralism, and post-structuralism, but rejects their contention that the work must be studied in isolation from its context. Context—historical, biographical, cultural, psychoanalytic—is relevant to the understanding of the text. Reader-response criticism, furthermore, rejects the post-structuralist claim that texts are meaningless. Texts may be incomplete in themselves, but the reading of them makes them potentially reflective of the real world—or at least the reader's experience of the real world.

Some reader-response critics, most notably the German critic Wolfgang Iser, agree with Derrida that works contain "gaps"—not necessarily because of the slippage between signifier and signified but because of the incompleteness of works. Authors always leave something unsaid or unexplained and thus invite readers to fill the resulting spaces with their own imaginative constructs. Iser argues, therefore, that many equally valid interpretations of a work are possible. Interpretations of a work will vary from person to person and even from reading to reading. Critics who agree with Iser often attempt to study how readers fill the gaps in works. These critics are more interested in mapping the process of reading than in explaining individual works.

Perhaps the most prominent group of reader-response critics focuses on how biographical and cultural contexts influence the interpretation of texts. These critics argue that reading is a collective enterprise. The American critic Stanley Fish says that a reader's understanding of what "literature" is and what works of literature mean is formed by "interpretive communities"—groups to which the reader belongs. These groups could be very small (a circle of friends) or very large (a region, country, or cultural entity like "Western civilization"). Fish rejects the idea that a text has a core of meaning that everyone in any age would agree upon. Rather, any shared understanding of a text's meaning comes from the beliefs of a community of readers, not from the text. Each reader's preconceptions actually "create" the text. If, for example, a reader believes that a miscellaneous collection of words is a religious poem, the reader will perceive it as a religious poem. If a reader believes that the work will fit a particular theory, the reader will find facts in the work to support the theory. The theory, in a sense, "creates" the facts.

Because of the influence and provocative nature of reader-response criticism, writings about it abound. *The Reader in the Text: Essays on Audience and Interpretation,* edited by Susan R. Suleiman and Inge Crosman (Princeton: Princeton University Press, 1980) provides an introduction to reader-response criticism as well as readings from prominent critics. Stanley Fish's *Is There a Text in This Class?: The Authority of Interpretive Communities* (Cambridge: Harvard University Press, 1980) is a collection of lively and sometimes funny essays.

## NEW HISTORICIST CRITICISM

New Historicism emerged in the late 1970s as a "new" way to use history to understand and evaluate works of literature. It shares "old" historicism's belief that the historical culture from which a work comes helps us understand the work. It drastically differs from the older historicism in its beliefs about the nature of literature, the nature of history, the ability of people to perceive "reality," and the purpose of literary studies. Its sympathy for disadvantaged or "marginalized" peoples gives it a political slant lacking in older historicism. This sympathy, along with its other beliefs and methods, has profoundly influenced other, more narrowly focused theoretical approaches such as feminist, Marxist, and ethnic criticism. Its breadth of inclusion has made New Historicism highly visible today in the teaching and study of literature. The term *New Historicism* applies to the American version of "cultural studies." The British version is called *Cultural Materialism*. Although Cultural Materialism is more overtly Marxist than New Historicism, both are heavily influenced by the French historian and philosopher Michel Foucault.

The key assumptions of New Historicism are embedded in its understanding of several related concepts: culture, text, discourse, ideology, the self, and history. These concepts, in turn, establish the New Historicist approach to the study of literature. Although some of these terms surface in the older historicism, New Historicists reconstrue them according to structuralist and post-structuralist theories of language. The first term, culture, is probably the most important. In an anthropological sense, "culture" is the total way of life of a particular society—its language, economy, art, religion, and attachment to a location. This way of life is the "tradition" of a culture, handed down from generation to generation, that marks its uniqueness, its distinctness from other cultures. For structuralists, however, and for New Historicists—culture is also a collection of codes that everyone in a society shares and that allows them to communicate, create artifacts, and act. These codes include not just language, the most obvious cultural "code," but every element of a culture—literature, dress, food, rituals, and games.

Because culture is made up of sign systems, it is also "textual." A *text,* traditionally defined, is a written document containing a symbolic system (words, mathematical symbols, images, musical notation). The structuralists, however, expand "text" to mean any system of codes. The post-structuralists go further by claiming that because everything we know is filtered through "language," *everything* is text. "There is nothing outside the text," Derrida says. New Historicists accept the structuralist concept of text but reject the post-structuralist concept. They argue that all aspects of culture are "texts" open to interpretation in the same way works of literature are. They agree with the post-structuralists that human thought is like language, but they disagree that thought can have no connection to reality outside the mind (outside language). Yes, cultures create "texts" and "discourses" and "ideologies" that influence people, but people can become aware of the falseness and incompleteness of those structures.

At first glance, the term *discourse* seems similar in meaning to *text. Discourse* is commonly used to mean a verbal exchange of ideas. The structuralists expand its meaning to mean any system of signs, whether verbal or nonverbal. "Discourse," then, is analogous to language (Saussure's *langue*) and "text" to specific uses of language (*parole*). Foucault claims that groups of people, such as doctors, lawyers, priests, and sports players, create their own discourses. People in groups use discourses to communicate with one another and to distinguish their groups from other groups. Each discourse, Foucault says, has its own "discursive practice" that makes it different from other discourses. These practices include such things as word choice, sentence structure, bodily movements, prejudices, rhetorical forms, and "rules" about where and when to use the discourse. Foucault claims that discourses always arise from historical situations and usually have "political" implications. People with power—social, economic, political, or artistic—use discourses to manipulate other people and maintain their own power.

Both texts and discourses help establish and communicate ideology. *Ideology* is a system of beliefs that governs a group's actions, its view of reality, and its assumptions about what is "normal" and "natural." It is communicated by discourse and represented by cultural texts, including literary texts. New Historicists typically see ideology in political terms. One group of people unfairly imposes its ideology upon others, devaluing and exploiting those who fail to fit its definitions of the "normal" and "natural." These groups are either people within a society—wealthy people, politicians, white people, males, Protestants—

or they are whole societies, such as countries that colonize and impose their ideology upon other regions. Ideology, the New Historicists claim, covers up and ignores the aspects of reality that inevitably contradict the ideology. "Bourgeois" ideology, for example, hides the inequities of race, class, and gender that supposedly allow some people to exercise power over others. When an ideology becomes so pervasive that most people are unaware of its influence, it is said to be "hegemonic." At that extent of influence, people, especially those to whom the ideology gives advantage, assume that it represents the way things really are. However, no ideology is comprehensive enough to extend fair and equal treatment to all people. As a result, some people are "marginalized" and made vulnerable to exploitation.

If texts, discourse, and ideology are so dominant in society, how does the individual, the "self," fit in? Old historicists see the *self* as clearsighted, autonomous, and self-directed. According to them, the self can make "objective" judgments about culture and history. New Historicists, however, see the self as much more limited in its ability to see reality and much more controlled by cultural codes. The self, they claim, is a "subject." Like the subject of a sentence, it performs actions and relates to "objects" (physical things, other people, literary texts). The self can also be a passive, rather than active, subject. It is "subject to" culture, to discourse, and to ideology in the same way that someone is "subject" to a law or a ruler. Because the self is so formed by its culture, it usually lacks the intellectual strength to see the inadequacies of dominant ideologies and discourses.

For this reason, people's ability to understand history is limited. Although *history* is the study and recounting of the past, people always see it through the lens of their own culture and their own "subjective" concerns. Any attempt, Foucault maintains, to tell a coherent story of historical events will fail. Historians can never know with certainty which events caused other events or which events are important. Rather, history is filled with inconsistencies, irregularities, and singularities that resist rational understanding. Events that are "trivial" from one person's point of view may be consequential to someone living at a different time or place. Historical narratives have political implications, Foucault says, because dominant groups create "official" histories, such as those taught in school and recounted in textbooks, to enhance their power. Dominant groups like to fabricate historical narratives that feature them as the engines of progress. But, according to Foucault, there is no such thing as "progress."

The New Historicist approach to literary study emerges from all of these concepts. Its beliefs about three things—literature, the author, and the reader—help distinguish it from other theoretical approaches. For other critics, such as traditional historicists, *literature* is a "work," not simply a "text." To them, a "work" is self-contained, complete, and coherent. It is different from other forms of written communication because it is "beautiful," it gives pleasure. Some works are finer than others and thus belong in a "canon" of great works that deserve appreciation and study. The work of literature, in short, becomes something like an icon, a mysterious, even spiritual, object that will stand the test of time. To old historicists, an *author,* especially of a great work of literature, is a "genius" who, although influenced by culture, transcends it. Authors intentionally craft works to convey certain ideas and create certain effects which can be understood and felt many years, even centuries, after the works were composed. A *reader* of literature, according to the old historicists, can respond spontaneously to the innate "beauty" of a work and can also use reason to discern how authors created their effects and what meanings they intended to convey.

New Historicists, in contrast, claim that *literature* is merely a "text" indistinguishable in nature from all the other texts that constitute a culture. They believe that there is really no such thing as "literature," at least as a discourse that transcends culture and time. Rather, literature is "socially constructed"; every society decides what "literature" is and what its conventions are, and these definitions always vary from society to society and age to age. Definitions of literature are, therefore, highly arbitrary. No one definition is better than any other, no single culture's concept of literature (or any art form) is better than that of other cultures. Equally relative are all judgments about literary value or merit. No author's works are better than those of other authors, no single work is better than others, no one culture's works are better than those of other cultures. All attempts to establish a "canon" of great works are inadequate, because they fail to take into account the complexity of cultural values. Rather, *all* texts, literary and otherwise (including "popular" texts such as films, television shows, advertisements, drugstore romances, westerns, and spy fiction), are worthy of study.

The *author,* for the New Historicists, is far less noble and autonomous than in other approaches. Like everyone else, authors are "subjects" manufactured by culture. A culture "writes" an author who, in turn, transcribes cultural codes and discourses into literary texts. Authors' "intentions" about the form and meaning of their work are largely unconscious or, at least, merely reflections of cultural codes and values. In addition, the *reader* is as passive as the author; culture "programs" readers to respond to its codes and forms of discourse. When readers read works of literature, they automatically respond to the codes embodied by them, just as they would to the codes in "non-literary" texts.

Not all New Historicists are so deterministic and relativistic as this description would indicate. There are those who reject Foucault's pessimism about a person's ability to understand historical reality, to read texts objectively, and to make changes in society. However, New Historicists do tend to share beliefs about the purposes of literary study. First, they believe that literature must be studied within a cultural context. Old-style historicists see historical facts mainly as a means to clarify ideas, allusions, language, and details in literature. New Historicists believe that literature *is* history; it refers to, and is "enmeshed," in history. When New Historicists study literature, they examine such things as how the work was composed, what the author's intentions were, what events and ideas the work refers to, how readers have responded to the work, and what the work means for people today. They draw upon many disciplines—anthropology, sociology, law, psychology, history—to show what role literature has played in history, from the author's time to the present. Second, New Historicists focus on literature as cultural text. They study the relationship between literature and other texts, including nonliterary and popular texts. They identify the codes that constitute literary discourse and ascertain how people use literary discourse to communicate with one another and to comment on society. Third, New Historicists scrutinize the relationship of literature to the power structures of society. They want to show how literature serves, opposes, and changes the wishes of people in power and therefore what ideologies literature supports or undermines. Finally, many New Historicists see criticism itself as an "intervention" in society. By marking literature's cultural roles, its ideologies, its effects, and the biases readers have brought to it, New Historicists aspire to diminish the injustices of race, class, and gender.

Since New Historicism is a fairly new critical approach to literature, its concepts and methods continue to evolve. Some general studies include Jerome McGann's *Historical Studies and Literary Criticism* (Madison: University of Wisconsin Press, 1985), Wesley Morris's *Toward a New Historicism* (Princeton: Princeton UP, 1972), and Harold Veeser's *The New Historicism* (New York: Routledge, 1989). Some of the best-known New Historicist criticism has focused on Renaissance literature, such as *Political Shakespeare: New Essays in Cultural Materialism* (Manchester, Eng.: Manchester UP, 1985), edited by Jonathan Dollimore and Alan Sinfield, and Stephen Greenblatt's *Renaissance*

*Self-Fashioning from More to Shakespeare* (Chicago: University of Chicago Press, 1980). Of special note in Dollimore's collection is Paul E. Brown's " 'This thing of darkness I acknowledge mine': *The Tempest* and the Discourse of Colonialism," which sees *The Tempest* as a reflection of colonialist malpractices. *Ideology and Classic American Literature* (Cambridge, Harvard UP, 1986) edited by Sacvan Bercovitch and Myra Jehlen deals with famous works of American literature. In *Orientalism* (New York: Pantheon, 1978), Edward Said offers a "postcolonial" version of New Historicism. He argues that Western culture has fabricated a distorted and unfair discourse about the East, manifested in countless works of literature and popular culture. Another postcolonial author is the Nigerian Chinua Achebe, who eloquently attacks the racism in Joseph Conrad's *Heart of Darkness* in "An Image of Africa: Racism in Conrad's *Heart of Darkness*," collected in Achebe's *Hopes and Impediments: Selected Essays* (New York: Anchor Books, 1990). Books expounding the New Historicist approach to popular culture are John Fiske's *Reading the Popular* (Boston: Unwin, 1989) and *Popular Fictions: Essays in Literature and History* (New York: Methuen, 1986), edited by Peter Humm, Paul Stigant, and Peter Widdowson. As for Michel Foucault, many of his works are excerpted in *The Foucault Reader* (New York: Pantheon, 1985), edited by Paul Rabinow. James Miller's *The Passion of Michel Foucault* (New York: Simon & Schuster, 1993) is a well-respected recent biography. David R. Shumway's *Michel Foucault* (Boston: Twayne, 1989) and Lois McNay's *Foucault: A Critical Introduction* (New York: Continuum, 1994) are succinct critical overviews of Foucault's work and thought.

# FEMINIST AND GENDER CRITICISM

Feminist and gender criticism have much in common with reader-response and New Historicist criticism, especially with critics who, like Stanley Fish, believe that interpretations of literature are influenced by communities of readers. With the rise of feminism in the 1950s and 1960s, feminist critics claimed that, over the years, men had controlled the most influential interpretive communities. Men decided which conventions made up "literature" and judged the quality of works. Men wrote the literary histories and drew up the lists of "great" works—the literary canon. Because works by and about women were left out of the canon, women authors were ignored, and women characters were misconstrued.

Since the 1960s, feminist literary critics have successfully challenged these circumstances. Far more women now teach, interpret, evaluate, and theorize about literature than ever before. Previously neglected works such as Zora Neale Hurston's *Their Eyes Were Watching God* (1937), Kate Chopin's *The Awakening* (1899), Charlotte Perkins Gilman's "The Yellow Wallpaper" (1892), and Rebecca Harding Davis's *Life in the Iron-Mills* (1861) are now widely read. Certain literary genres practiced by women, such as diaries, journals, and letters, have gained more respect. Numerous anthologies, literary histories, and interpretive studies explore women's contributions to literature. Recently, however, a new movement, "gender studies," has evolved out of feminist studies in order to address broader issues, notably the nature of both femininity and masculinity, the differences within each sex, and the literary treatment of men and homosexuals. Gender studies "complicates" feminist studies because, although they share many interests, they are not exactly the same. Both, however, are political in that they argue for the fair representation and treatment of people of all "genders."

A survey of the history of feminist and gender criticism helps spotlight their concerns. The first stage of feminist criticism began with two influential books, Simone de Beauvoir's *The Second Sex* (New York: Vintage, 1974; originally published in France in 1949) and Kate Millet's *Sexual Politics* (Garden City: Doubleday, 1970). Both authors criticized the distorted representation of women by well-known male authors. Their work laid the foundation for the most prevalent approach of this stage, the "images of women" approach. Following de Beauvoir and Millet, feminist critics called attention to the unjust, distorted, and limited representation of ("images" of) females in works of literature, especially works by men. They celebrated realistic representations of women and brought to light neglected works by and about women. They sought to expose the "politics" of self-interest that led people to create stereotypical and false images of women.

In the second stage of feminist criticism, beginning in the early 1970s, critics shifted away from works by males to concentrate on works by females. Elaine Showalter, a prominent critic from this period, called this approach "gynocriticism." Especially influential was the work of French critics such as Luce Irigary, Julia Kristeva, and Hélène Cixous. Their criticism, called *écriture féminine* (female writing) argued for an "essential" (biological, genetic, psychological) difference between men and women that causes women to think and write differently from men. Gynocritics urged women to become familiar with female authors and to discover their own female "language," a language that supposedly enters the subconscious before the "patriarchal"

language of the dominant culture. They tried to delineate a female poetics, a use of literary conventions and genres that seems typically "female." Some critics based feminist poetics on the possible connection
between writing and the female body. Because women's bodies have
more fluids than men's, they argued, female writing is more "fluid." It is
less structured, less unified, more inclusive of many points of view, less
given to neat endings, and more open to fantasy than writing by males.
It rejects or undermines the "marriage plot" and the "happy ending," in
which a strong female protagonist "capitulates" to a man by marrying
him. It seeks to understand why women authors seem to favor certain
genres (lyric poetry, novel, short story, tale, letters, diaries, memoirs)
over others (epic, romance, drama, satire).

The third stage of feminist criticism rebelled against the "essen-
tialist" assumptions of gynocriticism and is closely allied with New Historicism in its focus on the cultural creation of identity. Gayle Rubin, in
two influential essays—"The Traffic in Women" (*Toward an Anthropology of Women* [New York: Monthly Review, 1975] edited by Rayna
R. Reiter) and "Thinking Sex" (*Pleasure and Danger: Exploring Female
Sexuality* [New York: Pandora, 1992, originally published in 1984]
edited by Carole S. Vance)—distinguishes between "sex" and "gender."
Whereas *sex* is the biological difference between males and females,
*gender* is the cultural difference. Culture determines the traits and behavior that set masculinity apart from femininity and rules on "normal"
and "natural" gender distinctions. Western culture, for example, has
seen women as passive rather than active, irrational rather than rational, subjective rather than objective, at home rather than at "work,"
spiritual rather than material, and impractical rather than practical. It
has ruled that certain kinds of behavior are "abnormal" and "unnatural"
for females to practice, such as pursuing careers, doing construction
work, being pastors or priests, wearing "male" clothes, or being as-
sertive. Such gender distinctions, feminist critics claim, are arbitrary
and almost always give women less power, status, and respect than
men. In one sense, the feminist focus on gender is deterministic: Many
women are "trapped" by the gender traits assigned to them by culture.
In another sense, however, it offers hope. Culture, unlike biology, can
be changed—through education, social action, and politics.

All three of these "stages" of feminist criticism have overlapped
and coexisted. They continue to be practiced. But the focus on gender
in the third stage led not only to a new stage of feminist criticism, it also
helped to establish the broader movement of gender criticism. Until the
mid-1980s, many feminist critics assumed that all women were basically

the same in their biological nature, their gender traits, their shared history of oppression, and their aspirations. Most feminist critics, furthermore, wrote from the perspective of an elite group of people: Women who were white, Western, politically liberal, middle-class, and highly educated. Beginning around 1985, some feminist critics challenged these assumptions and this perspective. Feminist critics, they said, should look at the many ways in which women are different from one another. Factors other than gender, they said, give females identity, factors such as race, ethnic background, class status, and economic circumstances. These critics began studying the literary representation of women in minority cultures, in non-Western cultures, at various economic levels, and in different work situations. They began examining ways females themselves marginalize or "erase" other females. Perhaps most important, they began to pay attention to sex and gender differences among women, especially between heterosexuals and homosexuals.

Gender criticism, perhaps because it is so new, remains a nebulous, difficult-to-define approach to the study of literature. It covers almost anything having to do with "gender," including feminist criticism, theories of cultural influence, and crimes such as sexual abuse. One of the most important aspects of gender criticism is its exploration of the literary treatment of homosexuality. As with New Historicism, the theorist who most influences gender studies is Michel Foucault. The first volume of his three-volume study *The History of Sexuality* (New York: Vintage, 1980; originally published in France in 1976) states his basic ideas about sexuality. The Western concept of "sexuality," Foucault maintains, is not a universal category but was invented in the late nineteenth century. Before then, there was no distinction between "homosexuality" and "heterosexuality" in terms of gender preference. Although same-sex relationships occurred before that time, there was no concept of homosexuality as a "lifestyle" behavior. Modern Western views of sexuality constitute an "ideology" that benefits people in power, most notably bourgeois capitalists. This ideology, as with all ideologies, is manifested in discourses such as religion, science, politics, medicine, and literature. Although Foucault was himself apolitical, he was deeply sympathetic to "marginalized" people. He struggled with his own identity as a homosexual and felt personally marginalized. He attempted suicide in 1948 and died as the result of an AIDS-related illness in 1984.

Some gender critics disagree with Foucault's heavy emphasis on cultural determinism. They believe that sexual identity, including homosexuality, results from biological rather than cultural causes. Gay criticism (which deals with men) and lesbian criticism (which deals with women) share certain goals, primarily the struggle to eliminate homophobia. They call into question the Western assumption that heterosexuality is the only "natural" sexual identity and attempt to expose the politics of gender—how certain groups manipulate concepts of sex and gender for their own benefit. Gay and lesbian critics analyze all discourses, including literature, that reinforce or destabilize conventional concepts of sex and gender. They study the works and lives of authors who were admitted homosexuals and bisexuals or who seemed to have suppressed homosexual tendencies.

Perhaps the best place to begin reading feminist criticism is with an anthology of essays such as *The New Feminist Criticism: Essays on Women, Literature, and Theory* (New York: Pantheon, 1985), edited by Elaine Showalter. Showalter provides an introduction to feminist criticism as well as essays by other critics. Ellen Moers's *Literary Women* (New York: Oxford University Press, 1976), Sandra Gilbert and Susan Gubar's *The Madwoman in the Attic: The Woman Writer and the Nineteenth-Century Literary Imagination* (New Haven: Yale University Press, 1979), and Kate Millett's *Sexual Politics,* mentioned above, are among the best examples of "images of women" criticism. Virginia Woolf's *A Room of One's Own* (New York: Harcourt, 1957; originally published in 1929) and Hélène Cixous's "The Laugh of the Medusa" (originally published in English in *Signs* 1 [1976]: 875–94 but much anthologized) are well-known examples of gynocriticism. Gayle Rubin's essays, mentioned above, and Elaine Showalter's edited collection, *Speaking of Gender* (New York: Routledge, 1989), represent the shift of interest toward gender. Two texts that deal with the broadening of feminist criticism are Barbara Smith's "Toward a Black Feminist Criticism" in Showalter, *New Feminist Criticism,* (originally published in 1975) and *Wild Women in the Whirlwind: Afra-American Culture and the Contemporary Literary Renaissance* (New Brunswick: Rutgers University Press, 1989), edited by Joanne Braxton and Andree Nicola McLaughlin. *The Gay and Lesbian Literary Heritage* (New York: Henry Holt, 1995), edited by Claude J. Summers, is an excellent one-volume encyclopedia featuring articles on authors, terms, and theoretical approaches. *The Gay and Lesbian Studies Reader* (New York: Routledge, 1993), edited by Henry Abelove, et al., is an anthology of essays. Eve Kosofsky Sedgwick's *Between Men: English Literature and Male Homosocial Desire* (New York: Columbia University Press, 1985) deals with heterosexuality and homosexuality in literature before the twentieth century. For works by and about Michel Foucault, see the discussion of New Historicism.

# PART
## TWO

*Writing about Literature*

# 8

# *Writing about Literature*

## WHY WRITE ABOUT LITERATURE?

The answer to this question rests on two considerations: the writer's purpose and the writer's audience. You, the writer, may be so enthusiastic about a work that you write to your friends, urging them to read it. Or you may be so confused about a work that you write out your thoughts just to clarify them for yourself. Or you may use a work of literature to explain your ideas about some issue that's important to you personally. The common characteristic of these and most writings about literature is that they are interpretive. Most people write about literature to communicate their interpretations of it. The audience for such writing may be experts about your topic, or people who know you well, or your teacher, or your fellow students, or even just yourself. Whoever they are, they want to understand the works you write about. Your aim when you write about literature is to help them do so.

## HOW CAN WE WRITE ABOUT LITERATURE?

Writing about literature can take many forms. Your writings can be informal jottings, meant only for yourself. They can be effusions of praise or condemnation. They can be book-length studies of complex interpretive problems. The kind of writing emphasized in this book is the essay about literature. An *essay* is a piece of writing that has the following characteristics:

1. An essay is relatively short—from maybe two to no more than fifty pages.

2. An essay is somewhat "formal"; that is, it follows certain forms that have become conventional. It does not have to be stuffy and stilted, but it typically adheres to the rules of usage—punctuation, spelling, syntax, diction—expected in published writing. It has a thesis that unifies the whole essay. It follows an organizational pattern that emphasizes intellectual coherence.

3. An essay is aimed at a "serious" audience, one that cares about your subject and will take time to consider what you have to say.

4. An essay is "persuasive." Your purpose is to persuade people that your ideas are worthy of consideration. You might even want to convert readers to your way of thinking and to urge them to some action.

5. An essay is "dialogic." It often responds to other people who have written or spoken, and it assumes that its audience might talk back.

6. Most importantly, an essay is "argumentative." It develops a line of thought (a logically related series of claims) that relates to a thesis. It supports claims with evidence; that is, with facts and reasoning. It organizes its claims and evidence in a coherent and logical order.

## THE WRITING PROCESS

The remaining chapters of this book offer guidelines for writing essays about literature. The arrangement of the chapters follows the four stages of the writing process.

When you write essays, you typically think and write yourself through stages of a process in order to come up with a final product. Writers rarely follow this process in a neat and orderly fashion—first one step, then another, then another. Rather, they go back and forth among the stages and do many tasks simultaneously. But they inevitably follow the general outline of a process as they write essays. Understanding this process—the writing process—should help you plan how to go about writing essays. It should also help you reduce "writer's anxiety," that dreadful feeling that you have to come up with an essay all at once, to produce it, so to speak, out of thin air. Seeing writing as a process can help you relax and take writing tasks one step at a time. Even when you have to go back to earlier steps, as most writers do, you can feel sure that you are moving toward completion.

The writing process consists of four main sets of activities:

Inventing
1. Studying the subject. For essays about literature, the "subject," for the most part, is the work or works of literature you want to write about.

2. Identifying your audience (its needs and interests).

3. Recognizing any limitations placed on your essay (length, time in which you have to write it, specifics of the assignment).

4. Generating topics.

Drafting
1. Determining your thesis (or theses) and supporting claims.

2. Gathering facts from the works and, if necessary, secondary sources, to support your claims.

3. Creating a plan of organization for your first draft.

4. Writing the first draft.

Revising
1. Reading your draft critically. If possible, getting others to read your draft and make comments about it.

2. Rethinking your topic, plan of organization, and line of reasoning.

3. Gathering more support, if necessary, for your claims.

4. Writing further drafts.

Editing
1. Producing a final draft in the format expected by your audience.

2. "Publishing" the essay (by submitting it to a publication, such as a magazine or newspaper, by sending it out to a circle of readers, or by turning it in to your instructor).

# 9

# *Choosing Topics*

This chapter deals with the invention stage of the writing process. Probably the most challenging part of writing essays is answering the question: "What can I write about?" Choosing a good topic is a creative act, and like most creative acts, certain qualities of thought and circumstance must interact for it to occur. Although no set of guidelines can provide a foolproof formula for generating topics, the suggestions in this chapter should get you started.

## STEPS IN CHOOSING A TOPIC

### Be a Creative Reader

"Creative" reading—reading for interpretation—is the crucial first step toward choosing a topic for an essay about literature. As we have seen in Part One, when you do such things as reread a work, study formal elements in it, make connections between the work and your interests, assess what's good and bad about it, you move toward interpretations of the work. Reading creatively should give you ideas and questions about what the work means. Any of these ideas or questions can be topics for essays about literature.

### Identify Your Audience

After reading the work with care, your next step toward choosing a topic is to think about your audience. An essay is a communication.

With whom do you communicate? What do they want from you? What effect do you want to have on them?

When you write essays for college courses, you have two and possibly three audiences, One is the instructor. The effect you want to have on the instructor (one assumes) is to make him or her think well of your essay and give it a good grade. Make yourself aware, then, of the instructor's criteria for judging student essays. If the instructor is like most, he or she will want a well-crafted essay—a clear statement of thesis, logical and coherent organization, fluent and correct prose style, convincingly supported claims, and so forth. But the instructor will probably base his or her judgment on a more general criterion: how well your essay communicates to a general audience, an audience larger than just the instructor.

Several advantages result from writing for a general audience rather than for just your instructor. First, you practice skills of communication useful once you leave college. Your writing in the "real world" will usually be for groups of people, not just one person. A second advantage is that by meeting the needs of a general audience, you will almost certainly meet the requirements of your instructor. In fact, you will probably write a better essay if you write for a general audience than for just your instructor. The reason is that you won't take for granted—that is, leave out—the facts and reasoning needed by *both* a general audience and your instructor to understand and be convinced by you. When writing solely for the instructor, students often think, "The instructor already knows this, so I won't put it in." In fact, the instructor *does* want you to put it in. The instructor cannot read your mind. He or she must see how you arrived at the claims you make.

Who, then, makes up your reading audience? Two groups who probably will *not* are, first, experts on your subject and, second, people intellectually incapable of grasping your reasoning (children, for example). You could write for both of these audiences, but if you wrote for an audience of experts, you would have to be an expert yourself and, furthermore, have something to tell them that they do not already know. Most college students do not have enough time to master subjects that thoroughly. This, by the way, is another reason for not writing solely for your instructor. The instructor is an "expert" who, fortunately, rarely expects students to meet the needs of an audience of experts. On the other hand, if you wrote for the mentally immature, your essay would be too simpleminded for college courses.

Instead, write for an audience consisting of people who are intelligent, who have read or can read the work you want to discuss, and who want to understand it better. Assume that this audience consists of people who are your equals; they form a community of which you are a part, to whom you can talk with equal authority. They share your interests and eagerly await your comments. If it will help, visualize people you know— classmates, friends, relatives, students at other campuses, people anywhere who enjoy literature—as belonging to this audience. When you write, imagine yourself in dialogue with them, saying things that would interest them, responding to their questions and comments. Project an image of yourself as the conscientious searcher for truth. Let your audience know that you are doing everything possible, within the limits of your time and ability, to answer the questions you have raised.

A third audience is yourself. Writing essays is one way of satisfying your own intellectual needs and desires. Writing is not simply the product of thinking; it is a *way* of thinking. Some theorists argue that not until you write out your ideas can you be sure you have thought them through carefully. The process of writing essays, for example, underscores the need to use sound logic, to include all the steps in your reasoning, to state ideas precisely in order to produce arguments that will withstand the scrutiny of objective and intelligent people. It is easy *not* to do these things when you are just thinking to yourself or speaking to other people. Francis Bacon's maxim calls attention to this result of writing: "Reading maketh a full man, conference a ready man, and writing an exact man."

Perhaps the most important effect on you of writing is its ability to draw forth your ideas. One kind of essay about literature is the essay examination (discussed in Chapter 13). You may find essay examinations burdensome and even traumatic; but in writing them, students often discover ideas they never knew they had. The reason is that writing mates your knowledge of literature with the instructor's questions to give birth to new ideas. Essays about literature, then, can be journeys of self-discovery that lead you to new intellectual vistas. In this sense, you are part of your audience. You share your readers' curiosity and their desire to have puzzling questions answered. You write to convince them; but you write also to discover and clarify your own ideas and to convince yourself of their validity.

## Raise a Key Question about the Work

Related to the identity and needs of your audience is the *nature* of your topic. Your audience wants to understand the work you wish to discuss. They want to know your interpretations of it. But what will you interpret—everything in the work or just some part of it? Since essays are relatively short, rarely can you interpret everything in a work. You have to limit yourself to some part of it. But which part?

The answer: Write about a specific problem of interpretation. The "problem" should be a question about the meaning (the coherence, the sense) of an aspect of the work. Your essay should identify that question and provide an answer to it.

The topics of interpretive essays always refer to questions. You might announce your topic as "Hamlet's Indecision" or "Macbeth's Hunger for Power," but the audience knows that behind topics like these lie questions: Why does Hamlet hesitate to act? What propels Macbeth to seek power and to continue seeking it? The purpose of taking up such topics is to answer the questions that give rise to them. When you state your topics, you do not *have* to phrase them as questions, but good topics always *imply* questions of interpretation.

## Choose a "Good" Topic

What makes a topic good? One way to judge the quality of an essay topic is to ask yourself how easily your audience could answer the question that lies behind it. A useful criterion is that a topic is "good" if your readers could *not* answer the question after reading the work once. That is, readers could not answer it convincingly, either for themselves or for others, without reviewing and studying the work. In other words, the topic must be genuinely thought-provoking.

A second consideration is the meaningfulness of your topic. As the author, you should care about the topic, and your audience should be interested in it. To assess your audience's interest, imagine yourself as part of your audience. What would you want to know if you were reading your own essay? Common sense should tell you that one of the *least* interesting questions is, What happened in the work? True, the events and details of works are sometimes hard to understand and need clarification, but usually readers can understand a work's details after reading it one time. You do not need to provide information your audience already knows.

A third way to assess the quality of a topic is to ask if it is focused narrowly enough for the confines of your essay. Most of the essays you write for college literature classes will run from three to ten typewritten pages (900 to 3,000 words). Your topic is good if you can deal with it thoroughly within those limits. For example, "comedy in *Romeo and Juliet*" would probably be too broad for an essay topic; "the nurse as comic figure" would be more specific and manageable. "Love in *Romeo and Juliet*" would be too broad; "Juliet's mature love versus Romeo's adolescent love" would be better. "Values in *Romeo and Juliet*"—too broad; "Shakespeare's attitude toward suicide"—better. "Juliet as character"—too broad; "Juliet's change from child to young woman"—better.

Charlotte Brontë's novel *Jane Eyre* provides an example of an essay topic that meets these three criteria. Brontë grew up absorbing the superstitions of the English north country. These superstitions included beliefs in fairies, elves, and demons, and one does not have to read far into *Jane Eyre* before encountering references to them. Jane, the narrator and main character, says that as a child she looked in vain for elves "under mushrooms and beneath the ground-ivy" and concluded that "they were all gone out of England to some savage country where the woods were wilder and thicker, and the population more scant." After her first encounter with Mr. Rochester, he accuses her of being a fairy who "bewitched" his horse and caused it to fall. Her reply is that the fairies "all forsook England a hundred years ago." Throughout her relationship, he calls her "elf," "fairy," "dream," "changeling," "sprite." After she returns at the end of the novel, he reverts to his epithets, once again calling her "fairy," "ghost," "changeling," "fairy-born and human-bred."

If you spot this fairy-lore motif in *Jane Eyre* you might think, "Aha, why not write an essay on that?" You could title the essay "Charlotte Brontë's Use of Fairy Lore in *Jane Eyre*." The question underlying the topic would be, What significance does this lore have in the novel? The purpose of the essay would be, first, to raise this question; second, to show that the fairy lore actually does exist in the novel; and third, to provide an answer to the question. This answer would be the "thesis" of the essay. The topic is meaningful because fairy lore is prominent in the work and is consistently associated with the main character; the topic promises to lead to an interpretation of novel. Furthermore, the topic is complex enough so that a reader could not answer its implicit question fully and convincingly without rereading and studying the novel. And the topic is specific enough to be dealt with thoroughly in an essay of about 1,200 to 1,500 words. The topic, in short, is "good."

## Use Search Strategies to Generate Topics

For some people, finding good topics is easy and automatic. A student might be reading *Jane Eyre* and just happen to notice the references to fairies, and think, "Hey, that would be interesting to write about." For others, however, discovering good topics is difficult and frustrating, capable of inducing a severe case of writer's block. One writer can experience both situations. You might find that one work suggests all kinds of topics, whereas another, even when you have read it carefully, leaves you at a total loss. If you ever find yourself in the latter situation, try a search strategy.

A *search strategy* is a procedure for locating and examining important aspects of a work. It is a self-teaching device that helps you think about the work. As you examine the work, you become aware of areas you can raise questions about, questions that may lead to good topics. The following is a brief discussion of several of them.

**Analysis**   Analysis, the strategy of reading discussed in Part One, allows a systematic investigation of works of literature. In your search for a topic, you probably would not want to examine *every* component of a work, but analysis lets you focus on aspects you might otherwise overlook. Analysis, in other words, is a process of discovery, rather like shining a flashlight on different parts of a darkened room. You could even turn components of a work into essay topics: "Setting in Austen's *Pride and Prejudice*," "Meter and rhyme in Shakespeare's Sonnet 116," "Characterization in O'Neill's *The Hairy Ape*," "Irony in Poe's 'The Cask of Amontillado.' " Your purpose would be to show how the author uses these components and how they are important to the overall scheme of the work. All of the essays in Chapter 14 base their interpretations on an examination of literary components.

**Traditional patterns of thinking**   Traditional patterns of thinking or *topoi,* such as definition, structural analysis, process analysis, comparison, and cause-and-effect analysis—are useful for generating ideas about almost any subject, including literature, and for organizing essays. We discuss them in Chapter 10 (pages 186–189)

**Comments by critics**   Comments by literary critics are often a fruitful source of topics. Critics write about individual works, about an author's entire work, about the nature of literature itself, and about many other things as well. Your purpose would be to make a critic's whole approach or an isolated comment by a critic the starting point of your essay. Chapter 7 outlines several well-known critical approaches to literature, but consider for the moment how a student might use the following observation about narrative made by Terry Eagleton in *Literary Theory: An Introduction* (Minneapolis: U of Minnesota P, 1983):

> Watching his grandson playing in his pram one day, Freud observed him throwing a toy out of the pram and exclaiming *fort!* (gone away), then hauling it in again on a string to the cry of *da!* (here). This, the famous *fort-da* game, Freud interpreted in *Beyond the Pleasure Principle* (1920) as the infant's symbolic mastery of its mother's absence; but it can also be read as the first glimmerings of narrative. *Fort-da* is perhaps the shortest story we can imagine: an object is lost, and then recovered. But even the most complex narratives can be read as variants on this model: the pattern of classical narrative is that an original settlement is disrupted and ultimately restored. (185)

Here, Eagleton states a quality in narrative that many people have probably not thought about consciously: that there is a lost-and-found pattern and variations on it in many narratives. Examples abound: Homer's *The Odyssey,* Milton's *Paradise Lost,* Melville's *Moby-Dick,* Coleridge's *The Rime of the Ancient Mariner,* Keats's "La Belle Dame sans Merci," Shakespeare's *King Lear,* Jane Austen's *Pride and Prejudice.*

You could make Eagleton's comment the basis for an essay about a particular narrative—a novel, a short story, a poem, a play. You would try to explain how the pattern or a variation on it operates in your narrative. You would begin your essay by explaining Eagleton's idea, giving proper credit to him. (For when and how to give credit in your essays, see Chapter 11.) Then you would try to answer questions such as these: What has been lost? How was it lost? How are the protagonists trying to recover it? Do they succeed? What qualities allow them to succeed or cause them to fail?

Eagleton's comment covers many works of literature, but critics also write extensively about individual works. You could use a critic's idea about a specific work as a starting point for an essay. You could write your essay in support of the idea or in disagreement with it. For an explanation of how to find critical interpretations of individual works, see the treatment of sources in Chapter 11, pages 195–208. For a complete student essay based on a critic's comment, see the essay on Edwin Arlington Robinson's "Richard Cory" in Chapter 14.

When you think of literary criticism, you may think only of published works, but don't forget your instructor and the other students in your class. Your instructor is a critic who "publishes" comments in class, out loud to you, and students often give interesting responses to the instructor and to one another. All of these comments can provide excellent starting points for essays. An example of such an essay is the sample essay in Chapter 14 on Emily Dickinson's "Because I could not stop for Death."

**Your own knowledge**   Students at all levels of achievement often fail to realize that they know a great deal and are learning all the time. If you are a college student, you may be taking an English course, but you are most likely taking other courses in a wide range of disciplines. All of this knowledge interconnects, even though for practical reasons colleges chop it up into schools, departments, and courses. You can and may bring this knowledge to bear on works of literature. Subject areas such as psychology, sociology, philosophy, design, art history, history of science, religious studies, cultural history, political history, even landscape gardening shine beams of light on authors and literature. Ibsen's Hedda Gabler (in the play *Hedda Gabler*) is a deeply troubled person. Can you find in your psychology textbooks theories that would help explain her problems? Ernest Hemingway said in an early version of "Big Two-Hearted River" that he wanted to write the way the French Impressionist Paul Cézanne painted. Can you explain Hemingway's themes and methods by comparing his writing to Cézanne's pictures and theories of art? In the poem "Heritage," Countee Cullen conveys an ambivalent attitude toward Africa. How does the American understanding (or misunderstanding) of Africa at the time he wrote the poem (1925) both mirror his attitude and help explain his frustration? Anton Chekhov wrote plays at the turn of the twentieth century. What happened in Russia at that time, politically and socially, that clarifies the intellectual currents in his plays?

Another kind of knowledge students often overlook or discount is their own experience. Most students have developed expertise outside the academic world—through work, travel, family activities, personal experience of many kinds—and this expertise sometimes can illuminate works of literature. Have you done some sailing? If so, you might be able to explain the complex maneuvers the young captain makes at the end of Joseph Conrad's "The Secret Sharer" and suggest what this knowledge tells us about the captain. (Is he taking a foolish, irresponsible risk?) Speaking of Conrad, have you been to the Congo River, the setting of *Heart of Darkness?* If so, are vestiges of the colonialism he condemns in that novel still there? What can you tell us about the landscape and atmosphere of the country that would help us better understand this puzzling novel? Have you seen any bullfights? If so, you might help the rest of us understand the symbolic meaning of bullfighting in Hemingway's fiction. Have you been the victim of prejudice? If so, you should be able to give insights into the dynamics of bigotry dramatized in Bernard Malamud's *The Assistant* or Richard Wright's *Black Boy.*

## Use Talking and Informal Writing to Generate Topics

Talking and writing are themselves ways of generating ideas. When you talk with someone—or even to yourself—about a work, or when you write about it, you often come up with ideas you never knew you had. This is why the writing process often involves going back and forth among stages. As you write your first draft, for example, you often discover ideas that cause you to rethink your topic and major claims. Talking and writing, then, are themselves strategies for discovering topics to write about. The following are some specific suggestions about how to use these strategies.

**Conversing**   Imagine yourself talking to a friend about the work you want to write about. Or, perhaps better, find a real person to talk to. Talk out loud. Keep your partner clearly in mind. You really want to explain this work to her. Say anything you want about the work—what you like and dislike about it, what interests you or does not interest you. Make claims about the work—what it means, what motivates the characters, what the setting is like—and support your claims with evidence. Try to get your listener to respond to you. Does she agree or disagree? Listen to her counterclaims and reasons. You might even summarize the work for her and ask if she understands and agrees with your summary. As you exchange ideas—or imagine that you are exchanging ideas—see if you can get at some of the themes of the work. What points does the writer seem to be making? By talking out loud, you get your mind working and pushing yourself toward developing interpretations of your own.

**Outlining**   Make an outline of the work. The outline should not be formal (complete sentences, Roman and Arabic numerals, and so forth); rather, it should be a list or a series of statements that indicate important aspects of the work. You will probably want to write the outline down, mainly so you can remember everything you have put in it, but you can also outline works in your head. The outline could focus on the whole work or one element of the work.

There are many possibilities for the organization of the outline. The outline could follow the spatial order of the work; that is, it could represent the major aspects or events in the order presented in the work. Or it could follow a chronological organization; that is, the order in which the events occur in time. One thought-provoking organization is to outline the work according to the journalist's questions: who, what, when, where, why, how. The first four questions will help you get the facts straight. The last two will get you thinking about relationships among the facts. Who are the important characters in the work? What are they like? What are their values and beliefs? What has happened before the work begins? What do the characters do? When is the action set? Is the time of the action important? Where does the action occur? Does the author attach meaning to the place of the work? Why does the action happen? How does it affect the characters? How does it affect your attitude toward their beliefs and what they do? You might find that one of the journalist's questions will lead you to other questions and therefore further interest in that aspect of the work. And this line of thought and narrowing focus can give you the topic for an essay.

**Freewriting**   Choose a work or some aspect of a work and begin writing about it. Write for at least five minutes but no more than fifteen. During this time, don't stop writing. If you can't think of anything new to say, repeat your last sentence or something like "I can't think of anything else to say" over and over until something new occurs to you. Don't worry about sentence structure or correct usage. Write incomplete sentences if you wish.

The theory behind freewriting is that writing generates thought, even if some of what you write is repetitious or even nonsense. As you write, you may create ideas you never knew you had. These may enlighten you about what is most interesting about a work and what lines of thought you might take in an essay. You may even find that a piece of freewriting provides not only the topic but a rough organization for a full-blown essay.

**Brainstorming**   *Brainstorming* means thinking freely about particular works of literature—letting your mind flow where it will, but keeping it focused on the works and, after a point, upon some aspect of the works. To brainstorm you need pen and paper—lots of paper. As ideas come to you, jot them down. Think of this activity as play, a game in which you talk to yourself. As you write, don't worry about spelling, constructing complete sentences, putting ideas in order. Include even your craziest ideas. Channel the flow of your thinking with questions such as these: Among the works I may write about, which do I like best? (If necessary, jot down the possibilities. Choose one.) What interests me most about the work? (Jot down these.) What do I dislike about the work? (Jot down these.) Why do I like or dislike these particular things? (Jot down your reasons.) Are there aspects of the work I would like to write about? (Jot down these. Choose one. For example, if you want to write about characterization, begin brainstorming about the characters in the narrative. Some of the questions and exercises under "characterization" in Chapter 3 might help you get started.) If your ideas about one aspect of the work seem uninspired, move on to another aspect and brainstorm about that.

At a certain stage of the brainstorming process, you must shift from a noncritical to a critical look at what you have done. This is a process of organization—of subordination, arrangement, and elimination. You sort out, make connections, arrange your jottings into groups, and eliminate the unusable. Organization is still part of the play of brainstorming, even though it is a more controlled activity than the initial stages of brainstorming. Feel free, then, to try certain arrangements and relationships, then discard them if they do not work. Try even the strangest, most unlikely connections and see if logical relationships you had never thought possible actually emerge. If you have a list of ten items, see what groups of relationships you can establish within the list. If you see connections between some but not others (perhaps five out of the ten), keep the ones that connect and discard (cross out) the others. Then brainstorm about the qualities linking the remaining items. Try to summarize these qualities in one phrase or apply one question to them. This phrase or question could be your topic, and the five items, arranged in an order that seems to make sense as part of your developing argument, could provide the structure for a rough draft of the essay.

**Notes**   *Notes* are bits of writing you do for yourself. You can write them wherever it is most convenient and helpful: in the margins of books you own, on little slips of paper, or in a notebook. Since they are for yourself only, you need not worry about spelling, punctuation, or even coherence. Notes should almost always be short and pithy. Jotting down notes *as* you read stimulates interaction between you and the text. Writing notes *after* you read helps you think about the work, raise questions, state interpretations, and call attention to intriguing

passages and details. The following are notes made by a student after
she read Homer's *Odyssey:*

## NOTES ON THE <u>ODYSSEY</u>

Why does Odysseus want to leave Calypso's island? He's got such a good
deal there.

If he loves Penelope, why does he sleep with Calypso? And Circe? Is this being
"faithful"? I wonder what Penelope will think when he "confesses" (if he ever does).
Could she do the same thing--sleep around--and get away with it? Double standard.

Athene: Obsessed with tying up loose ends. Although a goddess, power limited. Poseidon. Are they rivals?

Nausicaa: my favorite. "where slept a girl who in form and feature was like
the immortal goddesses" (page 67). "white-armed Nausicaa" (69). "the lovely
Nausicaa" (69). Innocent but spunky.

"Zeus is patron of every stranger and every beggar" (72). Why doesn't Zeus
just zap the suitors?

Odysseus: A Greek Woody Allen (always worrying and down on himself).

At the end, Odysseus's treatment of the servant girls: horrible. Bloody and excessive. Sexist?

***Journals*** *Journals* are generally more coherent, more polished, and more developed than notes. You may be the sole audience
for your own journals, but sometimes they are for others as well. The
journals of authors like Ralph Waldo Emerson, Henry James, and F. Scott
Fitzgerald provide fascinating insights into their lives and works. Like
these authors, writers often use journals not only to try out lines of
thought, but also to get other peoples' reactions to them. If the audience for your journal is someone else, you should make your writing
and organization clear and concise. The root word for journal—*jour,*
the French word for "day"—suggests that they are more systematic and
regular than notes. You may write in your journal, if not every day, then
at least regularly. You may take more time developing your ideas than
for notes. The journal below is by the same student who wrote the previous notes on the *Odyssey.* Notice how her journal entry is more developed than her "notes" and less developed than her "essay."

## JOURNAL ENTRY ON THE <u>ODYSSEY</u>

Two things bother me about the <u>Odyssey</u>. One is the way Homer presents
women. Women are almost always more limited in what they can do than men
and are treated as inferiors by the male characters. As a female I resent this attitude. I will admit that females in the <u>Odyssey</u> are stronger--more admirable and

influential--than in some of the other things we have read this semester. If Athene weren't always helping Telemachus and Odysseus, where would they be? But Athene's femaleness seems unimportant. She isn't human, for one thing. And for another, when she takes human form, she almost always appears as a male. Penelope is admirable, I suppose, for being so loyal and patient, but she has to stay home and do domestic duties (for twenty years!) while her husband gets to roam the world, have adventures, and sleep with beautiful goddesses. What would the men of Ithaca have thought had Penelope had similar adventures? Probably lynched her. Finally, at the end, I think that Odysseus's treatment of the disloyal female servants is excessive. They are sentenced without a trial. Who knows, they might have been coerced by the piglike suitors. They don't deserve to die, especially in such a gruesome way. What threat to Odysseus and Ithaca could they be if left alive?

The other thing is Odysseus's attitude toward Ogygia, Calypso's island. I keep wondering why he wants to leave. Ogygia seems like paradise. Odysseus says he loves Penelope and wants to return to her, but is that the real reason? Ogygia strikes me as being similar to Eden in the Bible. It even has four rivers, just like Eden. In the Bible, Adam and Eve are kicked out of Eden as punishment for eating the apple. Yet, in the <u>Odyssey</u>, Odysseus *wants* to leave. Why? I think I might want to stay. Look at what he's got. He has a beautiful woman who loves him and takes care of him. He could have immortality. (Calypso promises to make him immortal if he will stay.) Ogygia is beautiful. All my life I have thought that losing paradise, as Adam and Eve did, would be terrible. Why would someone wish to lose it? As a person (character), Odysseus seems very restless. Maybe that's the reason. Once he returns home, you wonder if he will stay long.

## SAMPLE ESSAY ABOUT LITERATURE

The following essay is by the student whose notes and journal appear immediately above. It is a response to her reading of the *Odyssey.* Notice how her essay evolves out of her informal writing. In her notes she comments briefly on the *paradise* theme. She returns to it for more extended comment in her journal. She decides, finally, to focus an entire essay on this one theme. You can see from her notes and journal entry that she could have also written on other topics—the nature of the gods, Nausicaa, Athene, and gender equity. But, instead she chose to write on this one.

### PARADISE REJECTED IN HOMER'S <u>ODYSSEY</u>

After reading the creation stories in the Bible along with Homer's <u>Odyssey</u> this semester, I was struck by the similarity between the Garden of Eden and Calypso's island, Ogygia. Both Eden and Ogygia are paradiselike places. But even more intriguing is the difference between what happens to the people who dwell in these two places. Adam and Eve are expelled from Eden, whereas Odysseus chooses to leave Ogygia. I find his choice puzzling. All my life I have been taught to believe that Adam and Eve's expulsion from the Garden of Eden was a terrible thing. Yet here is Odysseus actually wanting to leave a similar place. Why does Odysseus make this choice?

Eden and Ogygia are similar in several ways. First, their physical features, which are almost identical, are pleasant. The Genesis account says that God caused trees to "spring from the ground," trees that were "pleasant to look at and good for food" (2:9). A river flows "from Eden to water the garden" and branches into four "streams," called Pishon, Gihon, Tigris, and Euphrates (2:10-14). Eden is a "garden," a pleasant place where all forms of vegetation and animal life exist together in harmony (2:19-25). Homer's description of Ogygia is more detailed than the description of Eden in Genesis, but otherwise Ogygia could be Eden, complete with the four springs:

> Around the entrance a wood rose up in abundant growth--alder and aspen and fragrant cypress. Birds with long wings roosted there, owls and falcons and long-tongued sea-crows that have their business upon the waters. Trailing over the cavern's arch [the entrance to Calypso's dwelling] was a garden vine that throve and clustered; and here four springs began near each other, then in due order ran four ways with their crystal waters. Grassy meadows on either side stood thick with violet and wild parsley. Even a Deathless One, if he came there, might gaze in wonder at the sight and might be the happier in heart. (56)

Ogygia is, furthermore, pleasantly fragrant: "Far and wide over the island was wafted the smell of burning wood, cloven cedar and juniper" (56).

Eden and Ogygia are similar in a second way: their inhabitants live in comfort and without pain. Adam, Eve, and Odysseus hardly have to lift a finger to get the necessities of life. Although Adam and Eve are forbidden to eat from "the tree of the knowledge of good and evil" (2:17), food is plentiful. It is true that God puts Adam "in the garden of Eden to till it and care for it" (2:15), but Adam doesn't seem to have to work hard. "Work" is what he has to do when he is cast out of the garden: "You shall gain your bread by the sweat of your brow until you return to the ground" (3:17). Adam and Eve, furthermore, seem free from pain in Eden. Only after they eat the apple does God give them pain. He tells Eve that he "will increase your labor and your groaning, and in labor you shall bear children" (3:16). He says that Adam will have to overcome the "thorns and thistles" of the earth (3:17). As for Odysseus, Calypso seems to provide all the food he could want: "Calypso put in front of him all manner of things such as mortal men eat and drink, then sat down herself facing the king while her handmaids served her with nectar and ambrosia" (59). We get the impression that, just as she provides food for Odysseus, she can protect him from pain. "Yet if you knew--if you fully knew--," she tells him, "what miseries are fated to fill your cup before you attain your own land, you would choose to stay here, to join with me in calm possession of this domain" (59).

A third similarity between Eden and Ogygia is that Adam, Eve, and Odysseus have companionship. After creating Adam, God worries that Adam will be lonely, so God first creates the animals and then Eve to keep him company. Adam and Eve are the first married couple, becoming "one flesh" and feeling no shame about being naked (2:18-25). Odysseus, of course, yearns to be with this wife, Penelope, but he has a loving companion in Calypso and seems to enjoy her company: "So he spoke; and the sun sank and darkness came; then the pair withdrew, and in a recess of the arching cavern they took their pleasure in love and did not leave one another's side" (60).

The most important similarity between Eden and Ogygia is that in both places there is no death. God tells Adam and Eve that if they eat of the tree of knowledge they will die (2:16-18). And, sure enough, after they eat the apple God tells them, "Dust you are, to dust you shall return" (3:19). We can infer, then, that before they eat the apple, they had eternal life. Odysseus is mortal, but he, too, has the promise of immortality. Calypso tells Hermes, "I welcomed him [Odysseus] and I tended him; I offered him immortality and eternal youth" (58).

In sum, Adam, Eve, and Odysseus seem to possess the essential benefits of paradise: a beautiful environment, an easy and painless life, loving companionship, and eternal life.

Yet Odysseus rejects this paradise? Why?

The obvious answer, I suppose, is that he loves Penelope and wants to be with her. We see Odysseus for the first time "sitting on the shore [of Ogygia] and weeping, breaking his heart with tears and sighs and sorrows" (57). Odysseus admits that Calypso is far more beautiful than Penelope. He tells Calypso that Penelope "is a mortal, you are immortal and unageing." Nonetheless, Odysseus says, "[My] desire and longing day by day is still to reach my own home and to see the day of my return" (60). At the end of the Odyssey, after many hardships, he does just that. For me, the climax of the story occurs when Odysseus and Penelope at last retire to bed to consummate their long-awaited reunion.

A less obvious explanation for Odysseus's rejection of paradise, however, has to do with the character of Odysseus. He is an incredibly creative and energetic person who seems to thrive on meeting challenges and devising stratagems. Early in the epic (40-41) Helen of Troy recounts the story of Odysseus's most famous stratagem, the Trojan Horse. But I feel that the entire Odyssey consists of a string of stories about Odysseus's successful attempts to overcome obstacles. Homer dwells on Odysseus's craftsmanship, his skill in making things with his hands. Odysseus tells with loving detail how he crafted his marriage bed.

> I was the maker, no one else. Inside the courtyard there was a bushy long-leaved olive tree in its prime and pride; it was as thick as a pillar is. Round this tree, using close-set stones, I built a bedroom from start to finish and carefully roofed it in above. I added faultlessly fitting doors. Then I

lopped the olive's leafy branches, rough-hewed the trunk from the root up-
wards, then trued the surface till I had made a bedpost of it; I handled the
bronze as a workman should, and where holes were needed I used my auger.
Working out from there, I shaped the frame complete, inlaying it with silver
and gold and ivory and stretching across it bright crimson oxhide. (281)
Homer gives a similarly detailed and admiring account of how Odysseus crafts
the raft on which he escapes from Ogygia (60-61).

Odysseus's main trait is that he is a craftsman, a maker, a builder. He crafts
the stratagem of the Trojan Horse. He crafts his escape from Polyphemus, the Cyclops: "So I countered him with crafty words" (105). He even laments the absence of craftsmen in the "Cyclops nation"; such "might have made this island
good to live in" (101). He crafts his way past Scylla and Charybdis (148). He
crafts his artful speech to Nausicaa that wins her help (70-71). He crafts the story
of his adventures for the Phaeacians. Alcinous compliments him for telling his
tale "as skillfully as a bard" (136). And, finally, he crafts the defeat of the suitors. In fact, he loves stratagems so much that at times he invents them for the
sheer pleasure of it. After telling Athene one of his elaborate lies, she says,

> Any man who met you--any god who met you--must indeed be crafty,
> indeed be cunning to go beyond you in varied stratagem. Shameless and all
> too subtle man, never surfeited with your trickeries--not even here, in your
> own land, will you lay aside the deceitfulness and the wily words that you
> love in every fibre of you. (161)

How satisfied would a maker and doer like Odysseus be with spending eternity in a place like Ogygia--in "paradise"? I think he would hate it. Ogygia, like
the Garden of Eden, provides everything one could possibly want. And that's the
problem with it. There are no challenges, no obstacles to overcome. People such
as Odysseus, whose love for overcoming obstacles is in their "every fibre,"
would be so bored and so restless that they would go crazy. That, I feel, is the
real reason Odysseus chooses to leave Ogygia. Yes, he loves Penelope. But he
loves, also, the very things that we usually think of as bad--the difficulty and pain
of life. He seems to have concluded that a life without struggle is no paradise.
Athene tells Zeus at the beginning that Odysseus "longs to die" (2). Odysseus
would rather die than live forever in the static eternity of "paradise."

Works Cited

Homer. The Odyssey. Trans. Walter Shewring. New York: Oxford University
   Press, 1980.
The New English Bible. New York: Oxford UP, 1971.

This essay represents the characteristics and interpretive quality
of essays about literature. The author begins by raising a question: Why
does Odysseus leave Ogygia? This is her *topic*. She follows the question
with claims about the nature of paradise and about Odysseus's motiva-

tion for leaving. She supports her claims with evidence. In her conclusion (final paragraph), she answers her question. Her answer is the *thesis* of the essay. Although the essay is "personal" (the author uses "I" and refers to her preconceptions), it deals with a serious issue that would interest thoughtful readers of the *Odyssey.* She shows them that the paradise theme is *meaningful* because of the light it sheds on Odysseus's values and motivations.

# 10

# Drafting the Essay

This chapter deals with the second stage of the writing process, drafting the essay. By the time you reach this stage, you should have chosen a topic and thought about what you want to say about it. Now your task is to draft the essay. How do you do this? To help you answer this question, we discuss the basic aspects of the interpretive essay and offer some guidelines for writing a first draft.

## THE ARGUMENTATIVE NATURE
## OF INTERPRETIVE ESSAYS

Essays about literature are almost always argumentative. Although they *can* be purely informational (that is, just give information) or be purely expressive (that is, just state opinions), they are usually argumentative. An *argumentative essay* has three main qualities. First, it persuades an audience of the validity of its ideas. Second, it uses evidence (facts, reasoning, and, when necessary, testimony) to explain and support its ideas. And third, it has at least one *thesis,* an overall claim supported by more specific claims.

The argumentative nature of essays about literature emerges from the relationship between the work and its reader. Good literature is complex. It communicates on many levels of meaning and by many methods. A single work may exist as a system of sounds, of symbols, of ideas, of images, of analogies, of actions, of psychological portrayals, of moods, of grammatical structures—all of which are separate entities, yet all of which interrelate. Furthermore, good literature also invites the reader to participate in creating the work. A work is not complete until it is read. The author leaves "gaps" in the work for readers to fill with the imagination. The completed work—the work that is read—is something more than the words on the page. It is a collaboration between text and reader. As a result, perceptions of a work vary from age to age, reader to reader, even reading to reading. This variability of perception occurs because no single reading, however careful, can take in all the elements of a work, or synthesize them into all their structural relationships, or include all the vantage points from which even one reader might experience a work.

Consequently, no single view of a work, whether your own or someone else's, can be the all-encompassing or final view. Cultures change, people change, and as a result, perception changes. It is a common experience for people as children to enjoy works—*Huckleberry Finn, Gulliver's Travels,* "Rip Van Winkle," *Alice in Wonderland*—and as adults to enjoy them again, but for very different reasons and with entirely new understandings of them. This does not mean that all interpretations of a work are equally valid. Interpretations of literature are subject to the same rules of human thought—accurate observation, sound reasoning, systematic procedure, thoroughness of treatment—as any other interpretive discourse. But no single interpretation can encompass the whole work.

Because literature is complex and can be perceived variously, essays about literature are usually arguments. You, the writer of the essay, cannot take for granted that your interpretation of the work is the same as your reader's. Your reader may have missed the very facts in the work you have found most compelling or most "obvious." Your reader may have a totally different understanding of the work than you do. If, therefore, you want your reader to grasp your interpretation or accept it as valid, you must explain and persuade. You must write an argument.

## THE STRUCTURE OF ESSAYS ABOUT LITERATURE

Argumentative essays have two interrelated structures: an argumentative structure based on logic and a rhetorical structure based on persuasion. The argumentative structure is really part of the rhetorical structure, because argumentation is a means of persuasion. But the two structures are not exactly the same, so we will talk about them separately.

## The Argumentative Structure

Syllogisms are the basis of an essay's argumentative structure. A *syllogism* is a unit of reasoning that consists of two claims that support a third claim. The two supporting claims are called *premises* and the third claim is called a *conclusion*. The *major premise* states a general concept. The *minor premise* is a specific instance of that concept. The *conclusion* connects the specific instance to the general concept:

MAJOR PREMISE: All complex characters are fascinating.

- MINOR PREMISE: Anna Karenina is a complex character.

CONCLUSION: Therefore, Anna Karenina is fascinating.

Although in formal logic all three parts of a syllogism are stated, in argumentative essays parts of syllogisms are usually left unstated. In an essay, for example, the above syllogism would probably be stated something like the following: "Anna Karenina is fascinating because she is so complex." Here, the major premise has been left out and is present only as an assumption. Such incompletely stated syllogisms are called *enthymemes*. Authors use enthymemes when they feel that the unstated premises would seem "obvious" or readily acceptable to their readers. But just because an author uses enthymemes does not mean that the syllogisms are not present in the author's line of thought. If the reader—or author, for that matter—wishes, he or she can recover all the parts of the syllogisms to understand more fully the author's reasoning.

The argumentative structure of an essay consists of a series of syllogisms that support a thesis. Consider, for example, the argumentative structure of the student essay on the *Odyssey* in Chapter 9. The student's thesis is that although at first glance Ogygia might seem like a paradise, Odysseus chooses to leave it because to him it is not. She supports this thesis with two sets of syllogisms. In the first set she reasons why Ogygia seems like a paradise:

1. Before reading the *Odyssey*, I thought that all places like Eden were paradises.
   Ogygia is like Eden.
   Therefore, Ogygia seems like a paradise.

This line of thought is "personal" in that it has to do with this student's own idea of paradise. In the second set of syllogisms, she reasons why Odysseus fails to find Ogygia a paradise.

1. All people who constantly scheme and love to overcome challenges are creative.
   Odysseus constantly schemes and loves to overcome challenges.
   Therefore, Odysseus is creative.

2. All creative people would hate living in a place that demands no creativity.
   Odysseus is a creative person.
   Therefore, Odysseus would hate living in a place that demands no creativity.

3. All places that anyone would hate are not paradise.
   Places that demand no creativity, like Ogygia and Eden, are places that some people (namely, Odysseus) would hate.
   Therefore, Ogygia is not, for Odysseus, a paradise.

These two sets of syllogisms—the "personal" syllogism about the nature of paradise and the ones about Odysseus—form the argumentative structure of this student's essay. If you read her essay carefully, you will see that she leaves parts of her syllogisms unstated. That is, she uses enthymemes. Such incompleteness is typical of argumentative essays. The point, however, is that the structure of all argumentative essays consists of a chain of syllogisms, whether fully stated or not, that lead to and support a thesis.

## The Rhetorical Structure

*Rhetoric,* simply put, is the art of persuasion. It consists of all the devices writers use to make their claims attractive and convincing. For argumentative essays, the most important rhetorical device is argumentation—the reasoning that supports your thesis. Reasoning, however, is not the only rhetorical device you can use in an argumentative essay. You need, also, to decide how you should organize the essay, where you should put your thesis, what parts of your syllogisms you should leave unstated, and which parts you need to emphasize and support with evidence from the text. All of these choices help create the rhetorical structure of the essay.

How should you organize your essay? The organization of any argumentative essay depends in part on the line of reasoning you develop, and this will vary from topic to topic. But the general structure of an argumentative essay is fairly standard and almost always contains the following units:

1. *A title* The *title* should tell enough about the topic of the essay to capture the interest of readers and let them know the focus of the essay. It helps to include the author's name and the title of the work you are discussing; for example:

The Jungle as Symbol in Joseph Conrad's *Heart of Darkness*

2. *An introduction* The *introduction* should state the topic of the essay and should be interesting enough to make the reader want to keep on reading. You may want to spell out your thesis here, but you could also announce it later in the essay. The introduction should be relatively short—one to three paragraphs.

3. *A body* The *body* is the place where you develop your line of reasoning. It consists of a series of paragraphs that contain claims (usually one claim per paragraph) along with supporting evidence. The body should be as long as you need it to be in order to make your argument convincing.

4. *A conclusion* The conclusion signals that the essay has come to an end. It should remind the reader of the problem posed at the beginning of the essay (the topic) and briefly summarize the solutions. It should state or restate the thesis. The conclusion should be brief, a paragraph or so.

The student essay in Chapter 9 illustrates these structural principles. The title—"Paradise Rejected in Homer's *Odyssey*"—gives enough information about the topic for readers to know, and perhaps be intrigued by, the focus of the essay. The introduction (the first paragraph) presents the topic as a problem to be solved: Why does Odysseus leave "paradise"? The body of the essay consists of a series of paragraphs spelling out the chain of syllogisms that make up the author's reasoning. The conclusion—the last paragraph—answers the question raised in the beginning.

Where should you put the thesis? You have three choices for the placement of your thesis: You can put it in the introduction, in the conclusion, or you can leave it unstated but make it implicit throughout the essay. You have to decide which is rhetorically most effective for the topic you want to discuss. If you state the thesis at the beginning, readers have the comfort of knowing what to look for as they read the rest of the essay. If you withhold it until the end, you create a sense of suspense that is climaxed by the revelation of thesis. If you leave the thesis implicit, you invite readers to infer it for themselves and to participate with you in the process of discovery.

The author of the student essay on the *Odyssey* puts her thesis at the end of the essay rather than at the beginning. Her rhetorical strategy is to intrigue us with an interesting question in the introduction and lead us to the answer—her thesis—at the end.

Which premises of your syllogisms must be supported with evidence from the text? Your syllogisms, and ultimately your thesis, will be believable only if your audience accepts the premises of the syllogisms. You do not have time to support all your premises with evidence, and you do not really need to. Your audience will accept most of them as true, but you will have to support some of them in order to make your argument believable. Which ones?

This, too, is a rhetorical question that you must answer topic by topic, essay by essay. You have to decide which premises your audience will accept as true and which ones they will want supported with evidence. For essays about literature, "evidence" consists of anything in the text or outside it that bears on your topic.

The author of the student essay on the *Odyssey* leaves many of her premises and conclusions unstated. The ones she emphasizes and supports with evidence are (1) that Eden and Ogygia are similar and (2) that Odysseus is creative. Is she right to have supported these claims and not some others? Only she and her readers can answer that question for sure. Some readers might say no, that she needs to support other claims as well. Others may say yes, that these are the key claims needing support. Arguing effectively depends on your ability to choose which claims to state and support. Where you present them—and how—becomes part of the rhetorical structure of your essay.

## GUIDELINES FOR WRITING FIRST DRAFTS

You are now about to begin writing. The following guidelines are suggestions about what to think about and do as you write.

### Keep in Mind the Needs of Your Audience

As you write the drafts of your essay, think of your audience and its needs. You will write better essays if you write for an audience that includes not just your instructor but anyone who enjoys literature and has ideas about it. Your goal is to convince them that your ideas have merit. Imagine yourself in conversation with your audience. In order to follow your line of thought, they will need to know certain things, they will have questions that need to be answered, and they will want complex points clarified. Try to anticipate and supply their needs, just as you would if you were talking with them in person.

One of their needs is clarity. They need a full and clear explanation of the points you are making. Your readers—including your instructor—cannot read your mind. Assume that they have already read the work or can read it; this means that you need only summarize and paraphrase those parts of the work that illustrate your points. But if you do not spell out your ideas, your readers may miss them altogether. In being fully clear, you may feel that you are being childishly obvious, but it is better to be obvious than risk having readers miss your points.

Your readers also need to be convinced. Assume that they want to learn from you, but don't expect them to surrender their views of the work just because you tell them to. Think of them as constantly asking, Why should we believe what you say? Your task is to explain and show them why.

## Draw Up a Rough Outline

Many people find rough outlines indispensable for drafting essays. A rough outline consists of the main points you want to make, including the thesis. If the author of the essay about the *Odyssey* had made a rough outline, it would look something like this:

Introduction
  Raise this question: Why does Odysseus leave Ogygia,
  which seems like paradise?
Body
  Claim #1: Ogygia is a paradise.
  Support this claim by comparing Ogygia with Eden (my standard for what
    paradise is). Give facts from the two texts.
  Claim #2: Odysseus leaves Ogygia because he wants to be with Penelope
    and because he is too creative to be happy there.
  Support these claims with facts from the Odyssey.
Conclusion
  Claim #2 is the answer to my question and therefore my thesis. I will make
  it my conclusion as well.

Rough outlines are *rough*. They include only the main points of your draft, not all the nuances. Their usefulness is to give you a general sense of your line of thought and rhetorical strategy and to help you make sure that all claims relate to your topic. When you start writing, you may discover new ideas or run into dead ends. If so, you can always redo your rough outline and go on from there.

## Begin Writing

Don't bog down. If you have trouble with the introduction (as many people do), move on to the body of the paper. Work on stating your claims clearly and supporting the key ones with evidence. Tackle the claims that seem easiest to support first. Once you get a draft written, it is easier to rearrange claims, to fill in gaps, and to decide for sure what your thesis is.

## Use Sound Logic

The logic of your essay is made up of the syllogisms and chains of syllogisms that reveal your reasoning. If one or more of your syllogisms is invalid, the whole of your argument is undermined. Logic is a complex topic that we do not have the space to discuss thoroughly here. (For more complete discussions, see "For Further Reading" at the end of this chapter.) But a general rule is to avoid *non sequiturs*. The Latin term *non sequitur* means, "It does not follow." A *non sequitur* results from the improper—that is, illogical—statement of a syllogism. For example, the conclusion of the following syllogism "does not follow" from the premises:

MAJOR PREMISE: All complex characters are fascinating.

MINOR PREMISE: Anna Karenina is fascinating.

CONCLUSION: Anna Karenina is complex.

Just because Anna is fascinating does not mean she is complex. She may be fascinating for many other reasons.

When you plan and write your essay, think about the validity of your most important syllogisms. After you finish the first draft, go back over it to make sure your syllogisms are valid. For practice doing this, identify some of the key syllogisms in one of the essays in Chapter 14 or in an argumentative essay in a newspaper or newsmagazine. Write the syllogisms down and see if they are properly stated.

## Support Key Claims with Facts

The believability of your argument rests not only on the validity of your reasoning but on the truth of your premises. The logic of your syllogisms may be perfectly valid, but if your readers do not accept your premises as true, they will reject your conclusions and, ultimately, your thesis. For example, look again at the correctly stated syllogism about Anna Karenina (p. 177). Your readers may not agree that "all complex characters are fascinating." If so, they would reject your conclusion that Anna Karenina, because she is complex, is fascinating.

One way of establishing the truth of premises is to support them with facts. For essays about literature, such facts come from two sources: primary sources and secondary sources. *Primary sources* are the works of literature themselves. If your essay is about *Hamlet,* then *Hamlet* is your primary source. If you are writing about all of Shakespeare's sonnets, then all of them comprise your primary source. Anything in your primary source is a "fact." Facts can be quotations, words, incidents, details of setting, descriptions of characters, conflicts within the plot, word sounds, or punctuation—anything in the work. Facts need not be just quotations; sometimes your facts will be more compelling if you summarize scenes or events in your own words, emphasizing what is most salient to your point.

Notice, for example, how the author of the essay on the *Odyssey* combines summary and quotation to support her claim that Odysseus is a craftsman:

Odysseus is a craftsman, a maker, a builder, in everything he does. He crafts the stratagem of the Trojan Horse. He crafts his escape from Polyphemus, the Cyclops: "So I countered him with crafty words" (105). He even laments the absence of craftsmen in the "Cyclops nation"; such "might have made this island good to live in" (101). He crafts his way past Scylla and Charybdis (148). He crafts his artful speech to Nausicaa that wins her help (70-71). He crafts the story of his adventures for the Phaeacians. Alcinous compliments him for telling his tale "as skillfully as a bard" (136). And, finally, he crafts the defeat of the suitors. In fact, he loves stratagems so much that at times he invents them for the sheer pleasure of it. After telling Athene one of his elaborate lies, she says,

Any man who met you--any god who met you--must indeed be crafty, indeed be cunning to go beyond you in varied stratagem. Shameless and all too subtle man, never surfeited with your trickeries--not even here, in your own land, will you lay aside the deceitfulness and the wily words that you love in every fibre of you. (161)

The only "long" quotation in this paragraph is the one at the end. Otherwise, the paragraph consists of the author's summary of relevant facts as well as brief quotations that she weaves into her own sentences. She also gives page references, so that readers can check her facts or get a sense of their context. Page references have a rhetorical function, as well. They say, in effect, "Reader, I know what I'm talking about. If you don't believe me, go check my references."

Facts from *secondary sources* come from places other than the work. Facts concerning the author's life, the period in which the author lived, the author's philosophy, literary history, other authors, the audience, the work's influence, similarities to other works—these come from secondary sources. Secondary sources are valuable for what they teach us about the work. They give information that helps us form our own opinions. When we study Hawthorne's fiction, our perception of his themes sharpens when we learn that he was deeply ashamed of his Puritan ancestors' dire deeds. When we learn that Jane Austen used an actual calendar to plot the events of *Pride and Prejudice,* we appreciate the care with which she crafted her fiction. When we compare Shakespeare's sources with his plays, we see his genius for deepening characterization and creating complex philosophical themes.

Use secondary sources, then, to learn as much as you can about a work. Use reliable secondary sources—accurate histories, biographies, autobiographies, memoirs, and interviews. When you include facts from secondary sources in your essay, cite them and your sources for them. Keep in mind, though, that secondary sources must be backed up by facts from primary sources. When you quote or summarize critics, make it a practice to buttress their claims with your own analysis of the primary source.

## Give Enough Facts to Support Your Claims

You need not report every fact in the work, but your reader should feel that you have given a thorough account of the work or the parts you discuss. Support your claims with facts that are representative of all the relevant facts rather than with facts that are isolated and atypical. Use important rather than trivial facts. Account for facts that contradict your thesis. If some facts fly in the face of your thesis, explain why they don't nullify it. Often when you deal with negative examples of your reasons, you make your overall argument more subtle and convincing. You discover nuances in the work that your readers— and you as well—may not have expected to find there.

## Define Key Terms

Learn the meaning of important words in primary sources. Look up words in a good dictionary when you have any doubts about their meaning. Doing so is especially necessary for poetry and earlier authors such as Shakespeare and Chaucer. See "For Further Study" at the end of this chapter for a description of different kinds of dictionaries.

## Organize Your Evidence According to a Coherent Plan

*Evidence* consists of everything you offer in support of your claims, especially your thesis. It includes both your reasoning and whatever facts you use to buttress your reasoning. The most important "coherent plan" for presenting evidence is your line of thought, the chain of enthymemes that lead to your thesis. It is hard to predict what that plan might be, since it will vary from topic to topic. You will have to work out a different plan of reasoning for each essay.

Nonetheless, there are several ways of presenting facts from works of literature that might help you think about how to make your reasoning coherent and easy to follow.

1. *Spatial organization* presents the facts as they appear in the work, from beginning to end.

2. *Chronological organization* takes up the facts in the order in which they occur in time. Often, spatial order is the same as chronological but not always. Many works employ devices such as stream of consciousness and flashbacks that make spatial sequence different from chronological. Detective fiction, which depends on a gradual revelation of past events, is a good example. One advantage of either organization is that you give the reader the sense that you are covering

all the important details of the work. The essay on "Young Goodman Brown" in Chapter 14 combines spatial with chronological organization.

3. *Organization by ascending order of importance* moves from the least important facts or claims to the most important. The primary advantage of this method is that it gives your essay an element of suspense by moving your readers toward a climax. Organizing from the least controversial claims to the most controversial is a variation on this plan.

The paragraph about Odysseus's craftsmanship (quoted on pp. 183–184) combines two of these plans of organization. The author arranges her facts *chronologically* by starting with the Trojan Horse and ending with the defeat of the suitors. Had she arranged them spatially—as they appear in the text—they would be out of chronological sequence. She also arranges her facts, at least roughly, in *ascending order of importance.* She ends with Odysseus's most important stratagem, the defeat of the suitors, and with his most surprising trait (his love of stratagems for their own sake). This plan provides an orderly review of Odysseus's career, makes her facts easy to follow, and gives her presentation a measure of suspense and drama.

## Use Traditional Patterns of Thought to Help You Analyze Literature and Organize Your Essay

Generations of communicators have recognized that certain ways of thinking—patterns of thought—are helpful tools for examining subjects and developing ideas about them. In his *Rhetoric,* perhaps the greatest book about writing, Aristotle called these patterns *topoi,* which means "places." Aristotle seems to have meant that these patterns are "places" to look when you need to find ideas. Several of the traditional patterns are especially useful—at times inevitable—for generating ideas about literature and for providing plans for explaining it. The following are descriptions of well-known *topoi.*

**Definition**   Definition is unavoidable in arguments, because premises often contain terms that must be defined. Quite often, these terms are not controversial or ambiguous and therefore need no formal definitions. However, when you have controversial terms, you must define them, and you must use all key terms in such a way that your readers know what you mean by them.

Apart from the necessity of defining terms in your thesis, definition can be useful in two other ways. First, your claims about the facts may rest on the definition of a particular word within the work. The student essays in Chapter 14 on Emily Dickinson and E. A. Robinson both contain such claims. Second, you may want to focus your whole essay on a definition. You might, for example, show that "imagination" is Isabel Archer's most admirable trait in Henry James's novel *The Portrait of a Lady.* Your whole essay would attempt to explain what James means by the term. Or you might argue that Jane Austen in *Pride and Prejudice* distinguishes between "good pride" and "bad pride." Again, you would discuss the novel in order to define these terms. Finally, you might claim that Emily Brontë uses "gothic" elements in *Wuthering Heights.* You would need a reliable definition of *gothic* to make your case convincing, and you would need to apply all parts of the definition to the work, showing which ones fit and which do not. Hugh Holman and William Harmon's *A Handbook to Literature* and the articles in encyclopedias such as *The Encyclopaedia Britannica* are helpful starting points for finding definitions of literary and philosophical concepts.

**Structural analysis**   Structural analysis identifies the parts of a "structure." A structure is something that has a definite pattern of organization. Works of literature always have a structure, sometimes more than one structure. Some works conform to established structures like the sonnet form. Many other works establish their own structures. Your purpose in writing about a work's structure is to identify the structure and explain its relationship to other elements such as theme and characterization. You might, for example, claim that the passage of the seasons provides the structure of William Wordsworth's poem "The Ruined Cottage"; or that the rhyme scheme of his "I Wandered Lonely as a Cloud" emphasizes the narrator's shift from feeling isolated to feeling connected to nature. The less obvious the structure or its effect on the work, the more revealing your essay would be. You might even argue that the work has several structures, an obvious structure and a less-obvious structure.

**Process analysis**   Process analysis identifies the stages in which things change—characters, states of mind, societies, settings, situations, conditions. Because literature often represents events occurring in time, it lends itself to process analysis: Characters change from weak to strong, societies from coherent to incoherent, settings from beautiful to ugly. The sample essay on Hawthorne's "Young Goodman Brown" in Chapter 14 is a process analysis of Brown's emotional state, from integration to disintegration.

When making a process analysis, be careful that you do not simply retell the plot. You should explain and illustrate clear *steps* in the overall process. The pattern of organization would almost always be chronological; you would explain the steps in the order in which they occur in time. Each step would be a unit—probably a paragraph—of your paper. The claim of each unit would be your proposition about what characterizes the step.

**Cause-and-effect analysis**   Cause-and-effect analysis helps you investigate the causes and effects of events. When you investigate *causes,* you are always dealing with events in the past. Why does Goodman Brown go into the forest? Why does Hedda Gabler act the way she does? What causes Pip to change? Two kinds of causes are relevant, the immediate or surface cause and the remote or deep cause. If someone has been murdered, the immediate cause is the murderer. The remote cause would be those forces—childhood experiences, parental models, heredity, financial situation, psychological state—that may have led the murderer to commit the crime. When you investigate *effects,* you may deal with events in the past or the future. In Faulkner's fiction, you could examine the effect of slavery on Southern society and on his characters. These effects are part of the historical past in his work. You could also try to predict what the South will be like in the future, given the way he depicts it. The student essay in Chapter 14 on "The Lottery" is a cause-and-effect analysis. It tries to predict what the villagers will do in the future by examining the causes of their actions in the past and present.

Because literature often deals with the actions of complex characters, cause-and-effect analysis is a fruitful source of essay topics. We constantly wonder why characters do what they do and what effects their actions have had or will have. Just as in real life, cause and effect in works of literature can be complex and subtle. Your task is to discover and communicate those nuances.

**Comparison**   Comparison means indicating both similarities and differences between two or more subjects. One use of comparison is to establish the value of something. You might argue that one of Shakespeare's comedies is not as good as the others, because it lacks some of the qualities the others have. To establish this judgment, you would compare the play to the other comedies. Another use of comparison is to reveal the elements of a work, such as theme, characterization, point of view, and setting. You could compare one character to another, or one set of circumstances to another, or one setting to another in order to expose the nature of these things. A comparison of the two sets of lovers in Tolstoy's *Anna Karenina,* for example, helps us understand his distinction between sacred and profane love. Comparisons of one work to another are also revealing. Sir Walter Raleigh's poem "The Nymph's Reply to the Shepherd" is a response to Christopher Marlowe's poem "The Passionate Shepherd to His Love." Raleigh not only disagrees in general with the premise of Marlowe's poem, but he also makes nearly every line of the poem respond to the parallel line in Marlowe's poem. A line-by-line comparison of the two poems helps make clear Raleigh's themes and methods.

Comparison is revealing also when the author of a work makes allusions. An *allusion* is a reference to another work, a historical event, a myth, or an author. An allusion is always an invitation to compare the work at hand to the thing alluded to. Wordsworth, for example, in his long autobiographical poem *The Prelude* often alludes to Milton's *Paradise Lost.* You could write a comparison of *The Prelude* and *Paradise Lost* to clarify Wordsworth's methods and themes.

When you use comparison, you may want simply to make brief comparisons to support specific points in your essay, but when you make extended comparisons, you need to organize them so your readers can follow them. You should, for example, cover the *same aspects* of all the things compared. If you compare two works and talk about metaphor, symbolism, and imagery in one work, you need to talk about these same things in the other work. You should also discuss the aspects *in the same order* for each thing compared. If you talk about metaphor, symbolism, and imagery in one work, keep this same order when you discuss the other work: metaphor first, symbolism second, imagery last. The outline for such a comparison would look like this:

Work #1

    Metaphor

    Symbolism

    Imagery

Work #2
    Metaphor

    Symbolism

    Imagery

For comparisons of more than two things or for long, complex comparisons, another method of organization may be easier to follow:

Metaphor
    Work #1

    Work #2

    Work #3

Symbolism
    Work #1

    Work #2

    Work #3

Imagery
    Work #1

    Work #2

    Work #3

Notice how the student essay on the Odyssey in Chapter 9 (pp. 169–172) uses this second plan of comparison:

Claim: Eden and Ogygia are similar.
    Reason #1: Their physical features are similar.
        A. Eden has certain physical features (described).
        B. Ogygia's physical features (described) are almost exactly the same.
    Reason #2: Their inhabitants live comfortable and pain-free lives.
        A. Eden
        B. Ogygia
    Reason #3: The inhabitants have companionship.
        A. Eden
        B. Ogygia

Reason #4: Both places are free from death.
   A. Eden
   B. Ogygia

There are other ways to organize a comparison as well as these. You could, for example, discuss all the similarities in one place and all the differences in another. But the general rule is to make the comparison thorough and orderly, so the reader can see all the lines of similarity and difference.

# FOR FURTHER STUDY

An explanation of the use of reasoning in arguments is Robert J. Fogelin's *Understanding Arguments: An Introduction to Information Logic* (San Diego: Harcourt, 1987). Fogelin discusses not only logic but also different kinds of argumentation such as legal, moral, scientific, and philosophical argumentation. For definitions of terms, the two most authoritative dictionaries are *The Oxford English Dictionary*, second edition, prepared by J. A. Simpson and E. S. C. Weiner, 20 volumes (Oxford: Oxford UP, 1989), and *Webster's Third New International Dictionary of the English Language*, unabridged, edited by Philip Babcock Gove (Springfield: Merriam, 1966). *The Oxford English Dictionary (OED)* is based on "historical principles"; it describes and gives examples of a word's use over the years. If you want to know what a word meant to Shakespeare or Chaucer, look it up in the *OED*. The *Merriam-Webster's Third International* is a "descriptive" dictionary; it describes how the word is used and spelled today. The college edition of the Merriam, abridged from the *Third New International*, is adequate for nearly all your needs, as are most hardcover "desk" dictionaries on the market. For definitions of specialized literary terms, such as *gothic* and *Naturalism*, see C. Hugh Holman and William Harmon's *A Handbook to Literature*, seventh edition (Englewood Cliffs: Prentice Hall, 1995) and M. H. Abrams's *A Glossary of Literary Terms*, sixth edition (Fort Worth: Harcourt, 1993).

# 11

# *Documenting Sources*

D ocumentation, or "giving credit," means identifying the sources
you consult when you prepare your essays. When you write essays about literature, you must use at least one source: the primary source, the work of literature itself. You may also want to use
secondary sources. (For a full discussion of primary and secondary
sources, see Chapter 10, the section on supporting your ideas with evidence, beginning on page 183)

## TESTIMONY

In Chapter 10 we discussed how essays about literature, like all
arguments, must support their theses with reasoning and facts. A third
kind of support is testimony. *Testimony* is commentary by experts. For
essays about literature, testimony is an expert's interpretation of works
of literature.

Of the three kinds of support in arguments, testimony is often the
least important. Sound reasoning and supporting facts are necessary to
the believability of an argument; testimony often is not. However testimony can add to the persuasive power of your essays: If you use testimony to show that certain experts or literary critics agree with you, the
reader may more readily accept your reasoning. Furthermore, you can
use testimony to show that your argument is part of an ongoing debate
about the work. You signal that you are aware of the debate and, therefore, of the different solutions already proposed to your problem. You
would explain the other solutions, identify the one that seems most reasonable, or offer a new solution of your own.

Use testimony, then, as a complement to your reasoning and facts, not as a substitute. If critics make especially good points or give especially good analyses, summarize their ideas and include particularly apt or telling quotations from their writings. Think of testimony as witnesses on your behalf.

## RESEARCH PAPERS AND THE USE OF SECONDARY SOURCES

The place to find both testimony and facts about literature is secondary sources. Most people associate the use of secondary sources with "research" and "research papers," so it is appropriate here to address what research papers are. In literary studies, there are essentially two kinds of research papers. The first kind is the informational paper. The informational research paper reports on background, publication, or biographical information that illuminates works of literature. When you write an informational research paper, you assume your reader wants to know the facts in your paper and will probably use them to interpret and to understand the works better. Otherwise you would have no reason to write the paper. Perhaps the most valuable informational research papers are those that present new facts, facts that you have turned up in your research and that no one else knows. Sometimes, however, instructors assign informational research papers to give you practice in writing them. For whatever reason you write an informational research paper, your job will be to gather the facts, to give order to them, and to report them accurately. You will also need a framing generalization—something like a thesis—to give focus to your material. This generalization will probably identify a reason for presenting the information, perhaps a problem of interpretation that the information will help solve. You might write a paper, for example, on a work's critical reception or on an event in an author's life, such as the financial crisis that struck Mark Twain late in his career and that helped cause the increased bitterness of his writing.

The second kind of research paper does more than simply present information; it offers an interpretation of a literary work or works. The writer searches through secondary sources to find facts and opinions that will help establish a reasonable interpretation or lead to a new one. Some research papers try to represent as many different views on a work as possible. Others use only a few secondary sources, either as support and illustration for their own ideas or as springboards for alternative interpretations. The sample essay on E. A. Robinson's "Richard

Cory" in Chapter 14, for example, takes issue with one critic's opinion in order to present another view.

The most important point to remember about this second kind of research paper is that, for all its use of sources, it is still an *argumentative essay*. Here, the terms *research paper* and *research essay* become synonymous. Like all arguments, a research essay presents opinions about a subject. A research essay, then, should be a synthesis of *your* discoveries about a topic and *your* evaluation of those discoveries. The reader should hear *your* voice speaking throughout the paper and should be constantly aware of *your* intelligence and consciousness shaping the essay. The paper should not be a mere anthology of facts or of other people's ideas. It should have what all good argumentative essays have: a unifying idea expressed directly and emphatically in a thesis, an introduction and a conclusion, and paragraphs that relate to the essay's thesis and that follow a logical plan. The sample essay at the end of this chapter exemplifies these traits.

# GUIDELINES FOR FINDING INFORMATION AND OPINIONS ABOUT LITERATURE

## Getting Started

Your research needs will vary from writing project to writing project. Some projects will require minimal research, others more elaborate research. Let's say, however, that you want to write an essay about one work, "Porphyria's Lover," a well-known poem by Robert Browning. Your instructor asks only that you use the primary source (the poem), but you want to read some secondary sources to get yourself thinking about the poem. Go to the *card catalog* or *online catalog* of your college library, find where the author's works are in *the stacks,* and browse among the books in that section. Most college libraries will have many books about well-known authors. So choose a few of the books that look promising for your needs. Look up "Porphyria's Lover" in the indexes, and read what each book has to say about the work. A book that surveys all of Browning's works, for example, will have several pages on your poem. It should take you only a few minutes to read through that section.

Your purpose in doing this kind of exploratory reading is to familiarize yourself with critics' assessments of the characteristics and themes of the work. This knowledge should stimulate your thoughts and get you started on your essay. Sometimes, no matter how carefully you read a work, you may be at a loss for a topic. Doing some introductory reading in secondary sources should clue you in to some of the issues that critics have been debating about the work. You might decide to join the discussion by taking up one of these issues as your topic. If it turns out that you want to incorporate some of this material in your essay, then you need to read these sources carefully, take notes, and give credit for the sources you use.

However, what if there is very little in the stacks on your author, or what if your teacher asks you to do a full-fledged research paper? It may be that you will be lucky enough to find plenty of material in the stacks—biography, background information, criticism—but you will probably need to supplement that material with what you turn up in a second place in the library, the *reference room.* The reference room is especially helpful when books are missing from the stacks (lost or checked out) or when your library's collection on a particular author is small.

The reference room of a college library typically includes several kinds of materials. First, it contains books with background information. These include encyclopedias, literary histories, books containing brief biographies, books that describe and illustrate critical reactions to authors, handbooks to literary terms, surveys of contemporary authors and their works, and guides to works by ethnic minorities. The "Oxford Companion" series published by the Oxford University Press (the *Oxford Companion to American Literature,* the *Oxford Companion to English Literature,* the *Oxford Companion to the Theater,* and so forth) is an example of this kind of book. So, too, is the *Encyclopaedia Britannica,* which contains fine essays on authors and literary movements. Second, the reference room contains books that give specific and specialized information about primary sources. These include concordances and indexes to standard authors like Tennyson, Milton, and Shakespeare as well as books dealing with specialized qualities of works, such as author's use of allusions, Greek mythology, or the Bible.

A third kind of material typical of reference rooms is bibliographies. With these, you can make your research systematic and thorough. There are many kinds of bibliographies for the study of language and literature, but for the sake of simplicity I have divided them into six categories.

1. **General reference**

Baker, Nancy L. *A Research Guide for Undergraduate Students: English and American Literature.* 4th ed. New York: MLA, 1995.

*Book Review Digest.* New York: Wilson, 1905–.

*Book Review Index.* Detroit: Gale, 1965–69, 1972–.

*The Essay and General Literature Index.* New York: Wilson, 1931-.

Harner, James L. *Literary Research Guide: A Guide to Reference Sources for the Study of Literatures in English and Related Topics.* 2nd ed. New York: MLA, 1993.

*Humanities Index.* New York: Wilson, 1975-.

Marcuse, Michael J. *A Reference Guide for English Studies.* Berkeley: U of California P, 1990.

*MLA International Bibliography of Books and Articles on the Modern Languages and Literatures.* New York: MLA, 1922-.

*Readers' Guide to Periodical Literature: An Author and Subject Index.* New York: Wilson, 1901-.

Both Harner and Marcuse are selective but comprehensive guides to reference works for the study of literature in English. They cover just about every area of the study of literature. Harner, for example, has chapters on, among other things, research methods, libraries, manuscript collections, databases, biographical sources, genres, national literatures in English (English, Irish, American, and so forth), and foreign language literatures. Marcuse covers the same ground but is more thorough on some areas, especially foreign language literature and literature related topics such as folklore. Harner and Marcuse are most valuable for access to *areas* of study rather than specific authors. If, for example, you are interested in the English Renaissance, find the section on the Renaissance in either book and locate the reference works—encyclopedias and bibliographies—that will lead you to the information you need. The indexes in both works are very helpful for locating topics. Unlike Harner, Marcuse has brief bibliographies for major authors and inviting lists of recommended reading ("Some Frequently Recommended Works in Renaissance Studies," "Some Frequently Recommended Works in Fantasy, Utopian Fiction, and Science Fiction," and so forth).

Baker is an excellent brief introduction to research methods in English and American literature. The author, a reference librarian, provides a guide to the basic tools of the library. She discusses, among other things, research strategies and how to use bibliographies, library catalogs, and computer databases.

The *MLA International Bibliography* is published annually and covers nearly everything published each year on modern languages, literature, folklore, and linguistics. Since 1981 the bibliography has been published in five parts: Part 1 (British Isles, British Commonwealth, English Caribbean, and American Literatures), Part 2 (European, Asian,

African, and South American), Part 3 (Linguistics), Part 4 (General Literature and Related Topics), and Part 5 (Folklore). Most libraries will have all five parts bound together in a single volume. A very helpful feature of the bibliography since 1981 is a subject index for each of the five parts. You can use these subject indexes to locate works about topics and authors. Before 1981, you have to look up an author by country and period and look up topics under headings like "Esthetics," "Literary Criticism and Literary Theory," and "General and Miscellaneous."

The *Humanities Index* lists articles about all the humanities (including literature) in nearly 300 periodicals. It is organized alphabetically by topic and author and comes out four times a year. Its title from 1920 to 1965 was *International Index to Periodicals* and from 1965 to 1974 was *Social Sciences and Humanities Index.* (In 1975 the index was separated into two individual indexes—*Social Sciences Index* and *Humanities Index.*)

The *Essay and General Literature Index* lists essays that appear in books. Library catalogs and many bibliographies do not do this. Someone, for example, might have written an essay on Robert Browning's "Porphyria's Lover" for an anthology of essays titled *Psychotics in Literature.* If you were doing a paper on this poem, you might overlook this essay because it is "hidden" by the title of the book. *The Essay and General Literature Index,* however, would have it. This bibliography comes out twice a year and is easy to use. Authors and topics are listed alphabetically.

The *Readers' Guide to Periodical Literature,* the *Book Review Digest* and the *Book Review Index* list articles and reviews in newspapers and popular journals.

## 2. Genres

### Drama

Breed, Paul F., and Florence M. Sniderman, comps. *Dramatic Criticism Index: A Bibliography of Commentaries on Playwrights from Ibsen to the Avant-Garde.* Detroit: Gale, 1972.

Palmer, Helen H., comp. *European Drama Criticism: 1900 to 1975.* Hamden: Shoe String, 1977.

Salem, James, comp. *A Guide to Critical Reviews: Part I: American Drama, 1909–1982.* 3rd ed. Metuchen: Scarecrow, 1984. *Part II: The Musical, 1909–1989,* 3rd ed. (1991). *Part III: Foreign Drama, 1909–1977,* 2nd ed. (1979). *Part IV: Screenplays from* The Jazz Singer *to* Dr. Strangelove (1971). *Part IV, Supplement 1: Screenplays 1963–1980* (1982).

Novel

Adelman, Irving, comp. *The Contemporary Novel: A Checklist of Critical Literature on the English Language Novel since 1945*. 2nd ed. Lanham: Scarecrow, 1996.

Kearney, E. I., and L. S. Fitzgerald, comps. *The Continental Novel: A Checklist of Criticism in English 1900-1966*. Metuchen: Scarecrow, 1983.

———. *The Continental Novel: A Checklist of Criticism in English 1967-1980*. Metuchen: Scarecrow, 1983.

Palmer, Helen H., and Anne Jane Dysen, comps. *English Novel Explication: Criticism to 1972*. Hamden: Shoe String, 1973. *Supplement 1* (1976). *Supplement 2* (1980). *Supplement 3* (1986). *Supplement 4* (1990). *Supplement 5* (1994).

Poetry

Kuntz, Joseph, and Nancy Martinez, comps. *Poetry Explication: A Checklist of Interpretation since 1925 of British and American Poems Past and Present*. 3rd ed. Boston: Hall, 1980.

Short Story

Walker, Warren S., comp. *Twentieth-Century Short Story Explication: Interpretations 1900-1975, of Short Fiction since 1800*. 3rd ed. Hamden: Shoe String, 1977. *Supplement 1* (1980). *Supplement 2* (1984). *Supplement 3* (1987). *Supplement 4* (1989). *Supplement 5* (1991). *Index to Supplements 1-5* (1992). *New Series Vol. 1* (1993). *New Series Vol. 2* (1995).

Bibliographies that focus on genres of literature—drama, novel, poetry, short story—are good places to begin looking for secondary sources on authors and especially individual works. These bibliographies provide a *selected* list of books and essays about authors and works, which means that they include only those studies the editors deem important. The disadvantage of them is that they may leave out works on the very topics you want to research. To use these bibliographies, look up the author and the work in the appropriate bibliography; there you will find a list of critical essays on the work you are studying. These bibliographies undergo constant revision, so check for supplements that bring them up to date. You can bring them up to date yourself with the *MLA International Bibliography*. The works listed above are only a few of the ones available. Your library may carry these or others that are just as useful.

## 3. Regions and countries

### World

*Contemporary Authors.* Detroit: Gale Research, 1962–.

Klein, Leonard S., ed. *Encyclopedia of World Literature in the Twentieth Century.* Rev. ed. 4 vols. New York: Continuum, 1993.

### Africa

Herdeck, Donald E. *African Authors: A Companion to Black African Writing.* 2nd ed. Washington, D.C.: Inscape, 1974.

Zell, Hans M., et al. *A New Reader's Guide to African Literature.* New York: Africana, 1983.

### Ancient Greece and Rome

Gwinup, Thomas, and Fidelia Dickinson. *Greek and Roman Authors, A Checklist of Criticism.* Metuchen: Scarecrow, 1982.

Luce, T. James, ed. *Ancient Writers: Greece and Rome* 2 vols. New York: Scribner, 1982.

### Eastern

Lang, David M. *A Guide to Eastern Literatures.* New York: Praeger, 1971.

Nienhauser, William H., et al. *The Indiana Companion to Traditional Chinese Literature.* Bloomington: Indiana UP, 1986.

### Europe

Stade, George, ed. *European Writers.* 14 vols. New York: Scribner, 1983.

### Great Britain

Watson, George, ed. *The New Cambridge Bibliography of English Literature.* 5 vols. Cambridge: Cambridge UP, 1969–1977.

### Native America

Marken, Jack W. *The American Indian Language and Literature.* Arlington Heights, Illinois: AHM, 1978.

### Latin America

Fenwick, M.J. *Writers of the Caribbean and Central America: A Bibliography.* 2 vols. New York: Garland, 1992.

Sole, Carlos A., ed. *Latin American Writers,* 3 vols. New York: Scribner, 1989.

United States

Spiller, Robert E., et al., eds. *Literary History of the United States.* 4th ed. rev. Vol. 2. New York: Macmillan, 1974. 2 vols. (Vol. 1 is the literary history; Vol. 2 is the bibliography.)

Like the bibliographies on genres, these bibliographies provide *selected* lists of sources on regional literatures and on specific authors within regions. The *Literary History of the United States* and *The New Cambridge Bibliography of English Literature* are especially helpful in pointing to important studies done on American and English literature up to their dates of publication. Many of these bibliographies are more like encyclopedias in that they combine biography with bibliography. They provide information about regional literature and authors as well as a brief list of secondary studies on them.

The above list is itself a brief selection. Your library may have these bibliographies as well as others that are equally useful. New bibliographies come out regularly, and many existing ones are periodically updated. You can supplement and update any of these bibliographies with the *MLA International Bibliography.*

## 4. Authors

Weiner, Alan R. *Literary Criticism Index.* 2nd ed. Metuchen: Scarecrow, 1994.

Weiner is a bibliography of bibliographies. It is organized alphabetically by authors, and it keys their works to specific bibliographies. If, for example, you wanted to know where to find critical studies of Browning's "Porphyria's Lover," you would look for the title of the poem under "Browning, Robert." The entry would tell you what bibliographies contain lists of works on the poem.

For the most thorough bibliographies of works by and about authors, seek out bibliographies devoted entirely to individual authors. You can expect to find bibliographies devoted to major authors, but they sometimes exist for lesser-known authors as well. In contrast to the bibliographies listed above, these bibliographies usually contain *complete* listings of works by and about an author. These listings are complete—up to the publication date of the bibliography. For anything after that date, you would need to consult the *MLA International Bibliography.*

## 5. Computer databases available through purchase or subscription

Computer databases can often save you enormous amounts of time. Using a bibliography database, for example, is the same as going through print bibliographies, only the computer does it for you and is much faster. Computer databases are available on compact disc (CD-ROM), magnetic tape, diskette, and from online sources such as the Internet. Generally, for in-depth research in literature, the databases you have to purchase or subscribe to are more useful than the ones you get free via the Internet. You can, for example, gain access to the 1911 edition of *The Encyclopaedia Britannica* on the Internet, but in order to get the most recent edition of the *Britannica,* you have to subscribe to it. Because most people cannot afford to purchase or subscribe to the many excellent databases available for research, we are fortunate to have libraries that can. College and university libraries typically subscribe to a variety of databases, some of which you read at special terminals in the library, some of which you get through your library's online catalog or through your university's online network. Ask your librarian for guidance in choosing and using databases that would be the most help for your projects.

If you want to find out about *all* the databases available, even ones to which your library may not subscribe, consult the *Gale Directory of Databases* (Detroit: Gale). This publication is updated twice a year and comes in two volumes. The first volume focuses on online databases; the second on databases available on "portable" devices such as CD-ROMs, magnetic tapes, and diskettes. Both of these volumes have a subject index. You can, for example, look up "literature" in the subject index and find a list of all the databases having to do with literature. Information about the databases—what they contain, who publishes them, how to subscribe—is available in the main section of the volumes, where the databases are listed alphabetically. If you discover a database that would be especially helpful to you, but that your library does not own, ask your librarian to subscribe to it or help you get it through another library.

Of all the bibliography databases, probably the most useful for studying literature is *The MLA International Bibliography* (1964–present). Its coverage of works about literature is very comprehensive. Like most bibliography databases, you can search it by author, title, and subject as well as by key words. Several bibliography databases that cover outside subjects and their connection with literature are *Essay and General Literature Index* (1985–present), *Humanities Index* (1984– present), and *Arts and Humanities Search.* These allow you to research interdisciplinary topics (art and literature, psychology and literature, science and literature, and so forth). Some excellent content databases are *Contemporary Authors, The Encyclopaedia Britannica,* and *DiscLit,* all of which provide information about authors and movements as well as historical background. *DiscLit,* for example, reproduces the introductory books published by Twayne Publishers. These books cover major American, British, and world authors. Most libraries subscribe to the print versions of the Twayne books, but if someone has checked out the volume you want, you can get it through *DiscLit.*

Several other databases may be helpful as well: *Reader's Guide to Periodical Literature* (1983–present), *National Newspaper Index* (1979–present; an author and subject index to various newspapers, including the *New York Times, Wall Street Journal,* and *Washington Post*), *Book Review Index* (1969–present), and *Book Review Digest* (1983–present). Databases are constantly being expanded—and new ones created—so check with your library to see which ones it carries that might pertain to your area of research.

One more database is worthy of mention here: the online catalog of your library. Many online catalogs have the capacity to perform sophisticated and thorough searches of authors and topics. Your library's online catalog may be limited to the material in the library, but that may be all you need. Many online catalogs are now linked to other databases such as the catalogs of libraries nearby and databases of newspapers, scholarly journals, and popular magazines. Most libraries schedule regular information sessions about how to use their online catalogs. Try to attend one. You may discover a world of resources that will help meet all your research needs.

## 6. Research material available on the Internet

The Internet is an enormous, constantly changing, continuously growing collection of documents. It is, we read, like an "ocean" that somehow we have to "navigate." This ocean is so vast and changes so fast that almost anything published about it, including this book, is dated as soon as it comes out. What follows, then, are a few observations about how to begin using the Internet for doing research about literature. New material will, of course, become quickly available, but once you get the hang of using the Internet, you can catch up with new developments on your own.

More than anything, the emergence of the World Wide Web in 1993 has made the Internet easier to search than ever before. Most Web documents are hypertexts. *Hypertext* is a document containing *links* (also known as *hyperlinks* or *embedded links*), highlighted phrases that take you to other portions of the document or other hypertexts. Click on a link, and you may be transferred to a completely new site. That site will, no doubt, have links of its own, which can take you to new sites, which in turn connect to more new sites—many of which may link back to your original site. You can see why the World Wide Web is called a "web."

Because of the Web's ease of use, it is rapidly subsuming everything else on the Internet. The Web grows at the astonishing rate of at least twenty percent per month. If you have access to the Web, you can now get to almost anything on the Internet. You can gain access to the Internet through an *online service* such as America Online, Compuserve, and Prodigy. You can also log onto the Internet by means of a *browser* such as Microsoft Explorer or Netscape Navigator. These are available through companies known as *Internet service providers* (or *ISPs*). If your college or university already subscribes to a service, you can probably log on from your dorm room or computer lab. Once on the Internet, you can use a *search engine* such as Alta Vista, Webcrawler or Yahoo to scan Web sites. Most services offer a choice of search engines. Whichever one you choose, it will typically have a box, located near the beginning of the document, that allows you to search by typing in *keywords*. Doing this is one of the most effective ways of finding things on the Internet. You can type in any terms or combination of terms, you want: an author's name ("William Shakespeare"), a literary movement ("English Romanticism"), a geographical or national region ("Canadian literature"). The search engine will find documents related to your keywords, tell you how many documents it has found, and arrange them in descending order of relevance: the most relevant documents first, the least relevant last. If one search engine fails to turn up what you want, try another. Some are more detailed and comprehensive than others. A useful feature of most web browsers is the *Bookmark* option, usually located at the top of the screen. If you find a site you want to keep for future reference, you can click on "Bookmark" to store the site (*Uniform Resource Locator,* commonly known as a *URL* or web "address"). When you want to get to that site quickly, open your Bookmark file and go directly to the addresses stored there. Bookmarks save you from having to retrace your original search in order to get back to the site you want.

You can also go directly to any site on the Web if you know the address. Once on the Internet, you should see a box at the top of the screen that contains the address of the site where you are. The address for the search engine Yahoo, for example, is http://www.yahoo.com. The "http"part of the address stands for Hypertext Transfer Protocol, the program that establishes a common language between computers and allows the transmission of all documents on the Web. By clicking on the address, you can delete all or part of it, type in a new address, press Enter, and the browser will take you to the site of the new address. Two publications that describe useful Internet sites are *Cyberhound's Guide to Internet Databases* (Detroit: Gale) and *The Book Lover's Guide to the Internet* by Evan Morris (New York: Fawcett Columbine 1996). *CyberHound's* is published annually and is similar to *Gale's Guide to Databases,* discussed previously. It, too, has a subject index at the back and descriptions of the databases in the main body of the book. Much more comprehensive on matters relating to literature is *The Book Lover's Guide to the Internet.* Morris gives an excellent, non-technical introduction to the Internet: a brief history, definitions of terms, how to hook up, pathways through the Internet (Gopher, File Transfer Protocol [FTP] sites, Telnet, Internet Relay Chat [IRC]), and different ways of using the Internet (discussion/news groups, mailing lists, self-publication, e-mail, online resources). Especially valuable is his long list of addresses, arranged by category (authors, cultural studies, poetry, mystery literature, science fiction, humor, hypertext literature, magazines, bookstores, and so forth).

Generally, three kinds of Internet resources are useful for doing research in literature: databases about literature (authors, periods, regions), electronic texts (e-texts), and personal communications (e-mail, newsletters, discussion groups). All three of these resources have their strengths and weaknesses. Databases related to literature, for example, can be quite wonderful—thorough, clever, amazingly informative, fun—or quite shallow. These databases, furthermore, are often created and maintained ("owned") by one person. The quality and longevity of the database result from the expertise, energy, and health of the owner. You might visit one site and find everything you could possibly want for your project; you might visit another site and feel you have wasted your time.

Time, by the way, is always a factor in searching Web databases. Sifting through sites, following links, can be a very time-consuming process. If you are trying to get a research project done by a deadline, searching the Web may eat away your time and still leave you empty-handed.

Two literature databases should be especially helpful for doing research on the Web. Both sites survey and provide links to sites having to do with all areas of English studies: Jack Lynch's *Literary Resources on the Net* (http://www.english.upenn.edu/~jlynch/Lit/) and *Literature Resources for the High School and College Student* (http://www.teleport.com/~mgroves). Both arrange material by categories (Medieval, Romantic, Literary Theory, Mailing Lists, Calls for Papers, and so forth), and Lynch's site allows you to search by keyword. Both sites are excellent for browsing through Internet materials relating to literature and getting a sense of what is out there. For one of the best author sites, check out the *Jane Austen Info Page and* Pride and Prejudice *Hypertext* (http://uts.cc.utexas.edu/~churchh/). The *Pride and Prejudice* hypertext will give you a sense of how interesting and informative literary hypertext can be. Note, also, all the current Jane Austen jokes! *Native Web* (http://web.maxwell.syr.edu/nativeweb/), *Canadian Literature Archive* (http://canlit.st-john.umanitoba. ca/Canlitx/ Canlit_homepage.html), and *OzLit* (http://www.vicnet. net.au/~ozlit/ index.html) are just three of the many sites that take you outside the British and Anglo–United States traditions. Finally, *Beyond MLA* (http://falcon.eku.edu/honors/beyond-mla/) and *Electronic Sources: MLA Style of Citation* (http://www.uvm.edu/~xli/reference/mla. html) discuss how to document resources on the Internet and provide an MLA format for doing so. When you look for these and other Web addresses, keep in mind that addresses often change or disappear altogether.

A second kind of resource is electronic texts (e-texts). Yes, you can find, the complete works of William Shakespeare on the Web, but many—perhaps most—people would rather read literary texts from a book. Compared to a computer, a book is more portable, easier to hold and flip through, and markable (underlineable), not to mention less stressful to the eyes! E-texts, furthermore, vary in reliability. The texts available on the Internet are typically old editions. Almost always, the most reliable literary texts are recently edited, still protected under copyright law, and unavailable for free. Take, for example, the poems of Emily Dickinson. You can get versions of her poems on the Internet, but they are the ones published in the 1890s by editors who misguidedly altered them from the originals. The authoritative texts of her poems were published in 1955 and are still under copyright protection. In an important sense, the Dickinson poems available on the Internet are not quite "her" poems. Therefore, if you want to do research on Emily Dickinson's poems, you should almost certainly avoid using the ones on the Internet.

The easiest way to find e-texts is to use your search engine. Type in an author's name and see what comes up. To look at several libraries of e-texts, check out the following two sites: *The Columbia University Bartleby Library* (http://www.columbia.edu/acis/bartleby/ index.html) and *Project Gutenberg* (http://promo.net/pg/). Both Bartleby and Gutenberg are projects whose goal is to get as many literary texts on line as possible. But, again, if you use any such texts for research projects, be sure to note the source for the text and get a sense of how accurate the text is. Project Gutenberg, for example, makes no claims for great accuracy in transcribing texts. More than likely, for serious research, you will be better off using print versions of texts.

Finally, interpersonal communication by means of newsletters, discussion lists, and e-mail is a wonderful opportunity for people doing research. You can exchange opinions, share information, and keep up with recent trends. An annual publication that surveys such venues is the *Directory of Electronic Journals, Newsletters and Academic Discussion Lists* (Washington, D.C.: Association of Research Libraries). There is a subject index for the discussion list part of the book (but not for the other parts of the book). The description of each newsletter or list characterizes the subject matter of each and tells you how to subscribe. Jack Lynch's Web site, mentioned earlier, also includes a directory of literary discussion lists. Bear in mind that newsletters and discussion lists are most valuable for researchers who have *long term* projects. They are less helpful for people who need to get research papers done quickly, say within a semester. It is, for example, an extreme breach of "Netiquette" (etiquette for using the Internet) for someone to send out a message on a discussion list saying something like, "I have a paper due in three weeks on *The Sound and the Fury*. Can anyone out there help me think of a topic?" Sending such messages wastes scholars' time and would either be ignored or condemned roundly. There are many, many newsletters and discussion lists. Some titles are AMLIT-L (American literature), Chaucer, Brontë, Arthurnet (King Arthur), Childlit, DorothyL (mystery/detective), Horror, Jack-London, Tolkien, and Twain-L.

## Where to Find Materials

Now that you have drawn up a list of resources for your project—by consulting bibliographies, databases, and Internet resources—your next step is to find these resources. Does your library own them or provide access to them? To find out, use your library's online catalog to see which books on your list the library has. Then locate them in the stacks. For computer databases and Internet resources, use either the computers on campus (in the library or labs) or your own computer. As for journal articles, look up the title of the journal in the online catalog or in a "serials holding catalog." Either should tell you whether or not the library subscribes to it and where it is located. Recent issues of journals are usually stored in the *periodicals room* of the library, and back issues are kept in the stacks. To save space, some libraries also store past issues of journals on microfilm. If you have trouble finding the journal articles you need, ask the librarian in the periodicals room for help.

This discussion of how to find information about topics related to literature is basic. If you want more thorough guidance on a particular project, see Nancy L. Baker's *A Research Guide for Undergraduate Students: English and American Literature,* listed above under "General Reference." Perhaps the most valuable resource for doing research is the reference librarian. Reference librarians are experts on locating sources of information and opinion. They are usually eager to help and can save you time.

# GIVING CREDIT TO SOURCES

## Why Should You Give Credit?

There are several reasons for giving credit to your sources. One is to give readers information that allows them to find and read the same material you read. They may also want to check the reliability of your sources or your ability to use them fairly and accurately. Giving credit, to put it positively, is one more means of arguing. The more careful and honest you are in giving credit, the stronger your argument will be. Another reason for giving credit is to distinguish your ideas from those of others. The purpose of the essay, after all, is to express your ideas, to argue your position. You may use facts, ideas, and words from other sources to clarify and support your ideas, but readers are interested, finally, in knowing what you think. That is why they are reading your paper. By giving credit, both in your text and in footnotes, you show them exactly where your ideas begin and where other writers' ideas leave off.

The most obvious reason for giving credit is to adhere to an ethical standard. Student honor policies stress this reason heavily. Although the ethical principle is obvious, it is not always simple. The usual definition of *plagiarism* is "the presentation of someone else's ideas, work, or facts as your own." The moral judgment that follows is, "Plagiarism is stealing and therefore wrong." These judgments are adequate when applied to blatant plagiarism, cases in which someone copies, verbatim or almost verbatim, the work of someone else and claims it as his or her own. Most cases of student plagiarism, however, are not so obvious or so consciously criminal. The issue of plagiarism is clouded with some uncertainties. Everything you know, for example, comes from a "source." When is what you know "yours" and not someone else's? Another uncertainty is that when you summarize someone else's ideas, you will probably use some of that writer's words. How many and what kind of words can you use without plagiarizing? A third uncertainty is the nature of facts. Some facts, even when they appear in a source, do not need documentation. But which ones? Because of uncertainties like these, most students who "plagiarize" do so unconsciously. The following are principles and guidelines that anyone using sources in essays about literature should obey. They should help you to use sources usefully, clearly, and ethically.

## When Should You Give Credit?

1. **Give credit for primary sources.** Whenever you make a specific reference to an incident or words in a work and whenever you quote from a work, you need to give credit to the source from which you obtained the information. This is as true for primary as for secondary sources. You must do this for several reasons. Works of literature, especially famous ones, often go through many editions and even different publishing houses. Readers need to know which edition you are using, so they can refer to the parts of the work you discuss. You document your primary source, then, for their convenience. Another reason is that the edition you use may affect the validity of your argument. If the edition is unscholarly and contains misprints or omissions, your interpretations will be suspect. A well-known

example is Emily Dickinson's poetry. After the poet's death in 1886, Thomas Wentworth Higginson and Mabel Loomis Todd edited her poetry for publication. They published it (or some of it) in four volumes throughout the 1890s. Instead of printing it as Dickinson had written it, they "regularized" it for the tastes of nineteenth-century readers. They changed the meter to make it more conventional, changed words to make them rhyme, normalized punctuation, and altered metaphors that seemed illogical. Not until Thomas H. Johnson published his edition of her poems in 1955 did we have versions of Emily Dickinson's poetry as she wrote it. If you write an essay about Emily Dickinson's poetry, your readers will want to know that you used Johnson's edition (or reprints therefrom). By giving full information about the editions you use, you enhance the reliability of your essay.

Often the nature of a college course allows you to omit complete citations for primary sources. You may be writing about a work that appears in one of your course textbooks. If so, the number of the page on which each quotation or specific reference occurs is usually all the documentation you need. Give the quotation or reference and then follow it with the page number or numbers in parentheses, placing your final mark of punctuation after the closing parenthesis.

EXAMPLE (a quotation): Lawrence says that when she is with her children she feels "the center of her heart go hard" (125).

EXAMPLE (a specific reference but not a quotation): When she returns home from the party, she finds Paul riding the rocking horse. Lawrence contrasts her elegant, even icy dress with Paul's frenzied and exhausted state (134-35).

More formal usage, however, requires that you give a complete citation for the edition you are using. This practice is always necessary when you use a book that is not a basic text in your course.

2. **Give credit for facts that are not common knowledge.** "Common knowledge" facts are those the average well-read person would be likely to know. You assume that such persons have some familiarity with your subject, even though they may not. Common knowledge facts include very basic facts about history (say, that Woodrow Wilson was president of the United States during World War I, that the United States entered the war several years after it began), birth

and death dates, occupations, publication dates, basic biographical facts about famous people (that Ernest Hemingway began his writing career as a newspaper reporter, that he entered World War I as an ambulance driver, that in 1929 he published a famous novel, *A Farewell to Arms,* based on his wartime experiences, that just before the outbreak of World War II he published a novel, *For Whom the Bell Tolls,* about the Spanish Civil War). Facts that are not common knowledge have to come from sources (what Hemingway's parents thought of his newspaper career, where he saw action during the war, how he was wounded, the identity of the nurse he fell in love with while recuperating, his attitude toward his hometown when he returned from the war, what he actually said to people about the war), and those sources must be cited. Also, facts that are in any way controversial need to be documented. If you claim that Theodore Roosevelt was a secret Marxist, or had an affair with Emma Goldman, or conspired to assassinate President McKinley, you must give sources (assuming there are any!) for these assertions; otherwise your reader will write you off as a crank.

3. **Give credit for all direct quotes.** This kind of documentation is crucial, whether you quote from primary or secondary sources.

4. **Give credit for summaries or paraphrases of someone else's ideas.** Even when you don't quote directly from the work, you must provide documentation for the sources of your summaries or paraphrases of someone else's ideas. This includes ideas that are held by other writers, by your instructor, or even by other students. It also includes ideas that you arrive at on your own and then find expressed in print.

5. **Give credit for ideas not "assimilated" by you.** Once you have absorbed someone's ideas, thought about them over a period of time, added thoughts of your own or of others, you can assume that these ideas are now "yours." If, however, your memory is so good that these ideas remain in your mind exactly as they were when you read and heard them, then you must give credit to the original author.

A final word about when to give credit: The dividing line between facts that are common knowledge and those that are not is sometimes frustratingly vague. So too is the line between ideas that are assimilated by you and those that are not. *When in doubt about where that line is, give credit.* Doing so takes a little extra trouble, a little extra time; but the trouble and time are worth it to protect yourself against charges of plagiarism or simply to provide the curious reader with enough information to check your facts and ideas.

## CORRECT DOCUMENTARY FORM

Documentary form varies from discipline to discipline. For people writing about literature, the authoritative guide to documentary form has been the *MLA Handbook for Writers of Research Papers, Theses, and Dissertations.* (*MLA* stands for Modern Language Association, the preeminent scholarly organization devoted to the study of modern languages and literature.) In 1984 the MLA created a new documentary format, one that resembles the formats of the social and natural sciences. The guidelines in this chapter are from the most recent edition of the *MLA Handbook:*

> *The MLA Handbook for Writers of Research Papers.* Joseph Gibaldi. 4th ed. New York: MLA, 1995.

### Where Should You Give Credit?

1. **Give credit by introducing your source in your text.** When you use the ideas and specialized or controversial facts of another person, introduce them *in your own text,* not just in parenthetical references. To do this, use introductory phrases like the following:

   As Jane Tompkins says, "The ground for complaint . . ."

   One critic has called attention to "the absurdity of Huck's shore experience."

   Annette Kolodny suggests . . .

   Tuchman's second point is . . .

   Leo Marx's theory about technology in America is . . .

All of these introduce paraphrases, summaries, and short quotations. The following example introduces an indented or blocked quotation (that is, a long quotation set back ten spaces from the established margin).

EXAMPLE: Friedman's definition of plot focuses on the changes the protagonist undergoes:

> The end of plot, then, is to represent some completed process of change in the protagonist . . .

Acknowledgments for facts are necessary, too, when the facts are very specialized or controversial. For example, details about F. Scott Fitzgerald's love life in Hollywood during his last years can come from only a few people. You must mention such people *in your text* when you use them:

> Sheilah Graham claims that . . .

> Budd Schulberg saw that Fitzgerald was . . .

> Nathanael West said that at the party Fitzgerald concentrated his attention on . . .

Note, however, that facts available from many sources do not need textual acknowledgment. Details about English history, for example, are available in many textbooks and are not associated with any one person or group. You do, however, need to provide parenthetical references for such information and to cite your source in the "Works Cited" list.

2. **Give credit in the text of your essay by making parenthetical citations to the works contained in your "Works Cited" list.** See Guidelines for Parenthetical Citations.

3. **Give credit in a "Works Cited" list at the end of your essay.** The parenthetical citations and "Works Cited" list work together to give readers complete information about your sources and how you use them. Use parenthetical citations in your text to show when you draw upon sources for facts and opinion. Give enough information so readers can find the sources in your "Works Cited" list. The "Works Cited" list provides enough information to verify the existence of your sources and to enable readers to check out the sources themselves.

## Guidelines for Parenthetical Citations

1. Make a parenthetical citation
   a. whenever you refer directly to a particular part of a source,

b. whenever you use facts that are not common knowledge,

c. whenever you use direct quotations,

d. whenever you summarize or paraphrase someone else's ideas.

2. Give enough information for the reader to do two things: identify the work on the "Works Cited" list and find exactly where your reference is in the work itself.

3. To do this, usually it is enough to give the author's last name and the page number or numbers of the reference:

(Mast 116-17)

The author's name points you to the work in the "Works Cited" list, and the page number points you to the citation in the work itself. The above citation is to the following work in the "Works Cited" list:

Mast, Gerald. *A Short History of the Movies.* (Indianapolis: Pegasus, 1971).

4. Give more information when necessary to eliminate ambiguity. If you use several works by the same author, give the author's last name, a portion of the title, and the page number.

(Mast, A Short History 116-17)

If you have several authors with the same last name, give initials or the whole name to distinguish among them:

(H. Jones 58-60)

5. You can leave out the author's last name if you use it in your text. All you need to include in parentheses is the page number or numbers.

EXAMPLE: Gerald Mast says that D. W. Griffith's *The Birth of a Nation* is racist in its social attitudes but brilliant in its cinematic technique (80-81).

This usage is especially helpful when you cite primary sources.

EXAMPLE: In Shirley Jackson's "The Lottery" the people are at first reluctant to participate in the lottery. The men standing around waiting are subdued: "Their jokes were quiet and they smiled rather than laughed" (219).

The children, when called, come "reluctantly, having to be called four or five times" (220). Once the black box is brought out, the villagers keep "their distance" from it (221).

If, however, you use more than one work by the same author, be sure the reader knows which work you are discussing. Make this clear by introducing the references properly or by giving adequate information in the parenthetical references.

> EXAMPLE: Lawrence describes the two mothers differently. Elizabeth Bates is "a tall woman of imperious mien, handsome, with definite black eyebrows" ("Odour of Chrysanthemums" 248), whereas Paul's mother is simply "a woman who was beautiful" ("The Rocking-Horse Winner" 271).

Or,

> EXAMPLE: Lawrence describes the two mothers differently. Elizabeth Bates in "Odour of Chrysanthemums" is "a tall woman of imperious mien, handsome, with definite black eyebrows" (248), whereas Paul's mother in "The Rocking-Horse Winner" is simply "a woman who was beautiful" (271).

6. You may leave out a parenthetical reference in your text if you identify the author and refer to the whole work.

> EXAMPLE: E. M. W. Tillyard devotes a short book to explaining how the Elizabethans saw the structure of the cosmos.

If readers are interested in Tillyard's book, they can find it in the "Works Cited" list.

7. When referring to primary sources, use page numbers for prose works; line numbers and division numbers for long poems (more than about twenty lines); and act, scene, and line numbers for verse drama.

> EXAMPLE: In *Hamlet* the queen bids farewell to Ophelia by saying, "I hoped thou shouldst have been my Hamlet's wife" (V.i.211).

Here the reference is to act five, scene one, line 211. If your instructor prefers, you may use arabic numbers instead of roman numerals to cite acts and scenes.

EXAMPLE: In *Hamlet* the queen bids farewell to Ophelia by saying, "I hoped thou shouldst have been my Hamlet's wife" (5.1.211).

The following is an example of a quotation from a long poem:

EXAMPLE: In commenting on our growing distance from heaven, Wordsworth says in "Intimations of Immortality,"

Heaven lies about us in our infancy!
Shades of the prison-house begin to close
Upon the growing Boy. (66-68)

For references to the Bible, use arabic numbers separated by periods to indicate chapters and verses:

(Isaiah 29.3-15).

8. Use hyphens between line or page numbers to indicate material that lies within a continuous sequence of lines or pages (231–33). Use commas between line or page numbers to indicate interruptions in sequence (200, 219). Use colons to separate volume and page numbers (*Clarissa* 3: 451). (Leave a space between the colon and the page number.)

9. If your reference is to a work with more than one volume, indicate in your parenthetical reference to which volume you are referring.

EXAMPLE: Even on the point of death, Clarissa writes to her father asking his forgiveness. She begs him "on her knees" to forgive her for "all her faults and follies," especially "that fatal error which threw her out of [his] protection" (4: 359).

Here the reference is to the fourth volume, page 359. If you use only one volume from a multivolume work, you need not give the volume number in the parenthetical reference. Include it instead in the "Works Cited" listing.

10. If the author of a work is anonymous, give the whole title or the first few words of the title, plus the page number. (Anonymous works are alphabetized by title in the "Works Cited" list.)

EXAMPLE: Unlike the pilgrims, the Puritans remained members of the An-
glican church. But like the Pilgrims, they adhered to a Calvinistic theol-
ogy ("Early American Literature" 2).

11. You may refer to more than one work in a single parenthetical ref-
    erence by separating the works with semicolons.

    EXAMPLE: At least two critics have seen the similarity between Voltaire's
    character Candide and the young Benjamin Franklin in the *Autobiogra-
    phy* (Orkney 13; Scott 151-52).

    If, however, you want to refer to more than two or three works, use
    a footnote or endnote instead of a parenthetical reference. (See the
    discussion of footnotes and endnotes.)

12. When referring to a work with two or three authors, give all their
    names in the text or in the reference.

    EXAMPLE: One work makes the useful distinction between "representa-
    tional" and "illustrative" narrative (Scholes and Kellogg 84).

    Or,

    EXAMPLE: Scholes and Kellogg make the useful distinction between "rep-
    resentational" and "illustrative" narrative (84).

13. When referring to a work with more than two authors, you may
    give all their names or, more simply, give the first name and "et al."
    (abbreviation for Latin *et alii*, "and others").

    EXAMPLE: The trickster has been a traditional folk hero not just of Amer-
    ican "Yankee" narrative but of American Indian and African-American
    narrative as well (Spiller et al. 729).

14. If you find an author or someone else quoted in a book or article
    but cannot find the original source for the quotation, rather than
    abandon the quotation, cite the place where you found it. To do so,
    use "qtd in" ("quoted in").

    EXAMPLE: When Dreiser was a magazine editor, he would write on re-
    jection slips, "We like realism, but it must be tinged with sufficient ideal-
    ism to make it all a truly uplifting character" (qtd in Fiedler 46).

15. Use the following guidelines for parenthetical references: Place the reference immediately after the material that needs referencing. Usually this is at the end of a sentence or paragraph, but sometimes it can be within a sentence as well. Put the reference before the closing punctuation of the phrase or sentence (comma, period, semicolon, colon, exclamation point):

> EXAMPLE: James Joyce, as Arnold Kettle notes, was consistent about employing his artistic principles (301), but that does not mean his works are all the same.

The exception to this punctuation rule occurs when a quotation is indented. Then the reference goes outside the closing punctuation.

> EXAMPLE: At a crucial point in the story, Hawthorne admonishes Wakefield for cutting himself off from the warmth of human affection and companionship:

>> Go quietly to thy bed, foolish man; and, on the morrow, if thou wilt be wise, get thee home to good Mrs. Wakefield, and tell her the truth. Remove not thyself, even for a little week, from thy place in her chaste bosom. Were she, for a single moment, to deem thee dead, or lost, or lastingly divided from her, thou wouldst be woefully conscious of a change in thy true wife, forever after. It is perilous to make a chasm in human affections; not that they gape so long and wide—but so quickly close again! (932)

## Guidelines for Using Footnotes and Endnotes

1. Use footnotes or endnotes for citing several sources (more than two or three) all at once.

> TEXT: A host of critics agree that Swift does not share Gulliver's extreme condemnation of human beings and approval of Houyhnhnms at the end of *Gulliver's Travels.*[1]

> NOTE: [1]Abrams 23-28; Converse 55-70; Portnoy 150-65; Clore and Barchester 300-05; Kellerman 83; Soles 15-20.

2. Use footnotes or endnotes for further comments or information relating to something in your text. These comments or facts are not

necessary to your line of thought, but possibly they are interesting to your readers nonetheless.

TEXT: Irving adopts the stance of the ironic narrator in his comic masterpiece "The Legend of Sleepy Hollow."[2]

NOTE: [2] The ironic narrator was a common fictional device in eighteenth-century English fiction and was most notably present in one of Irving's favorite authors, Henry Fielding.

3. To set up a footnote or endnote, do the following:
   a. In the text of your essay where you want the reference to appear, place a number raised slightly above the line (*superscript*). (Note the examples above.)
   b. Place a corresponding superscript number just before the note itself. (Note the examples above.)
   c. Indent the note five spaces.
   d. Number the notes sequentially throughout the paper. In other words, don't restart your numbering (with "1") when you come to a new page. Rather, go from "1" to the final number all the way through the paper.
   e. Place your notes either at the bottom of the page (footnotes) or at the end of the paper (endnotes). Many people put them at the end because it's easier.
   f. Single-space footnotes and place them three lines below your text. (Space three lines from the text and begin the footnote.) Double space between footnotes.
   g. If you use endnotes rather than footnotes, put them on a separate page or pages and position them between the text of your essay and the "Works Cited" page. In other words, the body of your paper would end on one page. The next page would have the endnotes with the title "Notes" centered at the top. After the endnotes, on a separate page, would follow the "Works Cited" list, with the title "Works Cited" centered at the top.
   h. Double-space endnotes and triple-space between them.
   i. See the sample research paper (pp. 231–237) for an example of an endnote.

## Guidelines and Form for the "Works Cited" List: General Rules

The "Works Cited" list contains citations for all the resources, primary and secondary, to which you refer in the body of your paper. Your goal here is to give enough information so readers can find these same sources and verify their content and reliability. The guidelines below should help you accomplish this goal.

1. Arrange entries alphabetically by author. If the author is anonymous, list the entry alphabetically by its title.

2. Do not number entries.

3. In each entry, put the author's last name first. (The author's last name is printed first because the list is in alphabetical order.) If there is more than one author in an entry, put the last name first for the first author but not the others, and keep the authors in the order in which they were listed on the work's title page.

4. Put the first line flush with the left margin. Indent any subsequent lines of the entry five spaces from the left hand margin.

5. Include without exception every source—primary or secondary—cited in your paper.

6. When you include more than one work by an author, substitute three hyphens for the author's name after the first citation:

   Jewett, Sarah Orne. *A Country Doctor.* New York: Garret, 1970.

   ———. *A White Heron and Other Stories.* Boston: Houghton, 1886.

7. Divide your entries into three main sections:

   a. author's name (last name first),
   b. the name of the article or book,
   c. information about publication.
   Sometimes more sections are necessary—for information about editors, about volume numbers, or about reprinted editions. But these three divisions are essential for all entries. Punctuate citations as indicated in the sample entries below.

8. If information seems missing from a source, provide as much information as you can.

9. Put the "Works Cited" list at the end of your paper, on sheets separate from your text. Double-space each entry and triple-space between entries.

## Sample Entries for Books

### 1. A book with one author

Hoffman, Daniel. *Poe Poe Poe Poe Poe Poe*. Garden City: Double-day, 1972.

The date of publication for books should be on the copyright page (the reverse of the title page) or, for some books published outside the United States, at the back of the book. If there is more than one date, choose the most recent one. If several cities are listed as places of publication, give the first one.

### 2. A book with two authors

Berry, Lester V., and Melvin Van den Bark. *The American Thesaurus of Slang: With Supplement.* New York: Crowell, 1947.

Reverse the name only of the first author.

### 3. A translation

Cervantes, Saavedra, Miguel de. *The Adventures of Don Quixote.* Trans. J. M. Cohen. Baltimore: Penguin, 1950.

### 4. A book that has three authors or more, has gone through several editions, and is one of several volumes in a set

Spiller, Robert E., et al. *Literary History of the United States.* 4th ed. rev. Vol 1. New York: Macmillan, 1974. 2 vols.

Using "et al." saves you from listing all the other authors of the work.

### 5. A work in more than one volume

Richardson, Samuel. *Clarissa; or, the History of a Young Lady.* Vol. 4. London: Everyman, 1932. 4 vols.

### 6. An introduction to a primary source

Charvat, William. Introduction. *The Last of the Mohicans.* By James Fenimore Cooper. Boston: Riverside, 1958

### 7. An edition of an author's work

Trollope, Anthony. *The Last Chronicle of Barset.* Ed. Arthur Mizener. Boston: Riverside, 1964.

8. **An anonymous introduction in an anthology of literature**

"The Middle Ages (to 1485)." *Norton Anthology of English Literature*. Ed. M. H. Abrams et al. Rev. vol. 1. New York: Norton, 1968. 1–25.

Here the reference is to the first volume, pages 1–25. Note that when you cite sections of books, you usually give numbers for the whole section. An exception is the introduction to an entire book, as in example six above. The abbreviation "Ed." after the titles in 7 and 8 above means "edited by;" *do not* add an "s" to the abbreviation if the book is edited by more than one person.

9. **A work from an anthology**

Chekhov, Anton. "The Lady with the Dog." *Norton Introduction to Literature*. Ed. Carl E. Bain et al. 3rd ed. New York: Norton, 1981. 55–70.

10. **A book with one or more editors**

Stevick, Philip, ed. *The Theory of the Novel*. New York: The Free Press, 1967.

Suleiman, Susan R., and Inge Crosman, eds. *The Reader in the Text: Essays on Audience and Interpretation*. Princeton: Princeton U P, 1980.

The abbreviation "ed." above means "editor;" *do* add an "s" to the abbreviation if the book is edited by more than one person.

## Sample Entry for Articles in Scholarly Journals

Leverenz, David. "The Last Real Man in America: From Natty Bumppo to Batman." *American Literary History* 3 (1991): 753–81.

In this entry, *American Literary History* is the journal, 3 is the volume number, 1991 is the year of publication, and 753–81 are the page numbers. Note that you give page numbers not just for the pages you cite but for the entire article.

## Sample Entries for Articles in Popular Publications

1. **A weekly magazine**

Troy, Judy. "In One Place." *New Yorker* 10 Sept. 1984: 42–43.

2. **A monthly magazine**

Malone, Michael. "Books in Brief." *Harper's* June 1977: 82-84.

3. **A book review in a weekly magazine**

Blake, Patricia. "Gingerly Removing the Veil." Rev. of *Josephine Herbst,* by Elinor Langer. *Newsweek* 3 Sept. 1984: 80.

4. **An article in a newspaper**

Coneroy, Herman. "*David Copperfield* Revisited." *New York Times* 19 Aug. 1962, late ed: F23.

When citing newspaper articles, indicate if possible the edition of the paper ("late edition," "national edition," "city edition"). The edition is usually indicated in the newspaper's masthead. The content of articles may vary from edition to edition.


## Sample Entries for Computer Databases

The documentary format for computer resources continues to evolve along with the resources themselves. The fourth edition of the *MLA Handbook,* for example, includes elaborate instructions for documenting databases but has scanty information about documenting certain kinds of Internet resources. The forthcoming fifth edition will have such information, but that information will inevitably be supplemented in future editions. When you are faced with the sometimes puzzling problem of documenting computer resources, keep in mind the reasons to document *anything:* You want to verify the existence and reliability of your resources. You want to help readers find these resources. You want to show that you have conscientiously sifted through the relevant evidence and opinion. So, if the guidelines for documenting a resource are unclear or incomplete, use common sense. Give the information necessary to accomplish the above goals, and you will be all right. I have compiled the following guidelines from three sources. Most important is the *MLA Handbook for Writers of Research Papers,* 4th ed, the official source for most documentary procedures in literature studies. The other two sources are World Wide Web sites: *Electronic Sources: MLA Style of Citation* (http://www.uvm.edu/~xli/reference/mla.html) and *Beyond MLA* (http://falcon.eku.edu/honors/beyond-mla/). The editors of these sites make their best guesses at MLA format for citing electronic sources not covered in the *MLA Handbook*. A book that does the same thing is *Electronic Styles: A Handbook for Citing Electronic Information* (Medford: Information Today, 1996) by Xli Li and N. B. Crane. *Electronic Sources* is the Web site for this book and gives information about other documentary styles as well as MLA. Check these three sources for a thorough treatment of how to document electronic resources. The information that follows is basic—what you are most likely to need and use.

1. **Portable databases published periodically** (that is, CD-ROMs, diskettes, magnetic tapes that are continually updated).

> Dolan, Marc. "The (Hi)story of Their Lives: Mythic Autobiography and 'The Lost Generation.' " *Journal of American Studies.* 27 (1993): 35–56. *America: History and Life on Disc.* CD-ROM. ABC-Clio, Inc. 1996.

> Earthman, Elise Ann. "Creating the Virtual Work: Readers' Processes in Understanding Literary Texts." Conference on College Composition and Communication. Seattle, Washington, 17 March 1989. *ERIC.* CD-ROM. SilverPlatter. June 1996.

These databases should include as much of the following information as you can find:

a. author's name. If the work is anonymous, omit the name.
b. publication information. If the work appears in print, use the same format for giving publication information as you would for the printed version. (See the sample entries for books, scholarly journals, and popular publications.)
c. title of the database (underlined or italicized).
d. publication medium (CD-ROM, diskette, magnetic tape).
e. name of the vendor. (You can usually spot the name of the vendor—the company that produces the database—somewhere on the first screen. If it's not there, check to see if you can press a key for "information about this database." If that doesn't work, the *Gale Directory of Databases* should tell you who the vender is. If nothing works, don't fret. You've done your best. Leave the information out and move on.
f. electronic publication date (when the database was released). The sources of information just mentioned should give you this date.

The first example above is an abstract of an article in a scholarly journal. If you wanted to summarize or quote from this abstract, you would cite the computer database (*America: History and Life on Disc*) that provides it. The second entry is a lecture available only from the computer database *ERIC*. If you want to use it, you would cite the database.

2. **Portable databases not published periodically** (that is, CD-ROMs, diskettes, and magnetic tapes published only once, like a book).

> "Mingle." *The Oxford English Dictionary.* 2nd ed. CD-ROM. Oxford: Oxford UP, 1992.

> Hallam, Walker. *Molière.* Boston: Twayne, 1990. CD-ROM. Boston: DiscLit, 1992.

For these databases, give the following information:
a. author's name (if given).
b. title of the part of the work (if given, in quotation marks).
c. title of the product (underlined or italicized). The "product" is the title of the "book" or work in which the part ("b" above) appears.
d. edition (if relevant, such as "2nd edition," "Revised edition").
e. publication medium (CD-ROM, diskette, magnetic tape).
f. city of publication.
g. name of the publisher.
h. year of publication.

The first example above is the definition of a word from *The Oxford English Dictionary.* The second is a book from the Twayne Publishers series of books about authors. For this second entry, publication information about the printed book is followed by information about the CD-ROM.

3. **Online databases accessed through a computer service and featuring material published in print.** (Such databases are available over the Internet, usually through subscription. You would typically gain access to them through your college or library computer network.)

> Halberstam, Judith. "Technologies of Monstrosity: Bram Stoker's *Dracula.*" *Victorian Studies* 36 (1993). 20. *Expanded Academic ASAP.* Online. Infotrac Online. 5 October 1996.

> Hutchinson, Mark. "In Defense of Fiction." *New York Times* 22 October 1995, late ed., sec. 7:30. *New York Times.* Online. First Search. 5 October 1996.

For these databases, give the following information:
a. name of the author (if given).
b. publication information for the printed source. Use the format for printed material. See the sample entries given above for books, scholarly journals, and popular publications.
c. title of the database (underlined or italicized).
d. publication medium (*Online*).
e. name of the computer service.
f. date of access (that is, the date you used the service to read this material).

In the first example above, the computer service, Infotrac Online, provides an abstract and the full text of an article that appeared in a printed scholarly journal. There are no page numbers in this document, but the information about it includes the number of pages (twenty) of the printed essay. In the second example, the service gives an abstract of a newspaper article.

4. **Online databases accessed through a computer service and featuring material with no printed source**

> "Courtly Love." May 1996. *Britannica Online*. Online. Compu-Serve. 5 October 1996.

For these databases, give the following information:
a. author's name (if available).
b. title of the article or chapter (in quotation marks).
c. date of the material (if given).
d. title of the database (underlined or italicized).
e. publication medium (*Online*).
f. name of the computer service. (If you gain access to the material from your college or library network, you could list that as your computer service.)
g. date of access (the date you used the service).

In the example above, the author is unknown (so not included) and the article came over the Internet by subscription to *Britannica Online*. Were you to look up "courtly love" in the printed version of the *Encyclopaedia Britannica,* you might find the same article as the one above, but the editors of *Britannica Online* claim they update their entries regularly, so their version of the article might be different from the printed version.

## 5. Internet resources: authors' comments in Websites and in electronic journals, magazines, and newsletters

> Atwood, Margaret. "Welcome to This Page." *The Margaret Atwood Information Web Site*. no date: 3 pars. Online. Internet. 5 October 1996. Available <http://www.io.org/~toadaly/Overview.html>.

> Coover, Robert. "The Titles Sequence from *The Adventures of Lucky Pierre*." *Postmodern Culture* 3 (Sept. 1992): 50 pars. Online. Internet. 23 September 1996. Available <http://jefferson.village.virginia.edu/pmc/issue.992>.

Many essays and commentaries are published only on the Internet in such places as Websites, journals, magazines (e-zines), and newsletters. For these resources, give as much of the following information as you can:

a. author's name (if available).
b. title of the article (in quotation marks).
c. title of the Website or publication (underlined or italicized).
d. volume number, issue number, or other identifying number (if available).
e. date of publication (if available).
f. number of pages or paragraphs (if given) or *n.pag.* ("no pagination") if not given.
g. publication medium (*Online*).
h. name of the computer network.
i. date of access.
j. electronic address of the site (contained within angle brackets).

In the first example above, Margaret Atwood makes a few introductory comments about her own Website. In the second example, Robert Coover's essay appears in the journal *Postmodern Culture*, which is published only on the Internet. The format for citing electronic journals is similar to that for print journals. Coover's essay appears in volume three of *Postmodern Culture*. The date of publication is September 1992. No page numbers are given, but there are fifty paragraphs.

## 6. Internet resources: electronic texts

> Keats, John. "La Belle Dame sans Merci." *The Poetical Works of John Keats*. London: Macmillan, 1884. Online. Columbia

Bartleby Library. Internet. 21 October 1996. Available <http://www.cc.columbia.edu/acis/bartleby/keats/keats 68.html>.

Milton, John. *Paradise Lost.* E-text created by Joseph Raben, 1964–65. Online. Project Gutenberg. Internet. 27 October 1996. Available <gopher://wiretap.spies.com/00/Library/Classic/parlost.txt>

For e-texts, give the following information:
a. author's name (if given).
b. title of the text. If the title is a work within a larger work, such as a poem or short story, put it within quotation marks. If the title is a self-contained work, such as a novel, play, or collection, underline or italicize it.
c. publication information about the printed source (to the extent available).
d. publication medium (*Online*).
e. name of the repository of the electronic text (for example, Project Gutenberg).
f. name of the computer network.
g. date of access.
h. electronic address of the text.

The first example above is a poem by John Keats which is located in a collection of his poems published in 1884. Information about the printed source for the poem is made clear at the beginning of the document. The second example is the complete version of John Milton's *Paradise Lost;* but information about its printed source is scant. The introduction to the text indicates who created the e-text and when he did it, but nothing else.

7. **Internet resources: discussion lists and newsgroups**

Singer, Bayla. <bayla@pbfreenet.seflin.lib.ft.us>. "Time Travel Fiction." 10 June 1996. Online posting. Discussion list. <darwin-1@ukanaix.cc.ukans.edu>. 12 June 1996.

Garland, John. <jgarland@morgan.ucs.mun.ca>. "Two Years Before the Mast." 12 August 1996. Online posting. Newsgroup. <sci.military.naval.rec.boats>. 23 September 1996.

Discussion groups abound on the Internet. For these resources, give the following information:
a. author's name (if known).
b. author's e-mail address (enclosed in angle brackets).

   c. the subject line from the posting (in quotation marks).
   d. the date of publication.
   e. the kind of communication (*Online posting*).
   f. the kind of information exchange group (discussion list, news-group).
   g. the name and address of the newsgroup (enclosed in angle brackets).
   h. access date.

The first example above came from a LISTSERV discussion group, the second from a USENET newsgroup. The format for each is the same.

8. **Internet resources: personal communications (e-mail)**

> Beale, Walter. <bealew@iris.uncg.edu>. "Time travel fiction." 11 October 1996. Personal e-mail. 11 October 1996.

For e-mail messages, give the following information:
   a. author's name.
   b. author's e-mail address (enclosed in angle brackets).
   c. the subject line from the posting (in quotation marks).
   d. the date of publication (the day the message was sent).
   e. the kind of communication (personal e-mail, office memo, distribution list).
   f. access date.

For *all* of these electronic-resources formats, you may find some of the information missing or difficult to come by. Don't be frustrated. Give as much of the information as you can, and leave out what you can't find.


## Sample Entries for Other Nonprint Sources

1. **An Interview**

> Rogers, Fred. Interview with Noah Adams. *All Things Considered.* National Public Radio. WFDD, Winston-Salem, North Carolina. 19 February 1993.

> Trillin, Calvin. Personal interview. 16 March 1993.

The basic information for interviews is, first, the interviewee's name; second, the title or nature of the interview and the interviewer (if known); and, third, the place and date of the interview. The first entry above indicates that Fred Rogers was interviewed on the radio program *All Things Considered* by Noah Adams. If you interviewed someone yourself, your citation would look like the second entry.

## 2. A lecture

> Gay, Geneva. "Ethnic Identity in a Diverse Society: The Challenge for Education." Temple University. Philadelphia, Pennsylvania. 30 March 1993.

> May, Marilyn. Class lecture. English 368: English Romantic Poetry. University of North Carolina at Greensboro. 10 April 1991.

For lectures, give the lecturer's name, then the title or nature of the lecture, and finally the place and date.

## 3. A television or radio program

> *Soundings.* NPR. WUNC, Chapel Hill, North Carolina. 7 March 1993.

> *Sixty Minutes.* CBS. WFMY, Greensboro, North Carolina. 24 January 1993.

> "Mistaken Identity." *Millennium: Tribal Wisdom and the Modern World.* Nar. Adrian Malone. UNC Center for Public Television, 12 February 1992.

Radio and television programs should contain the following basic information: first, the title of the program (underlined or italicized), the network (CBS, NPR), the local station where you heard or saw the program, and the date of broadcast. The first entry above is a radio program, the second a television program. The third entry illustrates how you can include other information about the program.

## 4. A recording

> Holbrook, Hal. "Journalism on Horseback." *Mark Twain Tonight.* Columbia, OL 5440, n.d.

> Thomas, Dylan. "Fern Hill." *Dylan Thomas Reading A Child's Christmas in Wales and Five Poems.* Caedmon, TC-1002-A, 1952.

> McKennitt, Loreena. "The Lady of Shalott." *The Visit.* Music by Loreena McKennitt. Lyrics by Alfred, Lord Tennyson. Warner Brothers, 9 26880—2, 1991.

For commercially available recordings, put the person cited first. Depending on your emphasis, this person may be the author, composer, performer, or director. Then list the title or titles, the artist or artists, the manufacturer, the catalog number, and the year of issue. If you don't know the year of issue, put *n.d.* ("no date").

5. **A film or videotape**

> *Star Wars.* Dir. and writ. George Lucas. Prod. Gary Kurtz. Music by John Williams. Perf. Mark Hamill, Harrison Ford, Carrie Fisher, Peter Cushing, and Alec Guiness. Twentieth Century Fox, 1977.

> *Crete and Mycenae.* Prod. and dir. Hans-Joachim Horsfeld. Videocassette. Kartes Video Communications, 1986.

When citing films, begin with the title (underlined or italicized), then give information such as director, writer, performers, and conclude with distributor and date. For videotapes (and filmstrips and slide programs, as well), include the medium right before the name of the distributor, as in the second entry.

## SAMPLE RESEARCH PAPER

The following sample student research paper illustrates the use of the MLA documentary style as well as the principles of the argumentative research essay. As in this paper, the first page of your paper should have your name and course information in the upper left corner the title centered just below this information, and the text just below the title. *The MLA Handbook* says that you do not need a title page, but you might ask your instructor for his or her preference. Usually, you do not need a title page. If you have endnotes, put them right after your text, beginning on a new page. Put your "Works Cited" list after the endnotes, beginning on a new page. For more detailed instructions on the format of your paper, see Chapter 12.

Joanna Briscoe
Professor Teleman
English 252-04
February 24, 1989

THE FORSAKEN SISTER:
RODERICK'S FAILURE TO RESCUE MADELINE IN
EDGAR ALLAN POE'S
"THE FALL OF THE HOUSE OF USHER"

Introduction. The author begins with the "obvious"— what most readers would

Perhaps the most obviously strange aspect of Edgar Allan Poe's "The Fall of the House of Usher" is the setting. The bleak landscape, dim tarn, crumbling mansion, and easily recognize as true—in order to get quickly to the less-than-obvious, the topic of the essay.

The topic of the essay (Roderick's unaccountable attitude toward his sister). The author chooses to state the topic as a question, a clear problem the author presents to be solved.

Body of the essay. The author opens the body or proof section of the essay with a brief survey of critical discussions of the story. By doing this, she places her essay within the ongoing debate about the story that has appeared in print for decades. She deals first with the least relevant approaches. She does so briefly—in one sentence and an endnote. She moves quickly to the approach (the symbolic) she thinks is most useful for solving the problem of Roderick's behavior toward Madeline. She summarizes two critics' views—Wilbur's and Hoffman's, blending quotations with her own words, and giving proper credit where needed.

In this paragraph, she turns to a critic who not only sees the story as symbolic but offers an answer to the question she poses at the beginning of the essay. She uses quotations and her own words to summarize the critic's (Davidson's) views.

miasmic atmosphere are nightmarish and inexplicable. They defy norms. But equally strange is Roderick's behavior toward his sister, Madeline. He claims to love her, and he grieves when she "dies." But when he hears her trying to escape from her tomb, he merely listens and waits. Why doesn't he rescue her?

The critical interpretations of the story are often as bizarre as the story itself. They range from incest, to vampirism, to madness.[1] But the interpretation that most meaningfully accounts for Roderick's treatment of his sister is the symbolic. This view holds that the story is symbolic of one person's deeply troubled mind. Richard Wilbur, for example, contends that the "typical Poe story occurs within the mind of a poet; and its characters are not independent personalities, but allegorical figures representing the warring principles of the poet's divided nature" (274-75). "The Fall of the House of Usher," he says, is a "journey into the depths of the self . . . a dream of the narrator's, in which he leaves behind him the waking, physical world and journeys inward toward his moi intérieur, toward his inner and spiritual self. That inner and spiritual self is Roderick Usher" (265). Roderick and Madeline, then, are symbolic of states of mind. Daniel Hoffman agrees with Wilbur and sees the story as "a terrifying tale of the protagonist's journey into the darkest, most hidden regions of himself" (302). Hoffman argues that the story is the narrator's dream (307).

Edward H. Davidson offers a lucid explanation of what this dream may represent. Like Wilbur and Hoffman, Davidson sees the tale as an allegory of one person's mental disintegration. And like them he sees the disintegration as caused by two warring sides of the same mind. Roderick, he says, "represents the mind or intellectual aspect" of the person. Madeline represents "the sensual or physical side" of this same person (197). Roderick "suffers from the diseased mind which has too long abstracted itself from physical reality; in fact, the physical world, and even the physical side of himself, fills him with such repugnance that he can maintain his unique world or self of the mind only by destroying his twin sister or physical side of himself" (197). He tries to bury her "in a place as far remote as possible from the place of aesthetic delight wherein the mind of Roderick lives" (197). But he cannot kill her, and she returns to kill both mind and body (198). The collapse of the house represents the collapse of "the

The author now begins her own interpretation of the story. Her purpose will be to show how the details of the story support Davidson's interpretation. Davidson, in other words, provides her with an overall interpretation that answers her question, but the analysis of how the story supports that interpretation is her own. She uses a quotation from Hoffman to remind us that the story is symbolic.

The topic idea of this paragraph is that Roderick's poem, "The Haunted Palace," is symbolic. She follows up testimony from Wilbur with evidence from the poem.

She uses Wilbur again to initiate her own analysis of the symbolic meaning of the Usher house. She supports her (and Wilbur's) claim with details from the story.

total being of this complex body-mind relation which Poe had studied in the symbolic guise of a brother and sister relationship" (198).

Davidson does not discuss the story specifically, but a careful examination of it supports his theory. Not only does the story have, as Hoffman says, "the fixated, tableau-like rigidity, the inexorability, of a dream" (307), but Poe hints that the story might <u>be</u> a dream. The narrator looks upon the house for the first time as if he were experiencing "the after-dream of the reveller upon opium" (Poe 397). As he examines the atmosphere enveloping the house, he tries to shake off from his spirit "what <u>must</u> have been a dream" (400). For several days after he first sees Madeline, the narrator listens to Roderick's "wild improvisations" on the guitar "as if in a dream" (404). And the climax of the story occurs in the middle of the night during a tempestuous storm, when the narrator cannot sleep and when his "fancy" becomes increasingly "excited" (414).

As a "dream," the story projects psychological phenomena; the characters, setting, and events represent aspects of the mind. One key detail that supports this interpretation is "The Haunted Palace," the poem that Roderick sings to the narrator during a moment of "the highest artificial excitement" and that represents "the tottering of his [Roderick's] lofty reason upon her throne" (406). "The Haunted Palace," as Wilbur points out, is the allegory of a man who goes mad. It represents two states of mind (263). In the first half of the poem, the palace is described as a "head" inhabited by the "monarch," "Thought." It is topped by "banners yellow, glorious, golden" (hair). It has "two luminous windows" (eyes). Out of its "fair palace door" (mouth) come sounds (speech) that represent the "beauty," "wit," and "wisdom" (artistic productions, sane and noble ideas) of the "king." But all changes in the second half, when "evil things" assail the "monarch's high estate." The windows become "red." Inside, "vast forms" move "fantastically/To discordant melody," and out of the "pale door" rushes "a hideous throng" that "laugh--but smile no more" (406-07).

A comparison of this allegorical house with the narrator's description of the Usher mansion, Wilbur says, leads to the realization that the Usher mansion "is, in allegorical fact, the physical body of Roderick Usher, and its dim interior is, in fact, Roderick Usher's visionary mind" (264). Details from the story support this claim. When the narrator sees the mansion for the first time, he describes it as having "vacant eye-like windows" (397-98), which make the mansion look like a head. He also thinks that "a mere different arrangement of the particulars of the scene, of the details of the picture, would be sufficient to modify, or perhaps to annihilate its capacity for sorrowful impression" (398), as if the house has the flexible quality of the mind, the capacity for rearrangement and thus for sounder mental health. The narrator then says the house is indeed symbolical; local peasants see it as an equivalent to the family. And the interior of the house, with its "many dark and intricate passages," its "feeble gleams of encrimsoned light," its rooms containing dark angles and recesses (400-01), resembles the complexity and mysteriousness of the mind.

The most important psychological phenomenon represented by the story is a mind at war with itself. Madeline is Roderick's twin, his mirror image: "her figure, her air, her features--all, in their very minutest development were those--were identically . . . those of the Roderick Usher who sat beside me" (404). As such, she seems to represent one aspect of the mind contained within the house, an aspect that Roderick wants to suppress and destroy. But what does she represent?

The author now examines the symbolic meaning of Madeline and thus why Roderick would want to suppress her.

An analysis of Roderick supports Davidson's claim that within the symbolic "house" two forces are at war. The character "Roderick" represents a desire to retreat from reality, whereas the character "Madeline" represents those qualities that make up reality--the physical, the sensuous, the bodily. Roderick's disease, for example, manifests itself as an extreme aversion to sensuous experiences--tasting, touching, smelling, seeing, hearing; that is, to all the ways the mind (through the body) receives and reacts to the physical world (403). It is as if the intellect is retreating from the body. Roderick seems, furthermore, to have a morbid fear of the physical, especially as it is embodied by the house. He confesses to a conflict between his "spirit" and "the physique of the gray walls and turrets, and of the dim tarn into which they all looked down" (408). His artistic products are further evidence of his escape from the physical world, from reality. Rather than paint real scenes, Roderick paints ideas, "pure abstractions," and "phantasmagoric conceptions" (405). Rather than sing about real people and situations, he composes songs that are "fantastic," "fervid," "wild fantasies," and "artificial" (406).

Roderick's apparently innate preference for the ideal over the real has led him to a practice that is the probable cause of his disease. He has increasingly isolated himself from the world outside his mind. The narrator traces the beginning of this process to Roderick's childhood, when his "reserve had been always excessive and habitual." Now the process is complete, for the narrator is his "best and indeed his only personal friend" (398). But the disease represents a further extension of Roderick's isolation from the exterior world. Roderick has reached the point where he wants to isolate himself from everything physical, and that means especially from his body. The result is that Roderick's body, although still whole, is near the point of disintegration, a fact symbolized by the "barely perceptible fissure" that goes from top to bottom of the mansion (400).

A logical extension of Roderick's tendency toward isolation is his obsession with death, the ultimate alienation from reality. When he plays his guitar and sings, he improvises dirges, most memorable of which is "a certain singular perversion and amplification of the wild air of the last waltz of Von Weber" (405), a piece of music that Von Weber was reputed to have composed on his deathbed (405-09). When among his books, Roderick's "chief delight" is perusing a "rare and curious" book detailing the last rites for the dead (409). His most memorable painting seems to represent total and final isolation. It is of a "vault or tunnel" at "an exceeding depth" with "no outlet" and no natural sources of light (405-06).

Roderick's treatment of Madeline, the nature of her disease, and her subsequent behavior seem to indicate that she represents the physical, bodily world from which he is trying to escape. Her disease links her directly to the bodily, for it consists of "a gradual wasting away of the person" (404). And after her first appearance, Roderick's <u>own</u> bodily strength diminishes: "a far more than ordinary wanness had overspread the emaciated fingers through which trickled many passionate tears" (404). After he announces her "death," Roderick buries her in a vault that corresponds not only to the vault in his painting but to the oppressive atmosphere surrounding the Usher mansion. It is "small, damp, and entirely without means of admission for light." It lies at

The author brings her essay to a climax by spelling out the implications of her analysis. She summarizes here what Madeline symbolizes and how Roderick tries to "bury" her.

a "great depth." It seems impregnable and inescapable because of its "massive iron" door and archway "sheathed with copper." Its oxygenless "oppressive atmosphere" half smothers the torches so that the light is lurid and dim (409).

All of these details suggest Roderick's obsessive, final attempt to isolate his bodily self, to separate it from his intellectual self. He even carries the entombment process further by putting Madeline in a casket, screwing down the lid, and locking the iron door. But one detail suggests that he will fail. Even though Madeline seems "dead," she retains a surprising physical vitality. She displays "the mockery of a faint blush upon the bosom and the face, and [a] suspiciously lingering smile upon the lip" (410). When she finally emerges from her tomb, her incredible physical strength is but a final detail linking her to the physical and the bodily. Her resurrection seems to show that repressing the physical side of the self results inevitably in its overwhelming and powerful reassertion at a later time.

Throughout the story, Roderick is pitiable. He seems to recognize that he is in deep trouble. As a last attempt to help himself, he reaches out to his only remaining contact with the outside world, the narrator. He also seems to recognize the importance of physical health and the tie of normal sensuous experience to mental health. He loves Madeline, and in the first half of "The Haunted Palace," he describes a healthy balance between the sensuous and the intellectual. But by the time we see him, he has carried the process of isolation too far to stop it. Against his better judgment, he acts out allegorically the final severing of mind and body. He buries Madeline, believing that she-- the body--is finally dead. When he realizes that she is still alive, he refuses to rescue her because he <u>wants</u> her dead. His mistake from the beginning was to think that the mind can operate independently from the body, the intellectual from the physical, the ideal from the real. In the end, he pays for his mistake with his sanity and his life.

**Note**

[1]Lawrence (84-85) and Spitzer (58) argue for the incest theory. A supporter of the vampire theory is Kendall (99-104). Hill (396-402) and Walker (585-92) claim that Madeline really dies and that both the narrator and Roderick go mad and hallucinate her resurrection.

---

**Marginal notes (left column):**

She summarizes the nature of Roderick's disease and his failure to bury Madeline and thus suppress the qualities she represents.

Conclusion. The author fully states the symbolic meaning of the story—the interior struggle of a mentally disturbed person—and the answer to the question she poses at the beginning. The answer is the thesis of her essay. For the sake of suspense, she states her thesis here rather than at the beginning. That way, she in effect retells the story, uniting the climax of the story with the revelation of her thesis.

This endnote allows the author to refer readers briefly to a wide assortment of critical discussions. Since she feels these discussions are not relevant to her thesis, she chooses to characterize them here rather than in the body of her essay. By including this note, she also lets readers know that she is familiar with other approaches and that if readers wish, they may explore these other approaches on their own.

Works Cited

The "Works Cited" list includes only those works the author uses in her essay. The citations conform to the MLA documentary style.

Davidson, Edward H. Poe: A Critical Study. Cambridge: Harvard UP, 1957.

Hill, John S. "The Dual Hallucination in 'The Fall of the House of Usher.' " Southwest Review 48 (1963): 396-402.

Hoffman, Daniel. Poe Poe Poe Poe Poe Poe, Garden City: Doubleday, 1972.

Kendall, Lyle H. "The Vampire Motif in 'The Fall of the House of Usher.' " Twentieth-Century Interpretations of "The Fall of the House of Usher." Ed. Thomas Woodson. Englewood Cliffs: Prentice, 1969. 99-104.

Lawrence, D. H. Studies in Classic American Literature. New York: Penguin, 1977.

Poe, Edgar Allan. "The Fall of the House of Usher." Collected Works of Edgar Allan Poe. Ed. Thomas Ollive Mabbott. Vol. 2 Cambridge: Harvard UP, 1978. 392-422.

Spitzer, Leo. "A Reinterpretation of 'The Fall of the House of Usher.' " Twentieth-Century Interpretations of "The Fall of the House of Usher." Ed. Thomas Woodson. Englewood Cliffs: Prentice, 1969. 56-70.

Walker, I. M. "The 'Legitimate Sources' of Terror in 'The Fall of the House of Usher.' " Modern Language Review 61 (1966): 585-92.

Wilbur, Richard. "The House of Poe." The Recognition of Edgar Allan Poe: Selected Criticism since 1829. Ed. Eric W. Carlson. Ann Arbor: U of Michigan P, 1966. 255-77.

## Analysis of the Sample Research Paper

Notice the way this paper begins. The writer raises a question about the story. She states that question in the first paragraph, her introduction. In the rest of the essay, the writer argues in favor of one answer to the question. The paper, in short, is an argumentative essay. It has a narrowly focused topic, a thesis, and a structure like other essays about literature. Its purpose is to enlighten and convince the reader. It is a "research paper" because it uses research as a tool to solve a problem, but it is nonetheless an argumentative essay.

In the second paragraph, the writer introduces the research part of the essay. After explaining that she surveyed literary criticism of the story, the writer passes quickly over interpretations that are not helpful to the thesis and lights upon one that is: the symbolic interpretation. The writer then accurately and fully explains that approach in the second and third paragraphs. These paragraphs contain the bulk of the references to research material. But the critical approach does not in itself answer the writer's question. It merely shows how the question might be answered. The writer proceeds to answer the question in the rest of the essay by analyzing the story in detail, using the critical approach as a guide. The transition sentence of the fourth paragraph ("Davidson does not discuss the story specifically, but a careful explanation of it supports his theory") signals the beginning of this part of the essay. In the last paragraph of the essay, the writer answers the question and, in so doing, states her thesis.

Not all research essays will be structured like this one, but this essay has a simple and functional organization that you might find useful when structuring your own research essays. First, it states the problem (question) in an introductory paragraph. Second, it surveys the pertinent literary criticism and fully explains what the writer believes is the most relevant approach. Third, it examines the work in light of this approach. This third part of the essay is the longest and most important. It represents the writer's use of the critical approach to solve the problem. In this section you might continue to draw upon secondary sources, as this essay does. But otherwise, you are on your own. Fourth, in a concluding paragraph, the writer states a solution to the problem, an answer to the question. This answer is the essay's thesis.

## FREQUENTLY USED ABBREVIATIONS

When you read essays and books about literature, you will often run into abbreviations. When you write your own essays, you may want to use some of the more well known and space-saving of these abbreviations. Here, then, is a list of them. Many pertain to essays that use secondary sources.

| adapt. | adapted by |
|---|---|
| app. | appendix |
| c., ca. | *circa,* "about" (usually used with dates when the exact date is not certain—for example, ca. 1594) |
| cf. | *confer,* "compare" (not the equivalent of "see") |

| | |
|---|---|
| ch., chs. | chapter, chapters |
| d. | died |
| ed., eds. | edited by, editor, editors |
| esp. | especially |
| e.g. | *exempli gratia,* "for example" |
| et al. | *et alii,* "and others" |
| etc. | *et cetera,* "and so forth" |
| i.e. | *id est,* "that is" |
| l., ll. | line, lines |
| ms., mss. | manuscript, manuscripts |
| NB | *nota bene,* "note well" |
| p., pp. | page, pages |
| pt. | part |
| rev. | revised by, revision; review or reviewed by (for reviews, use *review* where *rev.* might be confused with *revision* or *revised by*) |
| trans. | translated by |
| U, UP | university, university press (in documentation) |
| vol., vols. | volume, volumes |

# 12

# Revising and Editing

## REVISE THROUGHOUT THE WRITING PROCESS

The third stage of the writing process is revision. The term *revision* means "to see again." Revision takes place throughout the writing process. You constantly see your work anew, and you act upon that fresh understanding by rewriting.

For this reason, you not only produce better essays, but you also feel more comfortable, if you create the conditions that allow you to revise as you go. Assume that you will make several drafts of the essay, from scribbled lists to finished product—say, three to five drafts. Give yourself time—at least a week—to write the essay. You may be able to bring off an "all-nighter" every now and then, but few people can do so consistently. Work hard for a while, then put your work away; let the ideas percolate, then come back to the essay fresh.

## REVISE FOR THE FINAL DRAFT

Some people could go on revising forever, but you probably do not have that luxury. When you are ready to turn the essay in, you need to produce a final draft. The final draft is different from the earlier drafts, because readers will expect it to conform to certain "formal" rules (rules that govern a particular format). To help yourself prepare the final draft, think about what your audience will expect from it. They will, of course, want the qualities of a good argument we have discussed—an interesting topic, sound logic, thorough discussion of the works, good organization. These qualities are valuable because your readers want to learn from you, but they want something else as well: They want to think well of you. They want to feel that you are worth reading, that you are competent to talk about your topic, and that you can teach them something. Rhetoricians call this personal quality *ethos*. Ethos is the image that writers project of themselves. Ethos is unavoidable; you can't help projecting an image of yourself. Create, therefore, a compelling, trustworthy ethos.

The content and organization of the essay are the most important indicators of your ethos. By reasoning well, especially by presenting plenty of facts to support your claims, you make readers feel that you are conscientious and that your essay is intellectually sound. Other aspects of the final draft also help create a persuasive ethos. They are prose style, rules of usage, and physical format (the appearance of the essay).

## WRITE A CLEAR AND READABLE PROSE STYLE

*Style* is the way writers put words together in units of thought— sentences—and the way they link sentences to make larger units— paragraphs, essays, books. Closely related to style is tone. *Tone* is a writer's attitude toward the material and the readers. You convey tone through style.

You should adjust your style and tone to fit the occasion and audience. Sometimes the occasion and audience call for informal and humorous writing, such as for speeches made at parties or essays written for satirical magazines. At other times, they call for gravity and formality, such as for newspaper editorials and letters of application. The occasion and audience for essays about literature almost always require a measure of formality. Your audience is usually intelligent, literate, and serious. They are taking the trouble to read your essay because they want to learn. They wouldn't mind some levity, some lightheartedness, but mostly they want you to get down to business and not waste their time. They want to learn from you economically, to get through your essay with as little trouble as possible.

Your style for this audience, then, should meet these needs. Make your style clear, interesting, and readable: vary sentence structure, avoid the passive voice, emphasize active and concrete verbs, eliminate wordiness and unnecessary repetition, use words with precision, and base syntax on the natural rhythms of spoken English. Give your tone seriousness of purpose but avoid stiff formality: Stay away from incomprehensible words and long, complex sentences. Because essays about literature involve personal judgment, feel free to use "I," especially when you need to distinguish your ideas from those of others and when you want to stress the individuality of your views. But don't overuse "I"; otherwise, you will give the impression of being subjective and egotistical.

## HAVE OTHER PEOPLE READ AND RESPOND TO YOUR DRAFT

Writing is in one sense an isolated, individual task. We have to do it alone. In another sense, however, it can be collaborative. Other people's reactions to your writing can help you make it better. After all, your writing is *for* an audience. So, before you draw up a final draft, get some people to read your essay. Ask them to answer such questions as, Can you follow my line of thought? Do you agree with my reasoning? Can I support my claims more convincingly? Is my writing clear and fluent? Should I use different strategies of persuasion? Will my audience understand me? You may totally disagree with the responses you get, but even "wrong" responses can help you see "right" strategies. Your goal is to get fresh perceptions of your essay so you can make your final draft as good as it can be.

## EDIT THE FINAL DRAFT

The final draft of your essay is the one you will "publish." Publishing can mean printing the essay in a journal, newspaper, magazine, or book. It can also mean distributing it yourself to a group of people. For university courses, it means turning the essay in to the professor or to the rest of the class. The "published" draft of the essay should follow a certain format. What should that format be? What, for example, should the essay look like? What kind of language should it use? What kind of paper should it be written on? Where should you put your name? How should you number the pages?

The format of the final draft depends solely on what your audience expects it to be, so the format may vary from audience to audience. One of your tasks as a writer is to find out the appropriate format for your particular audience. The format described in the next few pages is typical of the writing done in a university setting and for many publications.

## Rules of Usage

*Usage* means the way English is used in most published writing—in newspapers, magazines, books, advertisements, brochures, financial reports, and scholarly journals. Although some rules of usage are arbitrary and seem to serve no purpose other than convention, most serve several important purposes. First, they often aid clarity. Punctuation, for example, represents parts of the sentence—pauses and inflections—that words do not. Marks of punctuation can be as important as the words. Misplace a comma, and you can change the meaning of a sentence. Second, rules of usage help communicate your ethos. Rules of usage are a form of etiquette; educated people are expected to follow them. By doing so, you communicate an image of competence and respect for your readers.

If you are not familiar with the basic rules of usage, they might at first seem bewildering. But they are not hard to learn. Study and practice using them, and you will learn them quickly. Get a handbook of usage, and refer to it when you write. A standard handbook of usage is *The Harbrace College Handbook;* another is the *MLA Handbook for Writers of Research Papers.*

Although all rules of usage are important for your writing, in this book we concentrate on rules common to essays about literature. One set of such rules governs documentary procedure (discussed in Chapter 11). Rules for handling documentation vary from discipline to discipline, but their purpose is the same: to help readers find your sources and to show readers you know your subject matter. Another set of rules applies to quotations. We describe these and other rules pertaining to essays about literature. The sample essays in Chapters 11, 14, and at the end of this chapter illustrate most of them.

## Quotations

Quotations serve two key purposes in essays about literature: They help exemplify claims, and they reproduce the language of the source.

1. **Introduce your quotations.**

   a. For primary sources, identify the author, the work, and the context of quotations.

WRONG: The woman tells her lover that the world "isn't ours anymore."

RIGHT: Near the climax of the lovers' conversation in Hemingway's "Hills Like White Elephants," the woman tells the man that the world "isn't ours anymore."

Readers need to know *where* in the text quotations occur. Otherwise, the quotation could seem meaningless.

b. Introduce quotations from secondary sources by giving the author's name or claim to authority.

WRONG: "A fully articulated pastoral idea of America did not emerge until the end of the eighteenth century."

RIGHT: Leo Marx claims that a "fully articulated pastoral idea of America did not emerge until the end of the eighteenth century."

RIGHT: A prominent American critic claims that a "fully articulated . . ."

There are several reasons for this rule. One is that giving the critic's name or claim to authority clearly distinguishes your ideas from the other writer's. Quotation marks help to make this distinction, of course, but introducing the quote by author makes the distinction emphatic. A second reason is that when readers see quotation marks, they are naturally curious about who said the quoted passage. Also, as they read your essay, they may want to keep track of the different approaches of the critics you are using. A third reason is that, by giving the author's name, you distinguish between secondary and primary sources. The distinction may not be clear from the quotation alone. A final reason is that it is a matter of courtesy to give credit in your text to the words and ideas of other people. It is as if you are standing before an audience making a speech, and for support of your argument you bring forth real people to speak on your behalf. In such a situation, you would always introduce them by name to your audience before they spoke. You are not just giving them credit; in a way, you are thanking them.

c. Introduce quotations with the correct mark of punctuation. Use a comma for brief, informal, grammatically incomplete introductions.

WRONG: Prufrock thinks "I am no prophet—and here's no great matter."

RIGHT: Prufrock thinks, "I am no prophet—and here's no great matter."

Use a colon to separate your own grammatically complete introductions or statements (complete sentences) from quotations.

WRONG: Edith Hamilton describes Hera perfectly, "She was the protector of marriage, and married women were her peculiar care. There is very little that is attractive in the portrait the poets draw of her."

RIGHT: Edith Hamilton describes Hera perfectly: "She was the protector. . . ."

The rules of usage here are to a degree arbitrary, and you may find that they vary from handbook to handbook. But their main function is to separate your thoughts from those of the quotation— that is, to eliminate ambiguity. Thus, the first examples above mean two different things. Without the comma, the reader might see the whole sentence as one complete thought: "Prufrock thinks [that] 'I am no prophet—and here's no great matter.' " With the comma, the reader sees that "Prufrock thinks" is merely the introduction to the quotation; the quotation is the complete thought.

2. **Integrate quotations into your own sentences.**

EXAMPLE: Because of this increasing darkness, Brown cannot be quite sure of what he does or hears. The devil's walking stick, for example, seems to turn into a snake, but this may be "an ocular deception, assisted by the uncertain light" (76). He thinks he hears the voices of Deacon Gookin and the minister, but "owing doubtless to the depth of the gloom of that particular spot, neither the travellers nor their steeds were visible" (81).

Once you introduce your source, you may want to integrate short quotations—words or phrases—from it into your own sentences, as in the above example. The quotations become part of your own thoughts rather than thoughts totally separate from yours. This technique allows you to summarize a source concisely and yet retain the language and authenticity of the source. If you use this method, you should obey several rules.

a. Keep all tenses the same. Change the tenses in the quotation to correspond to your tenses, putting your words in brackets. When writing about fictional events, for example, change quoted verbs to the present tense.

WRONG: While the legislators cringe at the sudden darkness, "all eyes were turned to Abraham Davenport."

RIGHT: While the legislators cringe at the sudden darkness, "all eyes [turn] to Abraham Davenport."

b. Make sure that sentences are complete.

WRONG: Yeats asks if "before the indifferent beak." [Incomplete sentence; makes no sense.]

RIGHT: Yeats asks if Leda "put on [the swan's] knowledge" before his "indifferent beak could let her drop."

c. Clarify pronouns that have no clear antecedents.

WRONG: Captain Wentworth says, "It had been my doing—solely mine. She would not have been obstinate if I had not been weak." [This quotation is wrongly handled if the antecedent of "she" is unclear.]

RIGHT: Captain Wentworth says, "It had been my doing—solely mine. [Louisa] would not have been obstinate if I had not been weak."

d. Make sure that subject and verb agree.

WRONG: Wilfred Owen says that the only prayer said for those who die in battle is war's noise, which "patter out their hasty orisons." [Subject: "noise"; verb: "patter." The subject is singular, the verb plural.]

RIGHT: Wilfred Owen says that the only prayer said for those who die in battle is the "rapid rattle" of guns, which "patter out their hasty orisons." [Subject: "guns"; verb: "patter." Both subject and verb are now plural.]

In short, when you integrate a quotation into your sentence, make it a grammatical part of the sentence. The whole sentence, including the quotation, must conform to the standard rules of usage. See item 4 below for methods of altering (interpolating) quotations.

3. **Quote accurately.** Copy exactly what the author has written.

4. **Make editorial changes in quotations correctly.** You may legitimately change the quotation in two ways:

   a. By using an *ellipsis.* The **ellipsis** (spaced periods) indicates material omitted. You may want to do this for brevity's sake. To indicate omitted material *within* a sentence, use three periods, with a space before and after each period.

   EXAMPLE: As one critic says, "Oedipus is guilty for two reasons: because of the deeds he actually committed . . . and because of his desire to commit them."

   To indicate omitted material at the *end* of your sentence, put a period with no space in front (the period that signals the end of the sentence) and then three spaced periods (the periods that signal the ellipsis). As in the example above, the spaced periods here indicate that you have left something out of the original sentence.

   EXAMPLE: In certain moods, Wordsworth confessed, he "was often unable to think of external things as having external existence. . . ."

   If, however, you make a parenthetical reference after the ellipsis at the end of your sentence, put the three spaced periods (the ellipsis) first, then the parenthetical reference, and then the sentence period. Note this revision of the above example:

   EXAMPLE: In certain moods, Wordsworth confessed, he "was often unable to think of external things as having external existence . . ." (175).

   In addition to using ellipses to indicate the omission of part of a sentence, you can use four periods to indicate the omission of whole sentences, a paragraph, or several paragraphs. The following example omits part of a long paragraph.

   EXAMPLE: Ruskin gives two reasons for his belief that to demand perfection of art is to misunderstand it: "The first, that no great man ever stops working till he has reached his point of failure. . . . The second reason is that imperfection is in some sort essential to all that we know of life."

b. By using *brackets*. Brackets indicate editorial changes that *you*, not the author, make to clarify the quotation or to make it fit the grammatical structure of your sentence. Do not use parentheses to indicate such changes; otherwise, your reader will see them as part of the original quote.

WRONG: Alceste says that "sins which cause the blood to freeze / Look innocent beside (Célimène's) treacheries."

RIGHT: "She looked carefully for the place where [Elizabeth] had entered the garden."

RIGHT: Flaubert says that "she [has] an excess of energy."

5. **Indent long quotations.** A *long quotation* has more than three lines of poetry or four lines of prose. Usually, your introduction to a long quotation will be a complete sentence. Conclude your sentence, then, with a *colon* (not a comma or a period). Double-space from your text. Indent ten spaces from the left margin. Do *not* put indented quotations in quotation marks. Double-space the quote.

EXAMPLE: The duke is chagrined that his own name and presence were not the sole sources of her joy:

> She had
> A heart—how shall I say?—too soon made glad,
> Too easily impressed; she liked whate'er
> She looked on, and her looks went everywhere.
> Sir, 'twas all one! My favour at her breast,
> The dropping of the daylight in the West,
> The bough of cherries some officious fool
> Broke in the orchard for her, the white mule
> She rode with round the terrace—all and each
> Would draw from her alike the approving speech,
> Or blush, or least.

As in this example, keep the first words of a quoted poem exactly where they come in the line. For prose quotations, do not indicate paragraph indentations unless you are quoting more than one paragraph.

## 6. Punctuate quotations correctly.

a. Use *double quotation* marks (" ") for quotations. For quotations within quotations, use double quotation marks for the main quote and single quotation marks (the apostrophe mark on the type-writer) for the inner quote.

EXAMPLE: After his interview with Hester, Dimmesdale sinks into self-doubt: " 'Have I then sold myself,' thought the minister, 'to the fiend whom, if men say true, this yellow-starched and velveted old hag has chosen for her prince and master!' "

b. Always put *periods and commas* inside quotation marks.

EXAMPLE: After performing her "duties to God," as she called them, she was ready for her "duty to man."

c. Always put *colons and semicolons* outside of quotation marks.

EXAMPLE: She had the "exquisite pleasure of art"; her husband had only envy and hatred.

d. Put *other marks of punctuation* (question marks, dashes, exclamation points) inside quotation marks when they are part of the quoted material, outside when they are not.

EXAMPLE: One critic asked, "Could the Pearl Poet really be the author of *Sir Gawain and the Green Knight?*"

EXAMPLE: But can it be, as one critic claims, that "the Pearl Poet really [is] the author of *Sir Gawain and the Green Knight*"?

e. *When quoting a line of poetry or part of a line,* make the quotation part of your sentence. Use a slash mark, with a space before and after the mark, to indicate line divisions.

EXAMPLE: Hopkins describes God's grandeur as gathering "to a greatness, like the ooze of oil / crushed."

*When quoting more than two or three lines of poetry,* indent the quotation ten spaces from the left margin. For indented quotations of poetry, do not use slashes to indicate line divisions and do not enclose the quotation in quotation marks. Type the lines and words in exactly the same position as in the original.

## Other Rules of Usage Related to Essays about Literature

Essays about literature obey the same rules of usage as other essays, but several rules deserve special mention.

1. **Tense.** Describe fictional events, whether in drama, poetry, or prose fiction, in the present tense.

2. **Authors' names.** Use either the full name (Charles Dickens) or the last name (Dickens). Some exceptions are Lord Byron, Mrs. Browning, and Dr. Johnson.

3. **Titles**
   a. Capitalize the fast letter of all words in a title except articles, short prepositions, and conjunctions. Capitalize the first word of a title and the first word after a colon.

   EXAMPLE: "How I Won the World but Lost My Soul to the Devil's Wiles"

   EXAMPLE: "Exile's Return: A Narrative of Ideas"

   b. Use quotation marks for titles of works included within larger works. This includes short stories, short poems; songs; chapter titles; articles in journals, magazines, and newspapers; and unpublished works such as dissertations and master's theses.
   c. Underline or italicize the titles of works published independently, such as books, plays, long poems published as books, periodicals, pamphlets, novels, movies, works of art, works of music, and radio and television programs. An exception is sacred writings such as the Bible, books of the Bible, the Koran, and the Talmud.
   d. Do not underline, italicize, or put in quotation marks the titles of your own essays.
   e. Many instructors prefer that your essay titles include full names of authors and works.

   WRONG: The Four Stages of Knowledge in Twain's *Huck Finn*

   RIGHT: The Four Stages of Knowledge in Mark Twain's *The Adventures of Huckleberry Finn*

f.  If your instructor approves, in the text of your essay you may use shortened titles for works you frequently cite: "Prufrock" for "The Love Song of J. Alfred Prufrock" or *Huck Finn* for *The Adventures of Huckleberry Finn.*

4. **Foreign language terms**
   a.  Italicize (or underline) foreign words used in an English text, such as *sans doute, et tu Brute, amor vincit omnia.*

   EXAMPLE: She objected to her son-in-law's behavior because it was not *comme il faut.*

   Reproduce, either by hand or in type, all marks and accents as they appear in the original language: *étude, à propos, même, übermensch, año, leçon.*
   b.  Some foreign words, like *cliché, laissez-faire,* and *genre,* have been naturalized (made part of) English usage and do not need to be italicized. Use your dictionary to determine whether the word or phrase needs italics. Foreign words in dictionaries are either italicized or placed at the back of the book in a separate section.

   EXAMPLE: Adam Smith advocated a laissez-faire economic policy.

   c.  Do not italicize quotations that are entirely in another language.

   EXAMPLE: Louis XIV once said, "L'état, c'est moi."

## Physical Format

As with rules of usage, the appearance of your essay also affects your argument. Your readers want an essay that is easy to read, pleasant to hold, and attractive to see. The more care you take with the appearance of the essay, the more competent your readers will think you are. Although your instructor may have specific preferences, the following are standard guidelines. Most of them come from the *MLA Handbook for Writers of Research Papers.*

1. **Typewritten and handwritten essays.** Some instructors may prefer that you type or print all your work, but sometimes you may also handwrite college essays. Whether you handwrite, type, or print your essay, use only one side of the page. For *handwritten* essays, use black or blue ink (which, unlike pencil, will not smear or rub

off). Use lined paper. Write on every other line if the lines are closely spaced. Above all, write legibly. If you *type or print* your essays, double-space. Use a good ribbon.

2. **Paper.** Use standard-size paper (8 ½-by-11-inch), not legal-pad size or notepad size. Use a sturdy weight of paper. Avoid "erasable" paper; it does not take correction in ink well, it is sticky, and in a warm place it is very unpleasant to handle. Do not hand in essays written on pages that have been ripped out of a spiral-bound notebook.

3. **Pagination.** Number *all* pages, beginning with the first page. Number pages consecutively, including pages for endnotes and works cited. Put the page numbers in the upper right-hand corner of each page. If you think a page might be misplaced, put your last name before each page number (with a space between the two).

   EXAMPLE: Caraway 16.

4. **Margins.** For typewritten essays, leave one-inch margins at the top, bottom, and sides. This gives the page a "frame" and a place for the instructor's comments. For handwritten essays, leave margins at the top, bottom, and left side.

5. **First page.** One inch from the top of the first page, on the left-hand side, put your name, the instructor's name, the course title, and the date, each on a separate line. Double-space between the lines. After the last line (the date), double-space again and center your title. If your title has more than one line, double-space between lines. Double-space between the title and the first line of text.

   Title pages for college essays—even research essays—are usually unnecessary; but if your instructor expects a title page, check with him or her for its content and form, or consult a handbook of usage.

6. **Corrections.** You may write corrections on final copies of essays— if the corrections are few and fairly inconspicuous. In typed essays, erase incorrect letters, and write or type in the correct letters. Draw a vertical line through an incorrect letter in a handwritten essay and write the correct letter just *above* the line. Separate run-together words with vertical lines (for example, made|a|mistake). To delete words, phrases, and clauses, draw a single horizontal line through them. Add words, phrases, and clauses by writing them in above the line. Use a caret (^) to show where inserted material should go.

7. **Putting the essay pages together.** Use a paper clip to join the pages of your essay unless your instructor specifies some other method.

8. **Copies.** Make a photocopy of your essay. If your instructor loses your essay, you can immediately present him or her with the copy of your finished essay. Or if your instructor keeps your essay indefinitely, you will have a copy for your files. When you turn in the essay the first time, however, turn in the original, not the copy.

9. **To fold or not to fold.** Leave you essay unfolded unless your instructor specifies otherwise.

## SAMPLE ESSAY IN TWO DRAFTS

The student essay below gives a brief idea of how the revising process works. Nearly all writers, no matter how experienced, go through several drafts of an essay before they produce the final draft. Printed here are an early draft of the essay and, after considerable revision, a final draft.

### Early Draft

A COMPARISON OF MARY AND WARREN IN ROBERT FROST'S
"THE DEATH OF THE HIRED MAN"

Robert Frost in "The Death of the Hired Man" presents two different views of how to respond to human need. Into the home of Mary and Warren comes the derelict hired hand, Silas. Mary and Warren disagree over how to treat him.

Mary tells Warren to "be kind" (7) to Silas. Warren, however, is upset with Silas for having run out on him the year before, when he needed him most. "There's no depending on him," Warren says (17). Mary shushes Warren so Silas will not hear him, but Warren does not care if Silas hears or not: "I want him to: he'll have to soon or late" (32).

In my opinion, Mary understands Silas much better than Warren. She is also much more sympathetic than Warren. Her sympathy is like that extended to all people by the Virgin Mary. This may be why Frost chose Mary's name, to underscore this quality. She reminds Warren, for example, of Silas's longstanding argument with the college student Harold Wilson. Warren agrees that Silas is proud of his one accomplishment, building a load of hay:

> He bundles every forkful in its place,
> And tags and numbers it for future reference,

So he can find and easily dislodge it
In the unloading. (89-92)

Mary then tells Warren that Silas has come home to die: "You needn't be afraid he'll leave you this time" (112).

One of the things that most upsets Warren is that Silas comes to them rather than going to Silas's brother for help:

Why didn't he go there? His brother's rich
A somebody—director in the bank. (127-128)

But Mary explains that probably there is some misunderstanding between Silas and his brother. Also, she says that Silas is "just the kind that kinsfolk can't abide" (141). He may be "worthless," she argues, but he "won't be made ashamed to please his brother" (145-146).

The climax of the poem comes when Warren seems to agree reluctantly with Mary that Silas should stay. She tells him to go inside and check on him. He quietly returns and catches up her hand. When she asks him what happened, he replies, simply, "Dead."

In sum, Warren has many qualities that Mary does not have. He is quick to blame, cynical, and even a little stingy. But most of all he lacks the sympathy, the kindness, and the understanding that Mary has. She seems also to be more imaginative than he. Finally, though, her kindness wins him over to her side. Even though Silas dies, Warren seems ready to do what Mary wants.

**Comments on the early draft**   This draft was one of several its author wrote before he produced the final draft. You can see from the first few paragraphs that he is moving toward a concept of how Mary and Warren are different. In the final paragraph he even states some specific ways in which they are different. You can see, also, how the details and quotations he gives between the beginning and end of the essay *might* be relevant to his claims about difference. But notice how almost all the paragraphs in the body of the paper lack topic ideas (topic sentences). Also notice how he never connects any of the poem's details to specific claims. As a result, although the paper begins and ends promisingly, it is more like a summary of the poem than an argument in support of a thesis. To make the paper better, the author needs to do several things. In the introduction, he needs to clarify and emphasize his thesis. If, for example, he put the thesis at the end of the introduction rather than at the beginning, he could more successfully show how all the sentences in the introduction relate to the thesis. In the body of the paper, he needs to state his claims about how Mary and Warren are different and support each with evidence from the text. Each claim could be the topic sentence of a paragraph, followed by supporting evidence. The claims he makes in the conclusion, for example, all support his thesis. He could use them for the body of the essay, making each the topic idea of a paragraph. In the conclusion, he needs to restate his thesis, summarize his reasoning, and offer some generalizing idea that pulls the entire essay together.

## Final Draft

### A COMPARISON OF MARY AND WARREN
### IN ROBERT FROST'S "THE DEATH OF THE HIRED MAN"

When Silas, the unreliable hired hand, returns to the farm owned by Mary and Warren in Robert Frost's "The Death of the Hired Man," Mary and Warren immediately disagree about what to do with him. Warren wants to send him packing. Mary wants to keep him on and care for him. In recounting their disagreement, the poem reveals fundamental differences between them.

*The most obvious difference is that Mary is compassionate and Warren is not.* The poem continually reveals Mary's pity for the sick and troubled Silas. She tells Warren that she discovered him

> Huddled against the barn-door fast asleep,
> A miserable sight, and frightening, too—.
> (35-36)

His physical weakness

> hurt my heart the way he lay
> And rolled his old head on that sharp-edged
> chair-back. (147-48)

She says that his prospects are bleak:

> Poor Silas, so concerned for other folk,
> And nothing to look backward to with pride,
> And nothing to look forward to with hope,
> So now and never any different. (99-102)

Mary's pity leads her to certain moral conclusions. She feels that they should not just take Silas in, but should try to protect his pride as well. "Be kind," she tells Warren (7). Warren, in contrast, is touchy about any hint that he has not done right by Silas. Mary's gentle request to be kind elicits an almost angry response:

"When was I ever anything but kind to him?" (11). He is impatient with Silas's shortcomings and unforgivingly judgmental:

> I told him so last haying, didn't I?
> "If he left then," I said, "that ended it." (13-14)

He expresses his bitterness loudly and clearly and does not care if Silas hears (32). He dismisses Silas's plans to "ditch the meadow" as the foolish promises of an insincere old man (43-46).

*What is not so obvious is just why Mary is compassionate and Warren is not. Frost offers three reasons, each of which reveals more fundamental differences between the two characters. First, they have a different attitude toward people in general.* Warren values people for their usefulness and wants to cast them off when they are no longer useful. This explains his bitterness about Silas's leaving the year before just when Warren needed him most. Now that Silas has returned, Warren wants no part of him:

> What good is he? Who else will harbour him
> At his age for the little he can do?
> What help he is there's no depending on. (15-17)

Even one of Warren's few positive comments about Silas concerns a useful skill, Silas's ability to load hay: "Silas does that well" (92). Warren believes, then, that one should be kind to people only if they are useful. Mary's compassion for Silas reveals a different view of people. She sees them as good in themselves. She admits that Silas may be "worthless" (144) as a hired hand:

> You'll be surprised at him—how much he's broken.
> His working days are done; I'm sure of it.
> (152-53)

But she insists that their farm is his "home," and it is their responsibility to receive him. Warren's definition of home is in keeping with his attitude toward people:

> Home is the place where, when you have to go
> there,
> They have to take you in. (118-19)

In other words, home is the place where, when you have become useless, people feel obligated to take care of you, not out of love but out of reluctant duty. Mary's counterdefinition is in keeping with her assessment of people as valuable in themselves:

I should have called it
Something you somehow haven't to deserve.
(119-20)

Mary believes that people should not have to earn tenderness. People at "home" give you tenderness no matter what you've done. Mary sees their farm as Silas's home.

A second reason for the difference in their attitudes toward Silas is that Mary is imaginative and Warren is not. Frost suggests this quality in the opening line of the poem: "Mary sat musing on the lamp-flame at the table." The word <u>muse</u> means "to ponder or meditate," "to consider reflectively." The word is associated with the Muses of Greek mythology, "each of whom presided over a different art or science." Because of this association, the noun <u>muse</u> means "the spirit or power regarded as inspiring and watching over poets, musicians, and artists; a source of inspiration" (*The American Heritage Dictionary of the English Language*, New College Edition [New York: Houghton, 1981]). Frost's use of the term introduces Mary as something of a poet. She at least has the reflective and imaginative capacity of a poet. By using her imagination, she can put herself in the place of others and experience what they feel. Her imagination allows her to "understand" Silas. She guesses why he says he wants to ditch the meadow, even though he probably knows he cannot:

Surely you wouldn't grudge the poor old man
Some humble way to save his self-respect. (49-50)

She understands why Silas remains troubled by his arguments with the college boy Harold Wilson:

I sympathize. I know just how it feels
To think of the right thing to say too late.
(76-77)

She realizes that "he has come home to die" (111). Warren, in contrast, lacks the imagination to see past his own practical and rather selfish needs. Frost does not suggest that Warren's needs are invalid or unimportant; he shows, rather, that Warren cannot see beyond them. And this limited vision causes him to be unsympathetic to people who hinder them. When Warren asks somewhat stingily why Silas's brother (a "somebody--director in the bank," [129]) cannot take care of Silas, Mary has to tell him that the banker brother may not want to take Silas in. When Warren wonders why, Mary has to tell him why. She uses her imagination to guess what the trouble may be:

He don't know why he isn't quite as good
As anyone. He won't be made ashamed

To please his brother, worthless though he is.
(143-45)

Their different imaginative capacities lead them to different ethical conclusions. Warren wants to do unto others according to their effect on his self-centered needs. Mary wants to do unto others as she would be done by were she in their place. Through her imagination she can feel what "their place" is like.

A third cause of their different attitudes toward Silas is that Mary is allied to nature and Warren is not. Frost directly connects Mary to nature twice. Just before Mary and Warren exchange definitions of "home," Frost describes nature in highly metaphoric terms:

> Part of a moon was falling down the west,
> Dragging the whole sky with it to the hills.
> Its light poured softly in her lap. (103 05)

It is indicative of the kind of person Mary is that she responds to this fanciful and beautiful quality in nature. And her response seems to cause or at least to fortify her compassionate impulses:

> She saw it
> And spread her apron to it. She put out her hand
> Among the harp-like morning-glory strings,
> Taut with the dew from the garden bed to eaves,
> As if she played unheard the tenderness
> That wrought on him beside her in the night.
> (105-10)

Frost's second connection of Mary with nature occurs at the end, when Mary sends Warren to see for himself how Silas is. She urges him once again to be kind and then says that as she waits for his return she will

> see if that small sailing cloud
> Will hit or miss the moon. (160-61)

Frost actually blends her in with nature: The cloud

> hit the moon.
> Then there were three there, making a dim row,
> The moon, the little silver cloud, and she.
> (161-63)

Mary's sympathy with nature, like her view of humankind and her active imagination, also leads to ethical conclusions. They should be merciful to Silas just as they would be to any other living creature:

> Of course he's nothing to us, any more
> Than was the hound that came a stranger to us
> Out of the woods, worn out upon the trail.
> (115-17)

Her point is that they should care for Silas for the same reason they cared for the stray dog: Both are living creatures. Frost does not say anything about Warren's attitude toward nature, but Warren's not saying anything is, in itself, suggestive that he lacks Mary's poetic love for nature. We can infer that, to Warren, nature is meant to be used. He is a farmer, and as such he seems to have reduced nature to its economic value, just as he has done with people.

We might wonder why, if Warren and Mary are so different, they ever got married. But as it turns out, Warren is not quite so different from Mary as he at first seems. It is true that he lacks her positive view of people, her imagination, her sympathy for nature, and thus her compassion. But he is not confined irretrievably in a hard shell of selfish indifference. He is persuadable. Who knows, he may have married Mary just for her imaginative and compassionate qualities. By the end of their conversation (and the poem), at least, he has come around to her view. He is now sympathetic to Silas and takes his side against the status-minded brother: "*I* can't think Si ever hurt anyone" (146). He even argues that maybe Silas's working days are not over after all (154). And when he brings news of Silas's death, he does so as Mary would have, with solemnity and tenderness.

Work Cited

Frost, Robert. "The Death of a Hired Man." *North of Boston*. New York: Henry Holt, 1914. 14-23.

***Comments on the final draft***   The final draft is much better than the early draft. The author opens with just enough information to give readers their bearings and get quickly to his thesis. In the body of the paper, each of the paragraphs has an unmissable topic sentence (italicized here for emphasis). Each of the topic sentences is supported with reasoning and facts from the poem. The last paragraph closes the essay with a summary of the differences between Mary and Warren and an explanation of how, at the end of the poem, they reach harmony. Notice how the final draft is more complex in its interpretation of the poem than the early draft. The rewriting process often has this effect. Good argumentative essays have a necessary structure: thesis clearly stated, claims supporting the thesis, evidence supporting claims, conclusion tying everything together. If there is a problem with an essay's structure—as there was in the early draft of this essay—it usually reflects problems with its reasoning and organization. Most writers struggle just to get ideas on the page. Their early drafts typically have gaps and inconsistencies. But during the rewriting process, writers force themselves to pay attention to the necessary structures of the essay. By doing so, they make their ideas, reasoning, and organization better.

# 13

## *Taking Essay Tests*

S o far, this book has dealt with essays written outside the classroom. Tests and examinations, however, are work that you do in
class, usually within a given time. When your instructor tests you,
he or she wants to know two things: how familiar you are with the
course material (the literature, the instructor's lectures, the secondary
material you may be required to read) and how creatively you can think
about this material. Tests fall into two categories, objective and essay.
Sometimes, the instructor may include questions or assignments from
both categories on the same test.

Objective tests ask you to account for, explain, and identify details about the course material. Essay tests ask you to state your ideas
about literary works and to support those ideas with facts. Some essay
tests call for short, one-paragraph essays; some call for long essays. The
same methods for writing out-of-class essays apply to test essays, short
or long. Your test essays are arguments: They should have a thesis and
should try to convince an audience of the validity of that thesis. They
should use sound logic and apt illustrations. Most of all, because of time
limits, they need good organization. Perhaps the most important general consideration to keep in mind is that your grade will depend on
how well you *perform* on a particular assignment, not simply on how
much you know. You may know the material very well, but if you do
not perform well, your grade will not reflect the abundance or quality
of your knowledge. The following guidelines should help you perform
well on essay tests.

# GUIDELINES FOR TAKING AN ESSAY TEST

1. **Prepare thoroughly.**
   a. First, learn the facts of the work or works on which you are being tested. Know who the characters are, what they do, and what happens to them, as well as the specifics of setting and so forth. When you are taking the test, you should know the details so well that they emerge from your memory almost automatically. This subliminal knowledge saves your creative energy for dealing with the interpretive problems the instructor gives you. If you have to dredge up facts from your memory slowly, you waste valuable test time.
   b. Systematically review the key problems or subjects relevant to the works, literary periods, or genres covered by the test. A good way to do this is to ask questions, as you would for finding essay topics. Here, however, you try to cover all the important questions. A knowledge of the elements of literature is especially useful for systematic questioning. How does the author handle setting? characterization? structure? theme? point of view? and so forth.
   c. Review class notes. But do so *along with* a review of the literary works. Reviewing your notes on the instructor's class comments will help you pinpoint important aspects of the works and should help you anticipate test questions. Remember, however, that memorizing class notes is no substitute for reviewing the works themselves. The two should be done together.

2. **Understand the assignment.** When you get the test, read all of the assignments carefully before you begin writing. If you do not understand any of them, ask the instructor to explain more fully. Sometimes instructors unintentionally write ambiguous assignments. You have a right to know exactly what you are supposed to do.

3. **Plan your answer.**
   a. Take a few minutes to make a short, topical outline. Making an outline frees you from worrying about being relevant or complete while you write. Instead, you can devote your whole attention to the creative development of each main point. If you have fifty minutes to write an essay, ten minutes making an outline will be time well spent.
   b. Exclude irrelevant topics.
   c. Arrange the remaining topics in a logical order. It may be that descending order of importance will be the most practical order for

your answer. That way, if you run out of time, you will still have covered your most important points.

4. **Address yourself to the assignment.** Anything irrelevant to the assignment wastes words and time.

5. **Give a direct response to the assignment.** One or two sentences somewhere in your answer should do the job. This way the instructor will know that you have kept the assignment in mind and that you have tried to deal with it. Your direct response to the assignment is the thesis of your essay and therefore usually should come near the beginning or end of your essay. Note the following example:

> ASSIGNMENT: Huck tricks Jim into believing that he dreamed they were separated in the fog. But Jim finally sees the trick for what it is. What does Huck learn from Jim's reaction?

> DIRECT RESPONSE: Huck learns that Jim has feelings and dignity just as white people do.

The complete answer, of course, would explain and illustrate this point, but the direct response connects the whole answer to the assignment. Without a direct response, your answer may seem irrelevant.

6. **Write in a clear, simple, and correct style.** The limited time and the pressure of the occasion make some mechanical slips likely, but you should be able to avoid most of them. Be especially careful to avoid serious errors such as sentence fragments, comma splices, ambiguous pronoun references, and subject-verb disagreement. If your handwriting is normally difficult to read, take care to make it legible.

7. **Develop your answer thoroughly.**
   a. Make claims that respond directly to the assignment. Often, these claims will serve as topic sentences for paragraphs.
   b. Offer specific details from the works that support and illustrate your claims.
   c. Represent the work or works adequately. The more thoroughly and appropriately you relate the work to your claims (and thus to the assignment), the better your answer will be.
   d. Your answer is an argument. You must back up your claims with evidence. Show your readers, don't just tell them.

8. **Be creative.** Some instructors want you to reproduce what they have said in class. Studying for their tests is simple. You just memorize what

the instructor has said and paraphrase it on the test. The more perfect your reproduction, the better your grade. Other instructors, however, want more—and they design their tests to get more. They want *your* thinking, not just their own. They want your creativity. But how can you be creative on tests? The answer is—think for yourself! Here are some ways to do so.

a. Use the instructor's points, but provide your own examples from the works. This shows that you are doing more than just memorizing lectures. It shows that you have thought through and applied the instructor's ideas on your own.

b. Find your own points. Although instructors try to cover the most important aspects of a work, limited class time makes it impossible for them to cover every aspect, even all the important ones. There are usually plenty of other points to be made. Study the work yourself, and come up with your own points. Read what others have said about the work, and discover points that way. Do not neglect points made by the instructor, but make other points as well.

c. Address controversies in works of literature, and take a stand. Often the instructor will discuss such controversies in class. In addition, controversies about works become apparent when you read literary criticism of them. Understanding these controversies will sharpen your perception of the work. Showing your awareness of them and taking a stand on them will demonstrate your creative involvement with the work.

d. Disagree with the instructor. This is risky but certainly creative. If you are brave enough to do this, have plenty of facts and logic at hand. Be diplomatic. Some instructors invite alternative interpretations and thus encourage a critical dialogue between themselves and their students.

e. Be detailed in your support and illustration of points. The more details you provide, the clearer your creative involvement becomes, especially if some of the details are those you have noticed on your own.

## SAMPLE TEST ESSAYS

All of the following essays respond to the assignment below. The writers had about twenty minutes to write their essays. Try to assess the strengths and weaknesses of each essay before you read its analysis.

ASSIGNMENT: Many stories contain symbols. Explain the possible symbolic importance of the rocking horse in D. H. Lawrence's "The Rocking-Horse Winner."

## Essay 1

Paul seems desperately to want his mother to love him. He senses that some-how she disapproves of him, that he stands in her way of achieving happiness. He seeks solace in the rocking horse. She has told him that "luck" means having money, so he rides the horse to get money. He hopes that by giving his mother money, he can buy his way into her heart. But, unfortunately, when he gives her an enormous sum of money, she is even more unhappy than before. Paul returns to the rocking horse to get more money for her. He frantically rides the horse one last time. But although he wins the jackpot, he dies from overexcitement and ex-haustion.

## Analysis of Essay 1

This is a mediocre essay because it does not directly address the assignment. It describes the action of the story accurately. It is clearly written. Its organization is easy to follow. It seems to have the assign-ment vaguely in mind, but nowhere does it say what the rocking horse symbolizes. The instructor may guess what the writer has in mind, but he or she cannot know for sure. The essay also omits important details. The writer does not say, for example, how Paul uses the horse to win money. The instructor may wonder whether the writer has read the story carefully.

## Essay 2

Paul's mother claims that she is "unlucky," and she explains to Paul that being unlucky means having no money. But the details of the story suggest that Paul's family does have money, because they live very well. The family has the trap-pings of wealth--a nurse, a large house, comfortable furnishings, and a gar-dener. The mother, then, isn't really poor but is obsessed with money. Her children sense this obsession. Most sensitive of all is Paul, who hears voices say-ing, "There must be more money." As a result, Paul sets out to win his mother's love by being "lucky." His means of achieving luck and thus his mother's love is the rocking horse. He finds that by riding the horse hard enough, he can predict winners of horse races. The rocking horse, then, symbolizes the love his mother has withheld from him. He even experiences something like the ecstasy of love when riding the horse to a winner. But his plan fails when his gift of 5,000 pounds only makes his mother's greed greater. He then becomes so desperate for love that he rides the rocking horse to his death.

## Analysis of Essay 2

This is a good essay. It not only accurately recounts details from the story but directly responds to the assignment, and it relates all the details cited from the story to that response. In other words, the details become "evidence." Because it deals directly with the assignment, it treats the story more specifically and thoroughly than does essay 1.

## Essay 3

The rocking horse symbolizes many things in "The Rocking-Horse Winner." Paul's mother complains that she has no money, and she tells Paul that to be "lucky" is to have money. Paul is very impressed by what she says and decides to prove to her that he is lucky. He wants also to stop the voices in the house that incessantly demand more money. He feels that the rocking horse can take him where luck is. Sure enough, when he rides the rocking horse and it takes him "there," he can predict the winners of horse races and make a great deal of money. So one thing the rocking horse symbolizes is luck, which, in turn, means money.

But the rocking horse also seems to represent a second idea. Paul's uncle says after Paul dies that he is better off being dead than living in a world where he had to ride a rocking horse to find a winner. The implication is that Paul was using the rocking horse to get what his mother never gave him: her love. So the rocking horse also symbolizes Paul's need for love and his parents' failure to give him affection.

Finally, the rocking horse symbolizes success. When Paul rides the rocking horse far enough, it brings him financial success. But this success is only ironic, for it never brings him the "success" he desperately wants--his mother's love-- and in the end it brings him death. Lawrence seems to suggest that some kinds of success are better than others; it is better to be loved than to be rich.

## Analysis of Essay 3

This is an excellent answer. Like essay 2, the essay directly responds to the assignment, and it plausibly and logically connects details of the story to its points. But it is more detailed and creative than essay 2. The writer makes a strong case for the complexity of the rocking horse as symbol and, by so doing, points to the multiple meanings and richness of the story.

# 14

## Sample Student Essays

This chapter contains six sample essays. Two are about fiction, two about poetry, and two about drama. All essays about literature, of course, are different; problems are different and writers have different methods of solving them. These essays, then, are not models to be slavishly imitated. But they do embody the main points of this book: that essays about literature are interpretations, that they are arguments, that their topics contain implicit questions, that their theses are answers to these questions, that they should convincingly support their theses, and that they should speak to a general audience of interested readers.

### ESSAY #1

#### CONFLICT IN SHIRLEY JACKSON'S "THE LOTTERY"

This is the central question of the essay.

The next sentence indicates the writer's *method* of answering the question.

Topic sentence. This paragraph deals with the first half of the conflict.

Shirley Jackson seems to want us to feel shocked and horrified at the conclusion of her chilling story "The Lottery." We see a group of human beings doing one of the worst deeds imaginable--cold-bloodedly murdering a defenseless person whom they all know and love. We wonder, Will the villagers ever stop doing such a terrible thing? The answer to this question seems to lie in the resolution of an important conflict--a conflict between the villagers' reluctance to participate in the lottery and their eagerness to participate.

Their reluctance to participate is evident from the beginning. The men standing around waiting are subdued: "Their jokes were quiet and they smiled rather than

First reference to the primary source (page number in parentheses).

A specific reference that is not a quotation but that needs a page citation.

Quotation introduced with a comma.

Quotation introduced with a colon.

An interpolation (put in brackets).

Transition sentence.

Topic sentence. This paragraph deals with the second half of the conflict mentioned in the last sentence of the first paragraph.

laughed" (437). The children, when called, come "reluctantly, having to be called four or five times" (437). Once the black box is brought out, the villagers keep "their distance" from it (437). The fact that people have made no attempt to repair the old black box suggests that when the box wears out, perhaps they will let the custom die. The ritual surrounding the lottery has also been neglected, so that only fragments are remembered and practiced (438). Once Mr. Summers begins the formal proceedings, Mrs. Dunbar is uneasy that her sixteen-year-old boy might even be thought eligible to stand in for his father (439). When Mr. Adams's name, the first name, is called, he and Mr. Summers grin at each other "humorlessly and nervously" (440). Mrs. Delacroix says to Mrs. Summers, "Seems like there's no time at all between lotteries any more" (440), as if the people find the lotteries unpleasant and put them out of mind as soon as they are over. She holds her breath as her husband goes forward to draw a name (440). We learn that there is some restiveness outside the village over lotteries: "over in the north village they're talking of giving up the lottery"; "some places have already quit lotteries" (440). The most obvious example of reluctance is Mrs. Hutchinson, who, as soon as her family is chosen, questions the fairness of the draw. She does not, it should be noted, question the fairness of lotteries, just of the particular draw: "You didn't give him [her husband] time enough to take any paper he wanted. I saw you. It wasn't fair" (441). Her reluctance to participate grows, of course, and reaches its apex at the very end, just before her death.

Throughout the village, then, people are generally reluctant to participate in the lottery. But their attitude toward the lottery is ambivalent, for they seem eager to participate as well. This eagerness emerges early in the story. Some of the children are apparently the most eager. They are on the scene first. Bobby Martin has "already stuffed his pockets full of stones," and the other boys soon do likewise; some even make piles of stones (437). Ironically, at first Mrs. Hutchinson is the most eager adult. She rushes disheveled to the square and tells Mrs. Delacroix that she "clean forgot what day it was" until she noticed her children were gone. Then "I remembered it was the twenty-seventh and came a-running" (439). Mrs. Delacroix assures her that she is "in time" since "they're still talking away up there" (439). Once the drawing begins, Mrs. Dunbar tells her son to "go tell your father" (441). Mrs. Delacroix picks up the largest stone she can find and tells Mrs. Dunbar, "Come on. . . . Hurry up" (443). Mrs. Dunbar has stones in both hands and, "gasping for breath," claims that she "can't run at all"; she will have to catch up. The children already have stones, and someone gives little Davy Hutchinson a few. Old Man Warner says, "Come on, come on, everyone" as they all close in on Mrs. Hutchinson for the kill (443).

**Topic sentence. The writer reminds readers of the essay's purpose by asking which side will win.**

Which of these two conflicting attitudes toward the lottery will become dominant? The villagers' reluctance to participate and the discontinuance of lotteries elsewhere suggest that the villagers want to stop having lotteries. But there is a weakness in the villagers' reluctance to participate. Their reluctance is purely self-interested. No one objects to the lottery on behalf of someone else. Only the victim is critical of it. It is true that some people exhibit uneasiness when loved ones and children might be victims. Perhaps the villagers are moving toward the belief that everyone's life is good in itself and must not be wantonly destroyed. But not until then will they be able to abolish the lottery as a communal evil. In contrast, the villagers' eagerness to participate is very strong. The lottery, we learn, is irrational. Only Mr. Warner, the oldest of the villagers, has an inkling of why lotteries are held at all: "Lottery in June, corn be heavy soon" (440). No one else remembers why they have lotteries. What everyone does remember is how to kill. The murder, which for the reader is the most horrible part of the lottery, is for the villagers the most important part, the part they most enjoy. So eager are they to kill that they risk being chosen themselves just to be there.

**Topic sentence.**

**Throughout the essay, the writer builds toward a conclusion while at the same time revealing details of plot. In this way the writer lends suspense to the argument. This paragraph reveals the writer's thesis and is the climax of that suspense. It also brings in an "expert" to resolve the conflict. Since the**

As the story draws to a close, Shirley Jackson seems to offer her own opinion about how the conflict will be resolved. The two people leading the attack on Mrs. Hutchinson are Mr. Adams and Mrs. Graves (443). The name "Adams" suggests the first sinner, Adam. The rural setting and the opening paragraph suggest an idyllic place like the Garden of Eden. The name "Graves" alludes to a consequence of Adam's sin, Cain's murder of Abel. If Shirley Jackson intended these connections, the lottery may be symbolic of Original Sin, which, according to Christian dogma, is ineradicable and universal. All writer's conclusions are clearly conjectural, she uses qualifying words such as "may," "if," "suggests," and "implies."

Thesis

people--women, men, children, the youngest and the oldest, even Christians (Mrs. Delacroix's name means "of the cross")--are tainted by Adam's fall. Thus, the villagers may give up lotteries in the form they now take, but Jackson implies that "lotteries" will always exist in some form or other and that human beings will always do evil just as eagerly as they do in this story.

Start a new page for the "Work Cited" section.

### Work Cited

Jackson, Shirley. "The Lottery." Perrine and Arp's Literature: Structure, Sound, and Sense. Ed. Laurence Perrine and Thomas R. Arp. 6th ed. Fort Worth: Harcourt, 1993. 436–45.

# ESSAY #2

### SETTING IN NATHANIEL HAWTHORNE'S "YOUNG GOODMAN BROWN"

The forest in Hawthorne's story "Young Goodman Brown" seems to represent sin. At least, the farther Goodman Brown journeys into the forest, the more he learns about the nature of sin and the more he suspects its presence in his village. But the forest also represents something else: Brown's psychological state during each stage of his journey.

Thesis. The implicit question answered by this thesis is, What does the forest represent?

Transition sentence. It announces the first stage of Brown's journey.

When Brown takes his guilty leave of Faith ("What a wretch am I, to leave her on such an errand!" [75]), the forest has three main characteristics. First, it is dark; the road Brown has taken is "dreary" and "darkened by all the gloomiest trees of the forest" (75). Second, it is hard to penetrate; the path is "narrow" and nearly obstructed by trees (75). Finally, it causes fear; Brown feels that something threatening "may be concealed by the innumerable trunks and the thick boughs overhead"--perhaps an Indian or "the devil himself" (75). The forest here represents Brown's recognition that he is entering the domain of evil (darkness is a traditional symbol of evil), that he cannot predict what will happen (he cannot see what lies ahead on the path), and that the consequences of his journey may be destructive (he is afraid).

Topic sentence. It announces what the forest represents during the first stage of Brown's journey.

Transition sentence. It announces the next stage of Brown's journey.

Once Brown has entered the forest, the devil joins him and initiates him into the knowledge of evil. One by one, the devil implicates individuals whom Brown particularly reveres: his grandfather, his father, Goody Cloyse, the

**Topic sentence. It states what the forest represents.**

**Transition and topic sentence.**

**Throughout the essay, the organization of the writer's evidence is spatial. Plot details are given in the order in which they occur in the story, and thus the essay has a measure of suspense. It builds toward a climax. All of the evidence, however, directly relates to the writer's thesis. The essay does not merely give a plot summary for its own sake.**

**Topic sentence.**

**A long blocked quotation, introduced by a colon and indented.**

minister, and Deacon Gookin. During this part of the story, Brown is confused about what really is true. The forest represents this confusion by its obscurity. It is sunset when Brown enters the forest, but when the devil appears, it has become "deep dusk" (76), and when Goody Cloyse appears it is "nightfall" (78). Because of this increasing darkness, Brown cannot be quite sure of what he sees or hears. The devil's walking stick, for example, seems to turn into a snake, but this may be "an ocular deception, assisted by the uncertain light" (76). Brown thinks he hears the voices of Deacon Gookin and the minister, but "owning doubtless to the depth of the gloom of that particular spot, neither the travellers nor their steeds were visible" (81). And he seems to hear "a confused and doubtful sound of voices," among whom are those of his fellow townspeople, "both pious and ungodly" (83), when the next minute "he doubted whether he had heard aught but the murmur of the old forest, whispering without a wind" (83).

After the deacon and the minister leave, the forest represents Brown's next psychological state: disbelief. The part of the forest into which the deacon and the minister travel is "the heathen wilderness" where "no church had ever been gathered or solitary Christian prayed" (82). Brown is on the verge of taking this road--"he looked up to the sky, doubting whether there really was a heaven above him" (82)--but resolves to go no farther. Suddenly he suspects that Faith herself, the person he most reveres, may be engulfed by this forest of evil. He fancies that he hears her voice, and he finds a pink ribbon that might be hers. On this faint evidence, he commits himself irrevocably to the forest: "My Faith is gone," he cries, and rushes headlong into the interior (82).

Because of his disbelief Brown now enters into a state of despair and insanity that the forest mirrors perfectly:

> The road grew wilder and drearier and more faintly traced, and vanished at length, leaving him in the heart of the dark wilderness, still rushing onward with the instinct that guides mortal man to evil. The whole forest was peopled with frightful sounds--the creaking of the trees, the howling of wild beasts, and the yell of Indians; while sometimes the wind tolled like a distant church bell, and sometimes gave a broad roar around the traveller, as if all Nature were

laughing him to scorn. But he was himself the chief horror of the scene, and shrank not from its other horrors. (84)

As he runs, Brown becomes a "demoniac" who brandishes his staff with "frenzied gestures" (84). His cries are in "unison" with the cry of the forest (85). It echoes his "horrid blasphemy" and is a "tempest" that drives him onward (84).

**Transition and topic sentence. The climax of the essay coincides with the climax of the story.**

At the climax of his frenzy, Brown sees the next and final step in his journey: complete alienation. Before him is a weird scene that represents the rejection of all belief in the goodness of human beings: a pulpitlike rock surrounded by four pine trees whose tops are on fire. Surrounding the pulpit is a "congregation" of all the inhabitants, past and present, of his village. The devil emerges to complete Brown's initiation. The devil has Faith brought in, and he asks the couple to accept the existence of evil in everyone's soul: "Evil is the nature of mankind. Evil must be your only happiness. Welcome, again, my children, to the communion of your race" (88). But Brown balks at this final step. He tells Faith to "look up to Heaven, and resist the Wicked One" (89). Immediately the forest changes. His frenzy has disappeared and so has the wild blaze of the forest.

**Transition sentence. It relates to the experience described in the preceding paragraph and also to the whole experience of Brown's journey.**

**Topic sentence. It summarizes the total effect of the journey on Brown's personality.**

**The writer makes one final point about Brown's mental state and the forest, saying that even here, in the last stage of the journey, the forest represents Brown's attitude.**

Hawthorne leaves us with a question of whether Brown's experience was a dream: "Had Goodman Brown fallen asleep in the forest and only dreamed a wild dream of a witch-meeting?" (90). But the question is probably irrelevant, since the effect on Brown is the same as if his experience had really happened. Brown is a changed man. He has, it seems, in fact taken the final step urged upon him by the devil. He sees all people as hypocrites who pretend to be good but secretly worship and follow devil. He even shrinks "from the bosom of Faith," scowling and muttering when he sees her at prayer. He has become a cold man, just as the forest when he awakens is "chill and damp" and "besprinkled . . . with the coldest dew" (89).

## Work Cited

Hawthorne, Nathaniel. "Young Goodman Brown." <u>The Portable Hawthorne.</u> Ed. Malcolm Cowley. New York: Viking, 1948. 75–89.

# ESSAY #3

## POINT OF VIEW IN EDWIN ARLINGTON ROBINSON'S "RICHARD CORY"

*The writer uses a critic's opinion as a point of departure. One question the essay addresses is, Is Winters right in his interpretation of the poem?*

*Thesis.*

*Topic sentence. This sentence connects with the thesis statement above because it establishes the poem's point of view—a first-person narrative by a citizen of the town.*

*Topic sentence. With the point of view firmly established, the writer now states the attitude of the narrator.*

*Since the poem is quite short, line numbers are not necessary to document quotations.*

*The writer interprets a key word to support the essay's argument. Such interpretations are often necessary in analyzing poetry, since the weight of a poem's meaning often rests on the nuances of words.*

Yvor Winters, a leading American critic, condemns Edwin Arlington Robinson's poem "Richard Cory" for containing "a superficially neat portrait of the elegant man of mystery" and for having a "very cheap surprise ending" (52). It is true that because Richard Cory fits the stereotype of "the man who has everything," his suicide at the end is surprising, even shocking. But the poet's handling of point of view makes the portrait of Richard Cory only apparently superficial and the ending only apparently "cheap."

In the second line of the poem, we learn that the speaker is not Robinson himself (the omniscient narrator), but someone with a limited view of things. He is one of the "people" of the town (38). It is as if he has cornered a visitor on a sidewalk somewhere and is telling him about a fellow townsman whose suicide has puzzled and troubled him. He cannot understand it, so he talks about it. Throughout this speaker's narration, we learn a lot about him and his peers and how they regarded Richard Cory.

Clearly they saw him as something special. The imagery of kings and nobility ("crown," "imperially slim" and "richer than a king") permeates their conception of Richard Cory. To them he had the bearing and trappings of royalty. He was a "gentleman," a word that suggests courtliness as well as nobility. He had good taste ("he was always quietly arrayed"). He was wealthy. He had good breeding (he was "admirably schooled in every grace"). He "glittered when he walked," suggesting, perhaps, that he wore jewelry and walked with confidence. Because of this attitude, the speaker and his peers placed themselves in an almost feudal relationship to Cory. They saw themselves as "people on the pavement," as if they walked on the ground and Richard Cory somehow walked above them. Even if he did not literally walk above them, they saw him as "above" them socially. They seemed to think it unusual that he was "human when he talked." The word "human" suggests several things. One is that the people saw Cory as somehow exempt from the problems and restrictions of being a human being (thus "human") but that when he talked, he stepped out of character. Another is that he, who was so much above them, could be kind, warm, and thoughtful (another meaning of "human"). They were so astonished by this latter quality that when he did such a simple and obvious thing as say "Good-morning," he "fluttered pulses."

**Transition and topic sentence.**

In the final stanza, the speaker brings out the most important differences between the people and Richard Cory. Most obvious is that he was rich and they were poor; they "went without the meat, and cursed the bread." But another difference is suggested by the word "light": "So on we worked, and waited for the light." "Light" in this context most apparently means a time when things will be better, as in the expression "the light at the end of the tunnel." But another meaning of "light" is revelation. Light has traditionally symbolized knowledge and truth, and it may be that this is the meaning the speaker--or at least Robinson--has in mind. If so, another difference that the people saw between Richard Cory and themselves was that Cory had knowledge and understanding and they did not. After all, they had no time to pursue knowledge; they needed all their time just to survive. But Richard Cory did have the time. He was a man of leisure who had been "schooled." If anyone would have had the "light"--a right understanding of things--then Richard Cory would have been that person.

**Interpretation of a key word.**

**Transition and topic sentence.**

Although Robinson does not tell us why Richard Cory killed himself, he leaves several hints. One of these is the assumptions about Richard Cory held by the narrator and the "people." Cory may have been a victim of their attitude. The poem gives no evidence that he sought to be treated like a king or that he had pretensions to nobility. He seems, in fact, to have been democratic enough. Although rich, well-mannered, and tastefully dressed, he nonetheless came to town, spoke with kindness to the people, and greeted them as if they deserved his respect. Could he even have wanted their friendship? But the people's attitude may have isolated Richard Cory. Every time he came to town, they stared at him as if he were a freak in a sideshow (lines 1-2). In their imagination, furthermore, they created an ideal of him that was probably false and, if taken seriously by Richard Cory, would have been very difficult to live up to. Cory did not, at least, have the "light" that the people thought he had. His sui-

**The line reference is necessary here because there is no easy-to-find quotation, but rather a reference to an event in the poem. Without the line reference, readers**

might find it difficult to spot the specific place in the poem that the writer has in mind.

The writer concludes by returning to the central issue raised at the beginning of the essay, bringing the critic's interpretation back into the essay.

cide attests to that. He was, in short, as "human" as they; but, unlike them, he lacked the consolation of fellowship. Ironically, then, the people's very admiration of Richard Cory, which set him apart as more than human and isolated him from human companionship, may have been the cause of his death.

Had Robinson told Cory's story as an omniscient narrator, Winters' complaint about the poem would be justified. The poem would seem to be an attempt to shock us with a melodramatic and too-obvious irony. But Robinson has deepened the poem's meaning by having one of Cory's fellow townspeople tell his story. This presentation of Cory's character, his relationship to the townspeople, and his motives for suicide open the poem up to interpretation in a way that Winters does not acknowledge or explore.

Works Cited

Robinson, Edwin Arlington. Tilbury Town: Selected Poems of Edwin Arlington Robinson. New York: Macmillan, 1951. 38.
Winters, Yvor. Edwin Arlington Robinson. Norfolk: New Directions, 1946.

# ESSAY #4

Like the "Richard Cory" essay, this essay uses someone else's ideas as a starting point.

Thesis.

Topic sentence. The writer keeps the opposite position in view and represents it fairly and fully.

This poem is a little longer than "Richard Cory." Line

## TONE IN EMILY DICKINSON'S "BECAUSE I COULD NOT STOP FOR DEATH"

One of the questions raised in class about Emily Dickinson's "Because I could not stop for Death" was whether or not its tone is optimistic. My feeling is that it is partly pessimistic and that Dickinson communicates that pessimism in the poem's imagery, its structure, its diction, and, in one crucial place, its rhythm.

The tone of the first half of the poem (the first three stanzas) seems optimistic. As was suggested in class, the speaker seems to feel a special and warm relationship to Death, perhaps even to the point of seeing Death as a groom. He comes in a carriage, "kindly" stops for her, rides with only her inside, and takes his time. She in turn seems to be putting away the things of childhood (her "labor" and "leisure") in response to his "Civility" (lines 7-8). She makes a symbolic journey through life with him,

numbers, even for quota-
tions, may thus be helpful.
Use "line" for the first
citation, line numbers only
for subsequent citations.

Topic sentence. The topic sentence in this paragraph is in
two parts. The second part is
at the end of the paragraph.

Topic sentence.

Transition and topic sentence.

Transition sentence.

The writer continues to represent the opposition.

just as she would with a husband. Her carriage passes
children at school (youth), "Fields of Gazing Grain"
(maturity), and the "Setting Sun" (old age) (9-12). Her
light, probably white, clothing (a gossamer gown and tulle
scarf, mentioned in lines 15-16) further suggests the marriage relationship. Altogether, in the first three stanzas, the
narrator seems to feel cozy in her relationship with Death.
She feels that Death is a friendly and kind companion. She
is optimistic about where Death is taking her.

The tone shifts, however, with the first line of the fourth
stanza (the beginning of the second half of the poem): "Or
rather--he passed Us--" (13). Several signals suggest this
shift. One is the narrator's loss of momentum. She is now
acted upon. The sun passes her. Since the sun traditionally
represents life and the sunset death, I take this to mean that
she has now died. Another signal is the change in rhythm.
Up to this point, the rhythm has been a very regular iambic
beat, almost a singsong. But the first line in the fourth
stanza completely distorts that pattern, almost as if the regular beating of the heart has been jerkily disrupted. In the
last part of the line, Dickinson substitutes one spondee (a
foot with two accented syllables) for the two iambic feet
that one would expect to be there. The result is that the last
three words, which she isolates with dashes, all have about
the same stress: "ŏr rátheř--hé paśsed ús--." For me, the
effect is as if something has come suddenly to a halt. No
longer is she certain of where she is going.

It seems logical to associate this halt with the narrator's
death, but I associate it also with her change of tone. Immediately after this line, she feels chilly. The sun has gone
down (she is dead) and her clothes, which formerly were
appropriate as wedding clothes, seem no longer adequate to warm her. Her gown is "only" gossamer, her tip-
pet "only" tulle (15-16). The chill of death is further
underscored by her current place of residence, her grave:

We passed before a House that seemed
A Swelling of the Ground—. (17-18)

In the final stanza, the narrator tells us that although
"Centuries" have passed, it

Feels shorter than the Day
I first surmised the Horses Heads
Were toward Eternity—. (22-24)

Several people in class concluded that the tone of this
final stanza is optimistic because the narrator is in "Eter-

Topic sentence.

Interpretation of key words in the poem.

Use of a reference work to bolster the argument.

Interpretation of another key word.

A summary of the writer's interpretation of the final stanza—put, appropriately, at the end of the paragraph.

The writer concludes by looking at the whole poem in light of the points established in the essay. The writer not only restates the thesis but offers an interpretation of the whole poem based on that thesis.

nity" and that time in an earthly sense passes very quickly for her. But this stanza may well have an ironic twist that suggests a pessimistic tone. At the end of the first stanza she says that the carriage held herself, Death, and "Immortality." But in the last stanza she says that she "surmises" the horses were headed "toward Eternity." It seems possible that the narrator sees a difference between the concepts "Immortality" and "Eternity." The <u>Oxford English Dictionary</u> defines "immortal" as meaning "deathless, undying," "living for ever," and as "pertaining to immortal beings or immortality." Almost all the historical quotations that follow these definitions in the <u>OED</u> associate "immortal" with life after death, particularly life in "heaven." The word "eternal," however, does not necessarily include this idea. Eternity is simply "infinite in past and future duration; without beginning or end." Eternity can exist even though one is dead. The word can also express weariness or disgust over something "that seems to be going on for ever." Thus "immortality" is a more optimistic concept than "eternity." Another nuance of the last stanza is provided by the word "surmised." The <u>OED</u> says that "surmise" means "to form a notion that the thing in question may be so, on slight grounds or without proof; to infer conjecturally." Thus the narrator does not know for certain where she is; she could (and can) only guess. The final stanza may be saying, then, that after her death, the narrator guessed ("surmised") that Death was taking her not to Immortality but only to Eternity. So traumatic was this discovery that although centuries have passed since then, they have not seemed as long as that day seemed.

By the end of the poem, we have learned from the narrator's tone that she is left in a bad way. Whereas before her death she thought that Death was kind, she is now cold and without adequate clothing. She is alone. And she is filled with doubt and uncertainty. She may in time gain "immortality," but it is also possible that she has only gained the bleak, cold wasteland of "Eternity."

Works Cited

Dickinson, Emily. "Because I Could Not Stop for Death." <u>The Poems of Emily Dickinson.</u> Ed. Thomas H. Johnson. 3 vols. Cambridge: Belknap-Harvard UP, 1955. 2: 546.

"Eternal." <u>The Oxford English Dictionary.</u> Ed. J.A.
Simpson and E.S.C. Weiner, 2nd. ed. 20 vols.
Oxford: Oxford UP, 1989.
"Immortal." <u>OED.</u>
"Surmise." <u>OED.</u>

# ESSAY #5

## OEDIPUS'S RESPONSIBILITY
## IN SOPHOCLES'S
## OEDIPUS REX

The writer identifies a problem of interpretation in the play.

One of the most puzzling aspects of Sophocles's play <u>Oedipus Rex</u> is that Oedipus at the end accepts full responsibility for what he has done. After horribly maiming himself by gouging out his eyes, he proclaims to the Choragos:

> This punishment
> That I have laid upon myself is
> just.
> If I had eyes,
> I do not know how I could bear the
> sight
> Of my father, when I came to the
> house of Death
> Or my mother: for I have sinned
> against them both
> So vilely that I could not make my
> peace
> By strangling my own life. (Exodos
> 140-47)

The method of documentation for classic verse plays is to identify the play's division, and its act, scene, and line numbers, when the play has them. The "Exodos" is the concluding section of the play.

The writer summarizes the meaning of the quote in his own words.

In other words, he declares himself a "sinner" and accepts full responsibility for what he has done by inflicting the worst punishment upon himself that he can imagine, even worse than death. Yet throughout the play it seems as if Oedipus was fated to do these things and actually did them in spite of his efforts to avoid doing them. How, then, can Oedipus justifiably accuse himself of wrongdoing?

The writer raises a specific question about the play.

Why doesn't he simply excuse himself by saying that he had done his best but fate was against him, that he had no control over what happened and therefore cannot be blamed? The answer to this question, I believe, is that although Oedipus may have been fated to do these actions,

Thesis. The thesis is the writer's answer to the question.

he nonetheless does them on purpose. It may even be that the oracle's pronouncements are more like forecasts or conjectures than prophecies. Knowing something about Oedipus's temperament would enable us to predict at least some of the things he did.

Transition and topic sentence.

We learn a lot about Oedipus's temperament in the first part of the play. In the opening scenes he appears as a proud and intemperate man. He enters treating his subjects as inferiors (he calls them "children") whom he, the one with the "famous name," will save (Prologue 8). He anticipates the moment when he can play the hero, just as he did when he solved the riddle of the Sphinx. To this end, he has sent Creon to the Delphic Oracle to learn "what act or pledge of [Oedipus's] may save the city" (Prologue 74). When Creon returns to say that the murderer of Laius, the previous king, must be found, Oedipus places an extremely harsh edict against the murderer; he must be "driven from every house," not spoken to, and his life "consumed in evil and wretchedness" (1.20-31). Teiresias, the blind seer, calls attention to Oedipus's intemperate nature (1.109), and Oedipus suddenly and irrationally accuses Teiresias of planning Laius's murder:

> You planned it, you had it done,
>    you all but
> Killed him with your own hands.
>    (1.128-29)

He rails at Teiresias--"You sightless, witless, senseless, mad old man!" (1.153)--and boasts that he is a better exorcist than Teiresias. Oedipus compounds his rash behavior by accusing Creon of the murder as well. Creon quite reasonably requests that Oedipus should at least present evidence against him, but Oedipus ignores him and says, "It is your death I want" (2.106). Throughout the first part of the play, in short, Oedipus overreacts passionately, even violently, to events, especially when they challenge his pride or authority.

The writer summarizes the meaning of the evidence presented in this rather long paragraph.

Transition and topic sentence.

The writer draws inferences from the sketchy evidence in the play, indicating the speculative quality of these inferences with phrases like "there is at least a hint."

It is possible to see Oedipus overreacting in the same passionate and violent way when he kills his father. When he tells Iocasta why he left Corinth, there is at least a hint that he had been coddled, perhaps spoiled as a child. He was adopted (he learns later in the play) by the king and queen, a childless couple who did everything in their power to protect him from the truth about his origins. And he says that he "grew up chief among the men of Corinth" (2.248). After he left Corinth (to escape the oracle's prediction), he came upon King Laius traveling with five attendants. The groom forced Oedipus off the road at Laius's command. At this point Oedipus became very angry and in his "rage" struck the groom back. Laius then hit Oedipus with his "double goad." With his club, Oedipus knocked Laius out of the chariot and onto the ground (2.275-87). Up to this point, Oedipus had acted as any spoiled, egocentric, and spirited person might act. He paid back in kind what he had received by way of insult. He might have behaved more humbly and temperately, but he at least gave back only slightly more than he had received. But what he did next was completely out of line with what had gone before. After saying that Laius "rolled on the ground," Oedipus says: "I killed him / I killed them all" (2.288). Assuming that Laius had not been killed by the blow that knocked him from the chariot, what Oedipus did was terrible. First he attacked an old man lying defenseless on the ground and killed him. Then he attacked all the rest, killing all he could (one, a "household servant," escaped). Because of Oedipus's pride--his sense of personal injury--he inflicted punishment on these people far in excess of what they deserved. And although Oedipus did not premeditatedly kill his father, he did so without just cause. He is guilty of murder. And he is close to doing the same thing at the beginning of the play, when he demands the death penalty for the innocent Creon.

Oedipus's high-handed way of meting out punishment brings up another flaw in his character, his inability to take the gods seriously. One might argue that had Oedipus taken the gods seriously, he would have remained in Corinth and awaited his fate humbly and courageously. Instead, he takes matters into his own hands, as if he could by his own actions escape the decrees of the gods. This feeling of independence, even defiance of the gods, is illustrated even more clearly when he and Iocasta gloat over having apparently outmaneuvered the gods' predictions. "Ah!" Oedipus says,

> Why should a man respect the
> Pythian hearth, or
> Give heed to the birds that jangle above
> his head?

*Here, as elsewhere in the essay, the writer not only summarizes the meaning of the evidence presented in the paragraph, but also ties the evidence to the main thesis of the essay.*

*Transition and topic sentence.*

They prophesied that I should kill
Polybos,
Kill my own father; but he is dead
and buried,
And I am here—I never touched
him, never,
Unless he died of grief for my
departure,
And thus, in a sense, through me.
No. Polybos
Has packed the oracles off with
him underground.
They are empty words. (3.917-26)

Transition and topic sentence.

The writer states an alternative interpretation and then argues against it. In other words, he anticipates the reader's potential objections and questions.

The most important result of Oedipus's refusal to take the gods seriously is his marriage to Iocasta. It is true that Oedipus would understandably have had his guard down when he came to Thebes. He thought he was far from the land where his father and mother lived. He came as a hero, the savior of the city, and was invited to be king. To seal his status as king, he married the former queen. But after all, Iocasta was old enough to be his mother--obviously. Even if he still thought that Merope was his mother, he might have considered the spirit of the oracle's pronouncement, not just the letter. It is possible to sleep with one who is like one's mother, even if that person is not literally so. In such a case, the sin of incest is no less a reality. Iocasta seems to recognize this possibility when she says, "How many men, in dreams, have lain with their mother!" (3.68). Oedipus's relationship with Iocasta, furthermore, is warm and close. It is more than just a state marriage entered into merely to secure power. And it is clearly sexual, since he has produced at least four children over a long period of time. The result, then, may be that Oedipus has committed incest in his mind long before it becomes a public, legal fact. The fact that Iocasta is his real mother can be seen as purely an accident. The existence of his incest would have been equally real without it.

The conclusion summarizes the points made in the essay and reemphasizes the validity of the thesis.

What I have tried to show in this essay is that although on the surface Oedipus seems a victim of fate, actually he participates in that fate enough to be responsible for it. He is impetuous, proud, violent, unjust, and heedless of the gods. As such, he is to blame for killing his father and committing incest with his mother. He finally and justly recognizes his blame, accepts responsibility for it, and punishes himself.

Work Cited

Sophocles. Oedipus Rex. Trans. Dudley Fitts and Robert Fitzgerald. New York: Harcourt, 1949.

# ESSAY #6

## CÉLIMÈNE'S COQUETRY IN MOLIÈRE'S THE MISANTHROPE

The writer raises specific questions about the play.

The instructor may prefer roman numerals for acts here.

Thesis. The thesis is the writer's answer to these questions.

Transition and topic sentence. Note the logic of the writer's organization. Before the essay can show that Célimène uses coquetry to defend herself, it must first show that something threatens her.

Transition and topic sentence. The essay moves to the next logical step in the organiza-

Célimène's coquetry is one of the mainsprings of action in Molière's play The Misanthrope. But why is she a coquette? Does she keep men on a string with her "most melting and receptive manner" (II.22) only to flatter her vanity? Is she merely the "beautiful woman without kindness"? My view of Célimène is much more sympathetic than this. I see her as a potential victim who must defend herself against a predatory world with the only weapon at her disposal, her coquetry.

That Célimène's world is predatory and that she is vulnerable seem clear by the time the play is over. In the first place, her world is one of constant struggle. Both she and Alceste are involved in lawsuits before the play begins, and Alceste becomes involved in a second (with Oronte) almost immediately. The causes of the first two lawsuits remain unidentified, but if they are anything like the cause of the lawsuit with Oronte, they are trivial. It seems as if one could end up at law over almost anything, even over words spoken in unguarded moments. The struggle in Célimène's society, however, is more than just legal. People are constantly gossiping with the sole intention of doing others harm. Of all the gossips, the most malicious is Arsinoé, who actually comes to Célimène's house to engage in a pitched battle of insult trading. Célimène herself is daily confronted with a struggle over her person and, presumably, her fortune. Her coquetry may exacerbate this struggle, but the struggle would still exist without it. Her suitors vie with one another for first place in her attentions and bombard her with jealousy and possessiveness.

Célimène's main need is for a protector. Normally, a family would shield a young woman from those who

tion. It must now show that Célimène has no means of protecting herself other than her coquetry. This paragraph eliminates one traditional means of protection: family.

would do her harm, particularly suitors who might turn out to be disastrous husbands. But Célimène has no family to speak of. Her cousin Éliante is the only relative we see, and although Éiante is "honest," she has no power to help Célimène. No one in her society, furthermore, is a fitting substitute for her parents, a fact that Célimène seems to recognize. Her gossip session in act II with Acaste and Clitandre may not show her in the best light, but it at least shows that she is clearsighted about her social peers. She describes them as blunderers, bores, social climbers, egomaniacs, paranoid fantasizers, and pretentious fools. She sees that hypocrisy dominates her society, and we see from Alceste's portrait of the man suing him that such hypocrisy can be dangerous:

Call him knave, liar, scoundrel,
and all the rest,
Each head will nod, and no one
will protest. (I.135-36)

Transition and topic sentence. This paragraph eliminates a second means of protection: marriage.

Note that even though it is a separate paragraph, it nonetheless continues to develop the major topic intro duced in the above paragraph: Célimène's need for a protector.

Cèlimène could provide herself with a protector by getting married. But her suitors are all a sorry lot. Acaste, Clitandre, and Oronte are vain and foppish. Her portraits of each in the letters revealed in act V accurately reflect what we see of them in the rest of the play. This leaves Alceste. Alceste has good grounds for criticizing his society, and it may be that because he does so he is more admirable than his passive and fatalistic friend, Philinto. Also, it may be that Célimène "loves" Alceste. At the end he is the only suitor to whom she feels a need to confess:

I've wronged you, I confess it;
and in my shame
I'll make no effort to escape the
blame.
The anger of those others I could
despise;
My guilt toward you I sadly
recognize. (V.304-07)

She even offers to let him marry her (V.347).

Topic sentences.

But Alceste would not be likely to give Célimène the protection she needs, a fact that she seems to sense. He has many flaws. One flaw is a lack of moderation. He takes extreme positions on everything. In the face of human error, he claims that "all are corrupt" (I.89). Rather than flatter others, he would hang himself (I.28). Rather

than work out his differences with society, he would re-
move to a "wild, trackless place" where he could "forget
the human race" (V.327-29). Rather than help Célimène,
he would force her to choose between him and other
human society; he would punish her with total separation
from other people. A second flaw is inconsistency. Even
though Alceste states his opinions in the strongest possible
language, he cannot act upon them. He claims to love
honesty, consistency, and plain dealing, yet he ignores
Éliante, who loves him and who fits his ideal. Instead he
pursues Célimène, who feigns indifference and seems the
opposite of his ideal. He threatens to withdraw his attentions from Célimène, but cannot do so when the crisis
comes. Even in trivial things he is inconsistent. In act II
(II.iv-v) he says that he will go, but he stays.

Transition sentence. Although
this paragraph develops the
topic introduced in the preceding paragraph, the writer
begins a new paragraph at a
logical break in the line of
thought in order to provide a
visual rest for readers.
Otherwise the paragraph
would be uncomfortably
long.

A third flaw is Alceste's lack of sound judgment. His attack on Oronte's poetry in act I, for example, seems
groundless. He produces little evidence to support his
opinions, and the poetry he offers as a model of good poetry seems little different from Oronte's. His accusation in
act IV that Célimène has betrayed him is based on an un-
signed, unaddressed letter that could have been written
by someone else and not necessarily to a man. He even
believes the person who gives him the letter, Arsinoé, although he knows her to be Célimène's bitterest rival.
Overall, his jealousy of Célimène is a self-fulfilling
prophecy. He is jealous before there is evidence of betrayal and thus helps to bring about that betrayal. A
fourth flaw is his willful and irrational contradictoriness.
Célimène says,

> He lives in deadly terror of
>    agreeing,
> 'Twould make him seem an ordinary
>    being.
> Indeed, he's so in love with
>    contradiction,
> He'll turn against his most
>    profound conviction
> And with a furious eloquence
>    deplore it,
> If only someone else is speaking
>    for it. (II.229-34)

Molière verifies the accuracy of this observation by having Philinte, the most moderate and reasonable man in

the play, agree with it. A fifth flaw is Alceste's failure to love Célimène truly as a woman would want to be loved. The love he offers only adds to the strife that threatens her. She tells him,

> If all hearts beat according to
> your measure.
> The dawn of love would be the end
> of pleasure;
> And love would find its perfect
> consummation
> In ecstasies of rage and
> reprobation. (II.261-64)

*Transition sentence.*

Rather, Éiante adds, men should "love their ladies even for their flaws" (II.284).

The flaw that most seriously undermines Alceste's ability to protect Célimène is his lack of practicality. If she is to have a protector, she needs someone who can win--or avoid--the battles that inevitably occur in this society. Yet Alceste seems to enjoy alienating everyone in sight, even his good friends. Such behavior will make him a magnet for every contentious crackpot who has the time, money, and power to battle and possibly destroy him. Even worse, he does not care about winning these battles. He would willfully and quixotically lose them just to make a point. He refuses, for example, to contest the unfavorable verdict of his lawsuit, no matter what "cruel penalty it may bring" (V.61), just so it can serve

> As a great proof and signal
> demonstration
> Of the black wickedness of this
> generation. (V.65-66)

*Transition and topic sentence. Having shown that Célimène has no traditional means of defense, the writer now can argue that she must defend herself with her coquetry.*

The corruption of her society and the flaws of the one man she cares for leave Célimène little choice about how to conduct herself. She seems unable at this point in her life to give up society:

> What! I renounce the world at my
> age,
> And die of boredom in some
> hermitage? (V.334-35)

She is, after all, very young--only twenty--and not fully cognizant of what she wants. "Her heart's a stranger to its own emotion," Éliante says:

> Sometimes it thinks it loves, when
> no love's there;

At other times it loves quite
unaware. (IV.50-52)

Topic idea completed.   She has no family and no reliable friends to protect
her. So her reaction, perhaps instinctual, is to gain power
by the only weapon at her disposal, her coquetry. With
this power she protects herself from those who would do
her harm. She tells Alceste, for example, that she keeps
Clitandre in tow because he can help her in her lawsuit
(II.45-46), and she encourages Acaste because he is a
gossip who, though "no great help," could do her "harm"
(II.100-01). Her encounter with Arsinoé is a tribute to her
power. Arsinoé comes to Célimène because Célimène has
the power to retain something that both want, Alceste's
devotion. And Célimène's victory in this scene shows that
she has learned how to maintain her power with other
weapons approved by her society, her tongue and her
wit. Another tribute to Célimène's power is paid by Alceste late in the play:

Yes, I could wish that you were
wretchedly poor,
Unloved, uncherished, utterly
obscure;
That fate had set you down upon
the earth
Without possessions, rank, or
gentle birth;
Then, by the offer of my heart, I
might
Repair the great injustice of your
plight;
I'd raise you from the dust and
proudly prove
The purity and vastness of my
love. (IV. 294-301)

In effect, Alceste is admitting that because Célimène's
power is equal to his, he cannot make her do what he
wants. And although he may regret this state of affairs,
we can see that Célimène's power gives her the option to
choose and that her coquetry is a means of testing and
thus weeding out undesirable suitors. Were she as weak
as Alceste wishes, she would have no options. She would
have to marrry the first protector who came along, no
matter how unsuitable.

Transition sentence. Rather than conclude by summarizing the points of the argument, the writer speculates about what will happen to Célimène in the future. But in order to do this, the writer reminds the reader of the thesis.

What will happen to Célimène in the future? Will her life turn out well or badly? The end of the play does not offer much hope for her. Alceste seems the same as he was at the beginning. And Célimène seems forced to follow the same course she followed up to now. Perhaps as she grows older she will become more mature and will help to stabilize the mercurial Alceste. But if Célimène cannot find a protector, she will ultimately have to discover some means of gaining power other than coquetry, for the strength of her coquetry comes from her beauty, and her beauty will decline as she grows older. Arsinoé is a graphic example of a woman who, because she has lost her youthful beauty, must grasp at power through hypocrisy, subterfuge, and slander. We can only hope that the youthful, charming, and beautiful Célimène will somehow avoid a similar fate.

### Work Cited

Molière. <u>The Misanthrope</u>. Trans. Richard Wilbur. New York: Harcourt, 1955.

# COPYRIGHTS AND ACKNOWLEDGMENTS

# INDEX OF CONCEPTS AND TERMS

# INDEX OF CRITICS, AUTHORS, AND WORKS